THE MOST BEAUTIFUL
PLACE IN THE WORLD

Also By Judith L. Mitrani

Framework For The Imaginary

Ordinary People & Extra-Ordinary Protections

Taking The Transference

Encounters With Autistic States

Frances Tustin Today

THE MOST BEAUTIFUL PLACE IN THE WORLD

A Memoir of a Psychoanalyst and the
Realization of a State of Mind

JUDITH L. MITRANI

Doctor of Philosophy in Psychology
Fellow of the International Psycho-Analytical Association
Founder of the Frances Tustin Memorial Trust

ISBN: 978-1-80227-031-0 (paperback)
ISBN: 978-1-80227-032-7 (eBook)

CONTENTS

Dedicated to my loving husband,
the fount of all encouragement and inspiration
and the best photo framer in the family

"They say that when good Americans die
they go to Paris . . ."
—Oscar Wilde (1890)

PREFACE

"HEY JUDE, DON'T MAKE IT BAD. Take a sad song and make it better . . ."

I reached over and grabbed my iPhone from the table next to the bed. I tapped the stop on its face to silence the alarm. Ted hated alarms, any alarm.

What time is it? Did we miss it?

I tapped the home button. It read 10:30, March 17, 2020.

Fall back, Spring forward. It wasn't daylight savings time yet. We couldn't have missed it, but we had. It was too late. We'd missed our flight to Paris. Maybe we could still make it if we called Sai San and asked him to return to pick us up, right away.

Ted would say, "You're chronically an hour early anyway. Don't pressure me."

I needed coffee before I could think. Something was wrong. I turned on the TV next to the coffee pot in the kitchen. That was all wrong. The TV hadn't been next to the coffee pot since we'd lived in the condo on Greenfield where I watched as the twin towers were struck by airplanes on 9/11.

Besides that, I was sure I had given the TV to Josefina before we packed. Now I watched as Joe Scarborough talked with Mika Brzezinski. She was wearing a crown with rubies around it. They were talking about President Macron and the people confined in France. The airports were closed, the country shut down because of the war.

Suddenly the electricity shut off. I swung open the door to the breaker switches Were we still in LA? Ted was still sleeping. There was nothing to be done. There was no telling when we would ever be able to travel again.

I began to sob.

Ted reached over, stroked my hair and asked, "What's the matter *Ma Petite Belle.*"

I opened my eyes and looked up. I always knew I was in Paris when I looked up and saw our bedroom ceiling with its 19th Century French moldings and the large double windows with a warm glow coming through the draperies from the courtyard below.

I was having a nightmare. But it wasn't a dream.

It was March 17, 2020 the day that the confinement took effect. We were at war with the Corona Virus. There was no date for an armistice, no word of a vaccine. Maybe by 2022.

Sadly, this story does not have a conventional ending. There is too much uncertainty. In a way, life seemed to stop after December 31st, 2019. However, the writing of this memoir has revived me, brought back memories of times before Covid-19.

This memoir was originally intended to tell the unlikely story of an American psychoanalyst who retires from her private practice in Los Angeles and moves to Paris, something everyone says that nobody does. But this book has become so much more than that.

My unconscious has linked everything since my retirement to so many things in the past, and in any order it pleases. My unconscious has interrupted the flow of my intended story and now all is in a jumble. At this point, I can only be certain about one thing. I cannot write about 2020, the year that never was, the year that might always be.

CHAPTER 1

EMERGING FROM THE VAN, I looked skyward into the deep azure of twilight. It would take time to get used to a ten o'clock sundown in early May, nearly two months ahead of the longest day of the year. Until then, we hadn't known where we'd end up as we searched on the internet for a rental apartment that allowed pets.

I felt a single tear in the corner of one eye.

There they were, just as advertised, three large arched windows on the noble floor pledging to open onto what promised to be a suite of relatively roomy living, dining and bedroom chambers, spacious for a small *pied a terre*. From the looks of the floor plan in the advertisement, the apartment appeared to wind around in a circle, with all paths leading to a bathroom with a door at each end, one to the kitchen and the other to the bedroom. Even the bathroom had what we in Los Angeles called French windows. They looked onto a bit of rooftop overhanging a modest courtyard. The photos revealed twin porcelain pedestal sinks, a huge free-standing claw-footed bathtub, a dressing table and cushioned seat next to the windows, and an oversized tile shower that was so deep and tall that it needed neither a door nor a shower curtain.

It was helpful to know in advance how we'd be able to negotiate our new digs. It seemed a long time since our departure from a world that had been so familiar, so organized, a world that I suspected we'd never see again. The future was uncertain, but we were here at last in the city of our heart, the most beautiful place in the world.

Ted had frequently likened L.A. to a Kibbutz in Israel, but the truth was that it had gradually grown more cultured and cosmopolitan over the past thirty years, which made it not quite as easy to fly away from, as we had originally anticipated. We would miss the Walt Disney Concert Hall, and the opera and ballet at The Dorothy Chandler Pavilion with its so-so acoustics. We would miss the museums and theatres that had so recently cropped up on the Westside and in the Valley NoHo district and the old war horses like the Los Angeles County Museum of Art in the Mid-Wilshire area, which had recently undergone major expansions and renovations, making it nearly competitive with some of the best in the country. Most of all, we'd miss our friends and Ted's pack of cousins, especially the ones who were too elderly or infirm to travel to Paris for a visit. We would surely pine for them regardless of any and all of the modern technology that could keep us connected, if only auditorily and visually.

We couldn't wait to get upstairs, to be released, to find relief, perhaps some refreshments, a deep breath, and a good spot in which to plunk down in the comfort of our new-if-temporary abode. The driver helped me down from the van as if I were some kind of antique doll. I hugged a sizeable package against my body. The way I held onto it, one would think it some kind of stolen treasure. Inside was our Bengal cat, Siegfried. It had been a protracted eighteen hours since I'd gently coaxed him into his canvas carrier in Los Angeles.

In the open porte-cochère, which had originally been built to accommodate horse drawn carriages, stood a stately stranger, quite tall, once blond, now greying and with a kindly smile on his attractive face. The man sported a subtly striped, navy blue, three-piece Brioni suit. He had an air of nobility on his high forehead, which was accentuated by a slightly receding hairline.

"Bonsoir, I am He."

Élie offered his hand to help me over the threshold and into the slightly shabby foyer of the building, while Ted remained curbside to supervise the driver as he unloaded multiple pieces of luggage, one large cardboard box completely swathed in duct tape, two carry-on bags, and two winter coats in hanger bags. All had been crammed into the back of the oversized SUV.

After depositing me and my purring parcel into an elevator scarcely the size of a coffin, Élie picked up two of the heaviest pieces of luggage and led the way for Ted and the chauffeur, up the sweeping staircase and through the door of the apartment into a vestibule. From there everything was rolled into the spare room just beyond. This room was decorated in dusty rose and green, with two cream-colored sofas on opposing walls, artisanal carved Vietnamese armchairs, a lacquered desk with a utilitarian black wooden chair, an oriental carpet, and a wall-to-wall built-in curio filled with Chinese porcelains under lock and key.

I arrived in synchrony with the men, stepping out of the elevator on the first floor of what we had affectionately dubbed mission headquarters. What was now a proper pursuit had been but a mere pipedream before the syzygy of events that occurred towards the end of 2014. As the stock market recovered, our lifesavings were restored to pre-2008 figures plus some. Meanwhile, the property values in Paris had become depressed due to the recession in Europe that lagged behind our own recovery.

Our home in Los Angeles was more highly appraised than ever before, our clinical practices were aging just like the two of us, and almost all our patients were nearing or well into a termination phase of their analyses. We were in our late sixties, witnessing the years pass as colleagues and friends our age and younger died of cancer, and elders in our profession continued to practice beyond what ethics would dictate, this perhaps because their identities as analysts were so deeply engrained. One colleague had announced at his 94th birthday party that he wouldn't know what to do with himself if he didn't work. He died suddenly three days after we left Los Angeles.

Those analysts just one generation above ours were already suffering with back problems, a frequent occupational hazard that was often quite severe. A number of others were dying sudden, unexpected deaths from strokes and heart disease. We observed as many of those still living to a ripe old age began to lose touch with their own mortality. Thus, they were sadly unable to deal effectively with their patients' unconscious fears of the imminent loss of one upon whom they still depended.

Meanwhile, our colleagues and friends in Europe were in or approaching retirement, and real estate in Paris had slid down to relatively affordable rates per square meter, something we had never thought we'd witness no matter how long we waited. We took a reasonable stance; If not now, when? It was clear that we'd never be able to retire in Los Angeles. The property taxes alone were prohibitive, and the cost of air travel was now more than a just a monetary drain on people our age. We also reached the realization that without being able to drive a car in our so-called golden years, getting around in Los Angeles would be unmanageable. We could foresee a future that was at best unappealing.

If we were to live long enough to be stuck in just one place, where would it be? Throughout our careers we'd been invited to speak and to teach in many wonderful cities throughout the world. I used to say that *we sang for our supper* when our travel expenses were reimbursed by our hosts, and the honoraria paid afforded us a prolonged holiday stay as well. But financially supported or not, we always came back to Paris. She was our favorite. She was sexy, her people were sexy, the sidewalk terraces overflowing with an affable, gregarious and vivacious society were sexy, too. Sensuality was contagious in Paris.

The fragrance of Her flowers, whether on display in street stalls or in large pots outside florist's shops, the irresistible aroma of Her fresh baguette barely out of the oven, the eye-catching decadence of Her pastries and chocolates that make ones' mouth water, Her fresh fish, fowl and meats exposing themselves in store windows throughout the city with and without feathers, feet, heads or tails, Her seductive shoes and fashion design that I'm certain only mannequins can bear to wear are just a few of Her many attributes that tickle and tease the senses.

Her beguiling bridges crossing over the river Seine, teeming with tourist-laden *bateaux mouches*, varied in size and style between the Renaissance elder *Pont Neuf*, the modest, love-locked *Pont des Arts*, and the gilded *Pont Alexander III*. The rose-colored air, the twinkling lights and the graceful shadows and clouds that dance day and night throughout the city skies are aphrodisiacs.

There are so many memories of Ted and me exploring Paris on our own, hand in hand, often pausing for a kiss especially while walking by the river *Seine*. We have native cousins our age and younger, and decades-long friendships with Parisian colleagues and comrades whose company we have never ceased to enjoy and who will continue to introduce us to their Paris, bit by bit. There are countless art museums, both grand and petit, divine music in venues commodious and diminutive, and alluring *Jardins* such as the formal *Tuileries* and *Luxembourg*, the more intimate *Parc Monceau* and *Place des Vosges*, and countless tiny gardens playing hide and seek and peek-a-boo throughout the city, adding color and vegetation to Her atmosphere. Most significantly, our lives together not only began in Paris, but our travels inevitably originated or concluded here in Paris. It was as if we couldn't stay away for very long, we were so enamored of Her.

On *rue du Mont Thabor*, a pizza joint appropriately named *Le Cosy* and a classy men's haberdashery, *Bespoke*, flanked the twin entry doors like two sentries on the ground floor of our building. Our narrow one-way street, although filled with small cafés and restaurants and a few chic women's boutiques, promised relatively light traffic and shady afternoons, compliments of the building across the rue that consisted largely of the back side of the Westin Vendome Hotel.

From our apartment on the French first floor, we could catch a glimpse of grand ballrooms lit by opulent crystal chandeliers that transform all at night. Each is decorated to the hilt for private functions. This tiny if well-known street on which we now lived was also a perfect spot from which to launch our home hunt. It was situated in the center of the right bank, embraced by the wide *rue de Rivoli* with its gracefully arcaded facades positioned directly across from the gardens of the *Tuileries,* just South of us.

We were familiar with all these sights from our many visits to Paris, but now they took on new significance, and I began to pay attention to them as landmarks that boosted my bearings and improved my sense of direction. The gardens were flanked on the east end by the *Louvre* and on the west by the *Place de la Concorde,* the largest square in the capitol. This impressive 21-acre rectangle, where Louis the XVI and Marie Antoinette had lost their heads, was embraced by two historical buildings, one on each of the two corners at the West end of the *Tuileries.* The *Musée de l'Orangerie* on the south had been named after the citrus trees it had originally sheltered in Winter, while the *Gallerie Nationale du Jeu de Paume* was named after a forerunner of the game of tennis, once played within its walls. These two landmarks, now famous art museums, had borne witness to crucial events of the French revolution.

Two mythical winged horses, one mounted by the god Hermes holding his *Caduceus* staff, the other straddled by the Angel Gabriel complete with his horn well known as a Torrecelli's trumpet, kept watch over the threshold of the gilt gateway that opened to welcome visitors to the *Tuileries* on its West end. Some witty Parisian claimed that Gabriel's horn would only be heard when at least one virgin woman was found in Paris

In the center of the *Place,* between two gold-trimmed bronze fountains, stood the famous *Luxor Obelisk,* a gift from Egypt. Two Marly Horses, rearing up high on their back legs as slaves held fast to the lead straps linked to their halters, heralded the entrance from the Concorde into the tree-lined *Avenue de Champs Élysée* on its western boundary.

Rue du Mont Thabor was paralleled on the north by the fashionable rue St. Honoré, filled with branded shops carrying designer clothing, jewelry and shoes for those with money, both old and *nouveau.* And at the west end of this tribute to commercialism flowed the rue Royale, which terminated on its North end at the steps of

L'Eglise de La Madeleine, the neo-classical home of the Archdioceses. Its construction, completed in 1842, was atypical of other religious buildings. Like the *Panthéon* in the 5th *Arrondisement*, it took the form of a Greek temple *sans* cross or bell-tower. It was said that Napoleon wanted the *Madeleine* to be a pantheon in honor of his armies.

Before entering through the two massive bronze doors of this church, I couldn't help but admire the Corinthian columns surrounding the building. Inside, there were sculptures, paintings, and famous neo-Byzantine mosaics created by Charles-Joseph Lameire. But my favorite was the magnificent pipe-organ, designed by Aristide Cavaillé-Coll, and mastered by famous French composers like Fauré and Saint-Saëns.

North Eastward, just steps from our abode, was the elegant octagonally shaped *Place Vendôme*, with its jaw-dropping openness, historic streetlights, and classical facades in the middle of one of the city's most glamorous quarters. Its centerpiece was an impressive obelisk that was surrounded by the Hôtel Ritz, many haute jewellers, and famous French houses of ready-to-wear clothing. Just North of this site was the *Palais Garnier* Opera house and two of the grand department stores of Paris, *Le Printemps* and *Les Galleries Lafayette*. All this and more were within walking distance of our short-term rental. There were only three words for the 'hood' in which we were taking up a transitory residence: Location, location, location.

I looked out the window of our temporary digs and in that moment I recalled so many of the events that had led up to this point in time, those events that had steered me to this most beautiful place in the world and the man whom I loved and with whom I would be grateful to be able to spend the rest of my life. This much I knew even then. Perhaps this feeling of enduring jubilation gave me the strength to recall and to live through other events in my life that had not been so blissful.

It might've been that this new path I was embarking upon also provided me with the opportunity to backtrack and to take the time to appreciate my life, including the wrong turns I had made, especially for the experience these turns had afforded me. Maybe, just maybe, this new course of existence might never have been discovered except by the route I'd previously taken. Perhaps what tasted like a rich dessert could only have followed the *entrée* and the *plat* that preceded it on the menu of events that had comprised my working life.

CHAPTER 2

SIEGFRIED WAS USUALLY EASY TO HANDLE in spite of his unusual size. He'd climb right onto the scale whenever he heard the vet say, "Let's see how much you weigh today." He graciously extended a paw toward the nurse as he watched the syringe in her hand approach him. One could swear that he recognized this gesture and was attempting to facilitate her endeavor to obtain a blood sample, to minister to him in some way.

Earlier this day, Siegfried had seemed uncharacteristically timorous and truculent. It was as if he could sense that whatever was going on, it wouldn't be nearly as easy or enjoyable as catching a mouse hiding under a kitchen cupboard. Perhaps this was because he felt my own distress.

I was not in a playful mood. I tried my best and whispered in his ear.

"It's OK, Siegfried."

He meowed loudly and unconvinced. I made a promise.

"We're going to the most beautiful place in the world."

I looked around the room; even I didn't believe me. We were hemmed in on all sides by scads of oversized luggage and ugly motel furniture in a junior suite where we three had been hunkered down bored to tears, until escrow closed after the movers packed up our belongings, finally driving off with nearly everything we owned.

I'm not religious, but I prayed.

We awaited our driver, Sai San. His name was pronounced like the painter's, but there was no relation. I had asked him. He would transport the tree of us, and all we still possessed, to The Los Angeles International Airport in his SUV. We'd surely miss him. He had been the one to see us off to wherever we flew, and he would never fail to fetch us upon our return for over twenty years. A kind and good soul was he.

Siegfried was not the only one who was fretful and fidgety. During our final visit to the vet to obtain the paperwork required by the Department of Agriculture, Doctor Lutz dispensed a stern warning, which was delivered with a somber stare. Siegfried had been hospitalized with acute kidney failure for an entire week at one-year of age, a congenital defect. After seven days of lying on the floor next to him, half in and half out of his oversized hospital cage, our little champ improved so much so that his numbers dumbfounded his caregivers. An aural doomsday prognosis accompanied his written discharge papers.

"I cannot emphasize enough the need to keep Siegfried well hydrated at all times. In any event, he probably won't live for more than a few months, perhaps only weeks."

We drove home with our purring kitten. I cried quietly all the way. Ted was as silent as a stone. It was unthinkable that this beautiful yearling faced the fate of a feline twenty-years his senior. He looked deceptively healthy and vigorous with bright bottle-green eyes and a dense shimmering coat.

From the day we'd adopted him, he'd been the perfect pal. Physically captivating with stripes circling his legs, around and about his tail, and across the top of his immature eight-pound body; he was additionally decorated with charcoal spots that speckled his fuzzy silver underbelly. His natural mascara was spectacular in the extreme. It adorned the sides of his face like war paint, anointed his forehead like holy oil, and resembled permanently applied eyeliner all around his huge peepers, set wide in his broadly masculine head with a noble black nose.

It was merely by chance that Ted and I adopted Siegfried. We'd lost our 19-year-old girl Squishy, an adorable five-pound female black and white mink-coated tuxedo. It was a year and a half later that our mourning for her was finally overridden by an intense longing to take on another feline friend. By December, we'd searched for weeks hoping for a freshly weaned female. About these two criteria we were in agreement. But as fate would have it, from across the room my eyes were drawn instantly to one particular cage. I could see, even at a distance, that it contained a beautiful, enormous, silver-striped tiger. Not very young, certainly not female, a real hunk. I spoke to myself like a Dutch uncle and silently plotted.

"Don't go there. It must be a male. Too old, too big, not at all what we want. Walk straight past him toward the others."

As I briskly marched by, this feline Don Juan swiftly stretched out his oversized paw through the bars of his cage, firmly grasped my coat sleeve, and forcefully pulled me toward him with a polite but unyielding meow. Simultaneously, he nuzzled my arm with the top of his head, a sure sign that he liked me and wanted me to like him, too. His purr was so loud that I could no longer hear my own consternation. So much for sensible resolve and good intentions. The capture was complete. In that instant, I belonged to him.

Ted looked on and smiled. He was also keen on this one. But would this kitten be able to meet Ted's criteria for adoption?

Ted's challenge consisted of placing the cat on his lap and attempting to clip each of its nails, one by one, front and back. The cat had to endure this audition without fussing, growling, hissing, nipping, spitting or pulling away. To our amazement, even though there were hordes of strangers roaming about the shop, and more than a few dogs barking loudly in nearby cages, this handsome Tomcat passed the test with dignity, purring like a diesel truck throughout the entire trial. It appeared that, for this not-so-little dude, any human attention was welcomed with grace, gratitude and humility, unusual qualities in a cat.

Ted and I looked at each other, nodding and winking in sync. Never having had a male kitten, let alone one that weighed over eight pounds at only eight months of age, our choice constituted a huge leap of faith. Only half the size he would eventually grow to become, this was quite a formidable feline. Nonetheless, we were both completely smitten.

Ted carefully carted our new family member upstairs in his carrier. Our bedroom seemed like a good place to acclimate him to civilized living, with an adjacent bathroom that included ample space for a litter box, and a counter long enough for his water and food plus a planter of *l'herbe à chat*. I liked the French name because 'cat grass' sounded like a contradiction in terms. After all cats are carnivores, not vegetarians.

When the travel bag was unzipped, our newcomer peeked out the front. A curious fellow, he looked this way and that, cautiously exited through the hatch, and abruptly made a mad leap for the top of our tall, king-sized four-poster bed. Alas, his eyes were bigger than his capacity to vault such heights; He fell back on the softly padded carpet with a look of dismay and embarrassment in his eyes.

Laughing affectionately, Ted lifted him up onto the quilt and our new kitty happily played with us in bed, accepting our affection for over an hour while we took turns with the camera recording this memorable day. He was a typical teenage boy appearing to believe that he could do more than his as-yet uncoordinated physique would allow. Right from the start he had demonstrated a certain recklessness and a courageous defiance toward just about everything in his environment, including but not limited to the laws of gravity.

As an opera lover, I was instantly reminded of Wagner's Siegfried, the cheeky, exuberant, inexperienced and naïve adolescent demi-god who simply knew no fear. I could never forget how he had ventured from his foster home, slayed the dragon, climbed great heights, and braved a wall of flames in order to rescue Brunhilde from her endless sleep. I too was awakened and cried out enthusiastically.

"That's what we should name him, Siegfried!"

At first Ted was bemused, finally surrendering to my whimsy. Although he wasn't quite convinced by the premise for my choice of name, I felt that he rather liked it anyway. He decided that if

Siegfried was going to be his first name, with such a loud purr his middle name ought to be Diesel.

"Is that a real name?"

Ted confirmed with confidence and without further debate, Siegfried Diesel he was, although we both wondered how this would fit with our Italian last name. But, before I could even begin to mull over the puzzle, my brilliant, multilingual and worldly husband came up with the perfect surname, Von Mitthausen and Ziggy as his nickname. Quite satisfied with and excited by our mythical new family member, we could hardly take our eyes off of him.

So, we didn't.

I brought a picnic supper upstairs on a tray while Ted spread our tartan plaid blanket over the bedroom carpeting directly in front of a glowing fire. We played a disc of Mozart piano sonatas and were reminded of dining at the Hollywood Bowl. We sat cross-legged enjoying our dinner, with Siegfried curled up next to us purring at full volume even as he slept. His purr seemed to express his appreciation for the warmth of the fire and our unwavering companionship. That night we slept soundly in bed, with Ziggy stretched out in between us. After Ziggy's death sentence had been pronounced, Ted and I didn't sleep soundly again for quite some time.

Our first and most daunting mission was to find an appetizing kidney diet. High-quality cat food with low phosphorous and low protein was unpalatable for a respectable meat-eater. We spent a full week buying up cans and bags of every brand of wet and dry kidney-friendly food in every conceivable flavor.

Ziggy continued on his hunger strike.

I studied everything I could find on the Internet, but it seemed that most people had little or no luck with processed or even home-made foods. Most of the time, their cats failed to thrive. Running out of inspiration and filled with despair, I called Ginger. She was my go-to gal for answers to all animal-related questions. Without skipping a beat, she suggested *Hill's Science Diet Prescription K/D* dry chicken kibble. I dashed out and back with the miracle meal that

Ginger had recommended, and I sat on the floor with the new bag in my lap. Ziggy came and sat next to me. He looked up as if to say, what-meow? I called him to attention with all the authority I could muster.

"Okay Mister, you are Siegfried, son of *Sieglinde* and *Sigmund,* grandson of the god *Wotan.* You are not just any cat. You are a hero."

As if lineage mattered to a cat, I pronounced my last exclamation with a full-throated conviction.

"Now, you just show all those pessimistic veterinarians that you can defeat the dragon, climb the mountain, brave the flames, and live the hero's life; a long one."

Still sitting by me in comfort pose, with paws folded up under his chest, Ziggy tilted his head to one side and then to the other as I spoke as if he were actually listening to every word with sincere interest and absolute comprehension. I took a deep breath and opened the bag. It smelled good. I filled his bowl while crossing my fingers, no easy task.

In disbelief and barely able to contain my joy, I watched as Ziggy snarfed up one mouthful after another of this newest nutritious offering. He munched loudly and with gusto as he ate. Clearly, he'd found these croquettes more than acceptable. Purring boisterously while he consumed every bit, Ziggy underscored his pleasure with an occasional chirp or trill, and once satiated he licked his chops and washed his whiskers with his paws.

We set up an electric water fountain, guaranteed to encourage maximum consumption of kidney-cleansing, life-giving liquid. He adored this new device that filtered, oxygenated, and chilled his drink to perfection. He lapped up more at one sitting than ever before, right from the spout. He even played with the water in the fountain's deep well, a true Bengal cat.

I happily mopped the floor.

Several years later, there we were with a fully-grown, healthy, happy and vigorous seventeen-pound Bengal cat who was accompanying us on our greatest adventure like the sport he'd always been.

It was only after we boarded the plane, and Ziggy fell sound asleep in his carrier, that I realized he hadn't had a drop of water to drink since we'd left the hotel. If I weren't already anxious enough, four hours into the flight, the pilot came onto the audio system and made a cheerful announcement.

"Good day folks! Just want to let you all know that we'll be making an emergency landing at Chicago's O'Hare Airport."

"Good grief," I muttered to myself.

Ted had been peacefully asleep since he'd buckled his seat belt, long before we were off the ground at LAX. Soon, word rippled throughout the cabin. The aircraft had a water leak. At least Ted was spared the news.

"Nothing to worry about," the pilot crooned.

The flight attendant tried to reassure me further when I seized his shirt sleeve as if for dear life.

"Depending on the source of the leak, time for repairs, and refilling our tanks, we'll be back on our way in no time."

Finally, near the crack of dawn, AF 069 was climbing back into a starry midwestern sky, only three hours behind schedule. While I sat upright wide-awake, checking on Ziggy throughout the flight, he and Ted were in the land of Nod during the announcements, the unplanned landing and second take-off. Ted's head, covered with shiny silver hair, was comfortably nestled into a breast of feather pillows, his body stretched out on a memory-foam mattress and, as if he'd never left home, he snuggled beneath a soft down-comforter pulled up under his chin. Ziggy's well-padded canvas safehouse, with netting on both ends and sides for air circulation, was a perfect fit for the warm cubby-hole that was intended for my feet to relax in my own lie-flat pod. The tradeoff, a minimum of peace of mind for the comfort of a long and deep sleep, was well worthwhile.

In my nearly vertical position I binged on movies, old favorites and never-before seen blockbusters. The Air France steward offered plenty of coffee and *Valrhona* dark chocolate to help stimulate consciousness in the darkened cabin. Ziggy continued to hibernate for much of the flight. He alternated between contented purrs and soft little snores that brought a smile to my face. I was pacified until we could make safe contact with French soil. It was only in the last couple of hours of our flight that Ziggy's inherent feline curiosity switched on. He peered out and scanned the cabin from the top of his carrier whenever I'd un-zip it to caress his warm furry head, an act intended to quell his angst and one that was certainly reassuring to me. As he perused his surroundings, it was as if he were aware of the plane's proximity to our destination, that most beautiful place in the world that I'd promised.

Ted woke up a little more than an hour before landing, smelling the coffee as it brewed. He looked over at me, smiled, took my hand in both of his and kissed it. He glanced at his watch.

"Almost there," he said, with a grin on his sleepy face, full of creases, imprinted by the pillowcase. I cooed back at him.

"You're sweet when you wake up. But you're no longer permanent pressed."

"Then I had better go wash-up."

Still smiling while raising his seat back, folding his mattress and blanket and stowing them along with his pillows in the compartment behind his seat, Ted stepped into his slippers, reached for his courtesy kit, and headed toward the lighted vacancy sign ahead. He was no different at home. Before I could make the bed, he would have already completed the task much better than I ever could. Ted was so orderly, well-rested and calm; I might have hated him if I hadn't been so in love. This whole thing, this move, was all his fault, or maybe not.

I'd been born and had spent nearly my entire life in Los Angeles, but I was damned if I was going to die there.

CHAPTER 3

I GRADUALLY SLIPPED INTO A DAYDREAM, one of the most effective moves in the art of self-defense, right up there with taking deep breaths. Maybe I was beginning to feel justifiably frightened about what we were doing? Was it the move to France that petrified me? Was it giving up a career for which I had fought to be recognized, one in which I finally had received the approbation that I craved, and the many surprising accolades I'd collected like souvenirs from foreign countries we visited by invitation?

Who would I become without my practice, my patients and supervisees, an audience, my publications, and the language I had invested so much effort to polish over my years of writing and formulating communications, both to patients and to colleagues? It had been just a little over a month since my swan song in the States; the penultimate flight on an airplane departing my birthplace. The occasion was the Windholtz Prize, which I'd been awarded for my last paper. I was flying to San Francisco in order to present my work in person to the Psychoanalytic Society and to collect my honorarium. Seated in the designated waiting area for the handicapped at LAX, I took out my compact mirror to refresh my lipstick.

"God, I look like my mother. When did I get to be a woman of a certain age?"

Even my new title, *Emeritus*, spoke to my being past it. All the accoutrements of my profession had been cleared out of my in-home office by March. My made to order analytic couch, its matching

17

oversized club chair, the diminutive wingback and its coordinated ottoman that had lived much of its life behind the couch, all gone.

Psychoanalysis, or at least the orientation in which I had been trained, had taught me that the room in which we work, both notably and observably represents the mother/analyst's body in the infantile, internal world of the patient. But I wasn't sure if anyone had ever written anything to support the probability that this same doctrine applies to the analyst herself.

After retirement and during the preparation for our move, sometimes I felt as if my body were being dismembered. Each item in my room held personal memories and significance for me. Each one told a story, bringing special characters and events to the forefront of my mind. The all-togetherness of this ensemble of things that had lived within the walls of the room in which I had worked, including the artwork and books, had been put in its particular place either consciously or unconsciously, or more likely owing to a bit of both.

Over time, I had come to realize that these things were a collective expression of who I was, what I had thought, and how I had felt throughout my lifetime. The room and its contents constituted a keepsake of desires and achievements, of failings and successes, a memoir. This relatively small chamber and its furnishings were as personal and tender to the touch as were my body and my soul.

The style of the furniture was French, of course. First came the couch. The elegant and understated floral pattern of the tapestry upholstery, a delicate and subdued dusty mauve and sage on a background of black, was something of me I hadn't known before. It was not until years after I'd chosen the fabric that I realized that I was no longer Daddy's tomboy daughter, the one who should have been a son.

I was no longer a tenant, subletting hours in a room that belonged to a male senior clinician. In those days, I had no choice but to work in a dark, wood-paneled, ultra-masculine office suite furnished with enormous, deep brown-leather everything that made me feel like a tiny tot seated in the huge recliner, my feet dangling above the floor behind the couch, none of which belonged to me. In those days, I was quite self-conscious in surroundings not my own; I was certain that my patients could sense it.

My own chair and its ottoman had originally been a part of my former life. They were already several years old when I had them re-upholstered for my office in a black, buttery, Italian leather. The club chair that I'd designed and ordered to match the custom-made couch, was a very deep feather-filled chair-and-a-half. Its arms were intended to enfold and comfort those who consulted with me, either with an eye toward beginning the process of analysis on my couch, or those who had decided to sit there as supervisees sharing intimate moments from their work with their own patients, confessing their own foibles and touting their own feats, disclosing moments of embarrassment and exultation experienced while they struggled through the process of becoming an analyst.

Alongside the chair was a lamp table with a replica of a verdigris *Tang Dynasty* horse that ported a black lamp shade with a gold interior, reflecting light without glare. Another table was placed between my chair and the head of the analytic couch. It was on this table that I kept a box of lotion-infused Kleenex well within a patient's grasp, and my telephone/answering machine, out of their way with the ringer and sound turned off. A green marble standing lamp also sported a black lampshade with a pink bulb for warmth. This was placed behind my chair, casting light over my shoulder; Light to help me see the truth, but not too harsh for a patient to tolerate.

My carpet, a soft dense mauve-grey wool, was as soothing to the eyes as the pale greyish-mauve walls, the off-white ceilings, and the all-encompassing crown moldings that seemed to embrace the room and everything in it. At the center of the wall nearest the foot of the couch was a three-piece, cherrywood bookcase. The two outer sections were gracefully curved and were comprised of deep shelves, top to bottom. The center section had cupboards across its lower third and below four broad shelves. Along with books, all related to my work, I had placed small pieces of porcelain, bronze and wood.

A wooden owl, that Ted had bought me on a road trip to Northern California, stood for the wisdom that I longed to carve out of my experience one day. On the opposite end of the same shelf sat a heavy, red, solid glass apple that a patient had once gifted me. It was a reminder to me of the learning we'd afforded each other during our years together. A bronze two headed bird, that decorated a small vessel in which I chose to store potpourri for its mild sweet scent, stood proudly in the center of the bookcase beneath a small, recessed light that reigned over the top shelf, which was made of glass. A tiny yet authentic *Han Dynasty* horse, also bronze with a greenish patina, was a gift from a respected colleague who lived in Rome. Representing the authenticity that I strived for, this piece occupied a prominent spot in the middle of the eye-level shelf in front of the books.

On one beveled shelf on the right side, always within my line of sight, was a hand painted porcelain plate resting in a wooden rack. The plate bore the image of two weanling fillies, galloping along, side by side. The plate had an inscription that read, *To have a joy, one must share it. Happiness was born a twin.* The plate was a duplicate of a gift of gratitude that I'd given to my oldest friend, Ginger, in what seems now like another lifetime, when I had bred Arabian horses. The bond between Ginger and me was made-up of many strands. I'd met Ginger by chance when my first husband Dennis and I had been inspired to visit an Arabian horse ranch.

The year was 1969.

Dennis and I were on campus at Moorpark College where we studied ornamental horticulture and turf-grass management in preparation for installing and caring for a garden of our own in our first and brand-new tract home in nearby Thousand Oaks.

The poster had read, *See the Fabulous Arabian Stallion Zarabo today at 5PM in the Quad.* The background was a photograph of a deep bay horse with a short head, big dark eyes and flared nostrils. His black mane and forelock were flying and a long black tail was held high over his back. He was depicted rearing precariouslsy over the head of his handler.

"Let's go," I said.

"What for," Dennis asked.

He never had any interest in horses. Didn't he know anything about me? How could I get through to him?

"I've always loved Arabians. You know Marly horse sculptures, and Delacroix, Landseer and Stubbs paintings. Arabian horses are living art."

The look on his face informed me that his was a lost cause. Dennis had no idea what I was jabbering on about, but he agreed to go. When we arrived, a small crowd had gathered in the Quad. Harlan Moehlman, the owner and trainer of Zarabo, was already putting his animal through its paces. It was a very impressive display.

"Please help yourself to a directory before you leave, visitors are always welcome," Moehlman declared, while loading his stallion into a trailer parked nearby.

Dennis was surprisingly enthusiastic.

"That was cool!"

He reached for one of the colorful booklets on the bench. I was thrilled to realize that he was hopelessly dazzled. His eyes were still glued to the page when he spoke.

"Here it is. A breeder in Thousand Oaks, not to far from our place. *Bo-Gin Arabians* on Colt Lane. Let's go see."

"This is it, now or never," I'd thought.

"OK," I faked complaicency.

We took Rimrock Road, the winding turn-off from one of the main drags intersecting with Thousand Oaks Boulevard, one that led to another world underneath and beyond the 101 freeway overpass. Between large rolling pastures and rocky outcroppings we climbed up and swirled around the rural switchback that circumnavigated the hilly terrain South of the ordinary suburbia in which we lived.

We turned left onto Colt Lane and immediately saw a sign that read Bo-Gin Arabians. Our Chevy clattered over the cattle-guard that separated the street from the circular drive. The car came to a stop at the halfway point, under an enormous old oak tree surrounded by a bed of colorful flowering plants, right in front of the entrance to a rambling, single-story ranchhouse. The lights came on automatically and the door opened before we had even mounted the steps.

"Hi," I said to the slight and wirey middle-aged woman who opened the door.

"Well, hi there yourself. What can we do for you," she asked with a smile brightening her face and a lilting twang in her voice.

"We thought you might have some babies," I squeaked.

After a brief and awkward introduction, I could feel my face as red as a beet. I was mortified that we'd actually shown up at a stranger's door, late in the evening on a week-night and without even a courtesy phone call.

"Well, as a matter of fact, we had a filly born just this morning. Would you like to see her?" Ginger asked, as her husband Bob, a tall and somewhat older man with greying hair, crinkled eyes and a craggy grin appeared in the doorway.

"Could we?" Dennis asked.

"Why sure. Right this way. But it'll cost ya," Ginger chortled and smiled some more.

Bob and Ginger didn't seem to be one bit surprised to see us, nor did they appear to be in the least put-out by our unannounced intrusion. I was dumbfounded as Ginger led us down a long driveway by the side of the house. It was adorned with colossally cultivated beds of six-foot tall rose bushes in solid and variegated colors and hues, each emitting a marvelous fragrance that permeated the air. We passed by a garage, a horse-trailer, and a stack of rectangular bales of alfalfa hay, at least a dozen feet tall and just about as wide.

With Ginger in the lead and Bob behind us we entered through the sliding door at one end of the aisle of a large cinder-block barn with a heavy, wooden, shake-shingle roof. Twelve hefty wooden sliding doors, with metal bars placed vertically on the upper half of each, led into stalls that flanked both sides of the concrete corridor. Off the back door of each stall there were individual pipe-corals, like quarter-acre playpens; One for each horse to stretch its legs.

Cats and dogs of all breeds and colors began to appear and join the group. Ginger introduced each one by name before she came to a halt at the entrance to one of the stalls, much larger than any other. She slid one of its two doors open as she spoke to its inhabitants, a lovely, almost all-white, grey mare and her dark bay filly, still wobbly on its spindly legs, its head butting mother's udder to encourage her milk to flow.

"Hello Lalla, and you too little Tenacitie," Ginger greeted the mare and her newborn as she stepped into the stall, filled knee-deep with straw.

"You have some visitors," she said, jubialantly.

The mare's ears were daintily curved inward toward one another and pricked forward with curiosity.Wide-set below her broad and convex forehead were two enormous coal-black orbs fringed with long, thick white lashes. With both ears and eyes attentive, but not in the least fearful, Lalla Kadija nickered softly to her filly as it suckled enthusiastically, ignoring the strangers as they came through the door of the stall.

Tears trickled down my checks as we stepped in. The beauty of the scene was moving. Dennis crouched down in the straw to get a better look, as Bob and Ginger stood proudly by without concern.

Within the year, Dennis and I had sold our orange 1968 Chevy Camaro convertible with the white racing stripes and a 450-horse-power eight-cylander engine, and in 1971 we were ready to sign the purchase contract for the two-year-old filly we had met on our second visit with Bob and Ginger. Divinitie, or Candy as she was called, had a sweet disposition, showing all the signs of her good breeding. She was another offspring of Lalla's. Candy had an animated personality full of mischief, a stunning copper coat the color of a newly minted penny, and four white stockings and a white blaze down her face. She dazzled us with her floating trot, appearing to levitate in midair. Her shiny black tail curled up over her croup and was a match for her flowing, silky, black mane that draped over her long neck with its fine throat-latch. Whenever she moved, her neck arched high, supported by the strong slope of her deeply laid-back shoulders.

She was a moving machine, the equine version of the Camaro.

"Be careful, there's invisable ink on that contract," Ginger giggled as she feined warning, while Dennis and I signed the two-year promisary note.

This was to be the beginning of a new chapter in my life. Ginger became one of my greatest role models, a teacher and mentor, and a lifetime friend. She not only permitted but even encouraged me to delve into the studbooks that she stored in the bedroom library, where I learned from the notations in the margins about the faults and fortes of each ancestor of every top individual breeding at the time as well as in the past, going all the way back to the Arabian desert.

Not long into our relationship, I discovered that Ginger was the third generation of Arabian horse breeders in the United States. Her grandmother, none other than the legendary Jeanette C. Morrill of the *Bear Claw Ranch* in Wyoming, was one amongst a first handful of breeders of Arabian horses in America, as well as some of the best beef cattle in the day.

I'd always fantasized that Mrs. Morrill might have been the prototype for the character that Barbara Stanwick played in the 1960's TV Series *Big Valley*, the one about a spunky, widowed, matriarch who, along with her three handsome sons and her beautiful daughter, had braved the ups and downs of livestock ranching in the late 19th Century.

While on the topic of significant maternal figures, in my office to the right of my chair, I'd hung a small black and white signed lithograph by George Ford Morris, one that I had purchased, with Ginger's endorsement, in the mid-seventies at an equine art auction for the benefit of the Morris Animal Foundation. At that time, Bob was on the Board of Directors, while they worked to discover a genetic test for equine Severe Combined Immunodeficiency Disorder (SIDS), a test that might aide in the process of selection within breeding programs, by making it possible to avoid carrier-to-carrier mating that would lead to the birth of clinically affected foals, likely to perish within their first six months after birth.

The lithograph I'd purchased depicted an Arabian mare who reminded me of Lalla Kadija, with her dainty curved ears, attentively directed in a straight-forward position as she watched over the young foal nestled just under her head and pressed snuggly against her long arched neck for warmth and comfort. The work was called *The Listening Mare of the Anazeh.*

I thought it appropriate to hang this print from a spot beside and just above my chair, as if she were overseeing my work as well as serving as a reminder, not only of two of the most important functions of an analyst—listening for and attending to the infantile anxieties and communications of our patients—but also, as I much later realized, as a memento of the influence of my friend Ginger, a true expert in the art of listening and paying attention to what she heard in the fifty-years that she'd watched over me.

I called her Ma.

CHAPTER 4

ON THE WALL ABOVE THE OVERSIZED CLUB CHAIR, I'd hung a mixed media piece. It had been executed on hand-embossed paper with a combination of pastels, colored pencils, a bit of gold leaf and watercolors. All combined to create the image of a beautiful rose, tied with cord in such a way that it couldn't fully open wide. At the same time, the cord afforded support on both sides, such that the rose was able to stay in an upright position, indefinitely.

It was a still life in more than one way.

Only years later did I realize that this *still life* was a mirror image of myself at the time: bound up and kept from blooming by those same strictures that protected and kept me from collapsing during much of my turbulent life. Later, as a psychoanalyst, I also became aware that those neurotic defenses, like the cords in the painting, functioned in a similarly protective way for my patients, while also inhibiting their emotional and mental growth. I came to appreciate and to respect these protections and my awareness was always reinforced by the sight of that *Bound Rose*, the title of that work that hung in my consulting room.

Further along that same wall, I'd placed a large museum copy of a frieze of the Roman woman *Gradiva* with her toga, strappy sandals and characteristic step. Written about by Freud in 1907, I was later to discover that he had a similar copy of the same frieze hanging in his own consulting room. My *Gradiva* was placed with a certain premeditation, perhaps to remind me of the moral derived from Freud's own analytic examination of Jensen's story of *Gradiva*.

In Jensen's 1903 novel the young archaeologist, Norbert Hanold, suffered from delusions and was finally helped to unravel the deeply repressed mysteries of his emotional life and mind with the aid of a woman whom he had insisted was *Gradiva*, a woman who must have survived the eruption of Vesuvius. This woman did not challenge Hanold's delusions, but rather 'stepped along' with Hanold, gradually helping him to disentangle his childhood reality from present-day fantasy via what Freud called the 'cure by love.'

Gradiva, originally felt to be the source of Hanold's malady, eventually became the agent of its resolution and of his gradual return to health and reality. This pattern could be found in any analysis that was on the right track. Freud used Jensen's work of fiction to make his famed analogy between the burial and excavation of Pompeii and the expulsion and re-emergence of early emotional experiences. He also developed a credible case for his argument that dreams and delusions were mental events imbued with meaning.

In my *Gradiva*, I saw the analyst who steps along lightly, tracking but not forcing the patient, enabling the development of the transference by taking it on the chin. While empathizing with and trailing along with the patient's imaginings, she loaned her understanding to the eventual revelations of the patient's unconscious psychic reality.

Directly over my analytic couch, I hung a pen and ink drawing with a white mat, simply framed in black. I had found it in Paris on Ted's and my December honeymoon in 1982. It depicted life as it was at the end of the 19th century, a lively scene taking place in the glorious *Place de la Concorde* in late Fall or early wintertime. It featured pedestrians in period dress, men in top hats, and women in graceful gowns sweeping the cobble-stone paved square.

There were also stylish horse-drawn carriages, all traversing the spaces between two lush greenish-bronze and gold-trimmed fountains, decorated in oceanic and river themes. These two stood on either side of the 3,000-year-old *Luxor* obelisk, and were surrounded throughout the *Place* by countless other monumental sculptures. Perhaps even then I had a faint dream of living in Paris.

It wasn't until I was in my fifties, that I realized that whenever I was disheartened by the work I was attempting to do, whenever I was close to despair, I'd glance at that etching above the couch that served to remind me of the fact of my good fortune. I was practicing my yearned for, freely chosen and hard-won profession, one that came complete with days that predictably rocked me between a sense of achievement and one of failure, very much like the sensation of driving a carriage on those Parisian cobblestones. Additionally, I have little doubt that even then I could have imagined that in my old age I might be able to retire to that wondrous spot, flagged on the atlas of my memory. Maybe the vision that hung on my wall in black and white, would one day become an everyday colorful reality.

On the foot of the couch, I had draped a mauve colored, knitted throw that I'd found after way too many shopping trips here and there. My search had largely been inspired by one patient who frequently expressed her longing for a blanket with which she might be able to cover-up and warm herself. I contemplated and shared with her my thoughts about what she may have been communicating, perhaps the fear of being exposed, seen by and vulnerable to me, and her need for my care and understanding, my sensuous warmth. This patient realized that she had infrequently been able to rely on the comfort and protection of Mother and others and had always found ways of providing the necessities for herself. She sincerely felt that, while lying on the couch, she risked opening up her soul to me and she feared that my response would be cold and ungiving, or that I would misunderstand her.

Although, over time and through experience, this young woman was relieved of her fantasies and fears, I remained aware of a simple reality that required action on my part: The physiological truth that a patient lying down may be and often is more sensitive to temperature than is the analyst sitting-up.

After my mental inventory, I found myself somewhat chilled and feeling quite naked and I harkened back to something akin to what Proust wrote about in *Remembrance of Things Past*. In the section

Swann's Way he wrote, *"Even when one is no longer attached to things, it's still something to have been attached to them; Because it was always for reasons which other people don't grasp."*

Unlike me, during this period in our lives Ted didn't show any sign of *schmaltziness*. His Chippendale treasures, including his Burgundy leather couch and a pair of overstuffed chairs, along with two artfully crafted mahogany accessory tables, had been lovingly carted off for a pretty sum by a somewhat senior colleague and old friend, whose own consulting room furnishings had been battered beyond repair, long past their shelf life.

Was I too nearing my use-by date?

Ted was fortunate. He, his body, and even the contents of his room were wanted, well preserved, useful, and still of substantial value, whereas my belongings were removed by my faithful housekeeper, who may have wanted them for sentimental reasons or perhaps just to disperse them amongst her many needy family relations.

Ted held onto his artwork, as did I, with the hope that all would find a place in the course of furnishing our new home in Paris. As for the books related to the field of psychoanalysis, books that we had collected for decades, these had been picked over weeks earlier by a flock of younger colleagues and students, perhaps expecting to discover the secrets of a successful career within their pages.

Whatever the motive, these secrets were complex. What we'd learned from books, from some truly superb instructors, from our supervisors and especially our own analyses played a significant role in our so-called success. Of course, a bit of talent, whatever that is, never hurt. Yet, all the more influential were those lessons learned in relationships with colleagues, friends, mentors, patients and supervisees.

Reading literature of the non-analytic variety, books that spark the imagination, as well as regarding films and live theatre, and listening to music that stimulated our minds and emotions were all sources of learning from experience. Last, but not least, was our sense of determination, our life experience and willpower shored up and fueled by our relationship with each other.

We decided, against our better judgement, to retain the *Standard Edition of the Collected Works of Sigmund Freud*, partly because it had been annotated and read over and over, reinforcing the foundations of our capacity for scholarship. These twenty-three volumes had been given to us by a psychiatrist who was the matron of honor at our wedding, which took place at her Malibu Beach home, perched on a bluff across the Pacific Coast Highway and overlooking the ocean and the colorful autumn sunset.

More memories and attachments.

We had also retained a few copies of the five books we had published, and it was out of the question for us to part with an assortment of other volumes, those that had been personally dedicated to us by their authors, esteemed colleagues and close friends. I read one of the dedications and felt tears, like silken slippers strolling down my cheeks, a sweet if poignant memory lane. It read, "As a down payment for your own books to come, 1985 Lexington."

This dedication was followed by a signature scrawled on the title page. It was a book written by one of our oldest and dearest friends, Harold Boris. He'd been gone too many years ago, even younger than we were on the eve of retirement. Hal had been one of the first authors whose work catapulted me beyond my shyness. I wrote him a long, hand-written letter about how much his very original ideas on *The Psychotherapy of Hope* had stimulated my thinking about those of my patients for whom 'the ideal had become the enemy of the good.'

"They simply cannot accept other than their personal 'ideal', an expectation of perfection that not only applies to those with whom they might otherwise build satisfying relationships, but also exacerbates their sense of themselves as unforgivably flawed, imperfect, lacking, and unlovable," I wrote.

"Their hyperbolic capacity for hope, normally a positive attribute, makes it impossible for them to accept anyone or anything that doesn't live up to the ideal. Isolation and despair can be found at the extreme ends of hope, since compromise is intolerable either with oneself or with others," I concluded.

Fortunately, I had been one of the lucky ones who had been helped by many to get beyond that otherwise impenetrable barrier to achievement and affectionate connection. That said, there were also those people in my life that gave voice to and reinforced such internal barriers to success. I'd never forget one voice in particular.

An elder, for whom I had great respect, once counseled me.

"Don't even bother to submit your paper to the International Journal. They never accept the work of Americans of our theoretical persuasion."

Listening to him, my heart dropped like a rock and shattered into small shards like shale. I felt doomed to ignominy. I would never succeed, especially since my 'persuasion,' although rooted in the work of the British Kleinians who had formed the foundations of our psychoanalytic society, was considered to be tainted by the extensions comprised of my own original thinking that served to exclude me from the food chain of referrals necessary for survival in what was already an anti-psychoanalytic climate in the United States.

Stalwart as I was, I pushed the nay-sayers aside or at least out of my mind long enough to submit my work. The subsequent acceptance of my original papers also encouraged me to write and to accomplish the publication of three books of my own work, and two additional volumes. The latter were collections of papers by other authors accompanied by Ted's contributions and my own, all of which we had co-edited. This body of work emerged over three decades.

These publications led to invitations to speak and teach in cities in the States and later to cities in Canada and Great Britain, several cities in countries on the European continent, as well as a variety of cities in Japan, Israel and Australia. Eventually, our work was enthusiastically sought-out in our hometown as well, even after retirement.

CHAPTER 5

IN APRIL 2016, I had pre-boarded an airplane to San Francisco with deference to my arthritic knees, just one month before our planned departure for France. A fellow passenger gallantly offered to hoist my carry-on bag into the overhead, one of the few perks that mitigated the loneliness of flying without Ted. I could always rely on the comfort of strangers, and in doing so, save Ted's back the wear and tear. He was also spared the boredom of hearing, yet again, another paper that he'd read and edited, and had happily played the role of sage sounding board while I rehearsed for my public readings.

"Slow down," I could hear him say. He was with me in my mind, always.

Flights from LAX to San Francisco seemed more like bouncing than flying; I was down before I felt fully up in the air. The taxi ride to the Intercontinental Hotel, where the conference was taking place and where I was being accommodated, was usually a 20-minute ride at most from the airport.

I wondered if POTUS, then Barak Obama, had followed me from Los Angeles, or if he had preceded me in taking off, since my flight was delayed for unstated reasons, which usually means POTUS was incoming or outgoing. I wondered, was the traffic thick with anticipation of Obama's arrival, or was this the usual San Francisco Friday rush hour?

"If this traffic is normal for Frisco, it makes LA look great."

"Yes Miss, it's normal, not bad."

"Not bad, huh," I thought, incredulously.

As we neared our destination, round and round the cabby drove, trying to approach my hotel in the face of a multitude of road closures. Finally, ninety minutes and one-hundred and fifty bucks later, we reached the corner of 4th and Howard Streets. I was dropped off along with my baggage and profuse apologies from my driver in the Northern California Spring rain.

I was ushered to a shelter under a pink canopy on stilts, surrounded by uniformed police and plain-clothes secret service agents. An improvised podium, branded with the hotel's logo, was staffed by a blond, perky and petite woman in official Intercontinental garb.

"Guess POTUS must be here," I said, as she opened her booking ledger.

The woman kept her eyes lowered into the book.

"May I have your name, Miss?"

"Doctor Judith Mitrani."

"And your reservation number."

"How the hell do I know? I didn't make the reservation," I muttered inaudibly.

"Just a moment," I said politely.

I pulled my laptop out of the large pocket of my carry-on. Placing it atop the adjacent table, I opened to the file for my lecture, where I kept the emails from the conference organizer. *Voila!*

"My reservation number is 4679A220C. It was made by Doctor Windholtz."

I was proud of my efficiency.

"Very good, Doctor. You may go."

She impertinently waved me on, already looking away.

"Excuse me young lady, but I have luggage and it's raining."

My tone reflected my serious irritation. The entrance to the hotel was half-way down the block.

"Well, I can offer a cart to take you, if you'll just wait a minute."

She gesticulated with her hand up in the air and within moments my chariot arrived, driven by a male hotel employee who looked like a very young Pat Boone. He took my bag in one hand and my elbow in the other, helping to seat me inside the covered electric phaeton with the fringe on its extended top. At the hotel, in front of the two revolving doors, stood no less than twenty policemen.

Inside I went through a miniature TSA, where one of them opened my bag, another my purse, while still another asked me a few questions.

"Did you pack your own bag? Have you kept it in sight? Has anyone asked you to carry something for them?"

"No, no, no, in that order," I answered.

The men smiled and waved me on. I walked to the front desk.

"Hello Miss, may I help you."

"I'd like to check in . . . for the second time," I responded with just a touch of sarcasm and nonchalantly I asked the question.

"Is POTUS really here?"

At first, she was mute.

"Your name, Madame."

Poor soul, it wasn't her fault. I decided to attempt to be helpful.

"Doctor Judith Mitrani, M-I-T-R-A-N-I."

"Of course, Doctor Mitrani, you'll be in room number 1502."

She handed me the key card.

"You have a lovely view, one of my favorite rooms. Breakfast is from 7AM to 10:30 in the dining room. Hope you enjoy your stay with us. Do you need help with your luggage?" she inquired, all in a single breath.

"Yes, please."

As a bellhop even older than I approached me, I noticed that the lobby was filled with six-foot plus, fortyish, mostly brown-haired men, dressed in suits of various shades of dark blue and grey, some with coiled-wire earpieces running down into their starched collars. None of them wore sunglasses.

"Is POTUS really here," I asked the one closest to me, as we turned toward the elevators.

He too wore a deadpan expression to match his charcoal suit.

The old porter pulled at the handle of my four-wheeler.

"Please follow me, Miss."

I did so gladly. I was eager to get into my room, to call Ted and to order room service for dinner. I was starved. I needed a soak in a hot bubble bath, and I wanted to try out the bed and check my e-mail.

The porter demonstrated how the lights, heat, TV and minibar worked. I handed him my sincere thanks in the form of a five-dollar bill.

"Good-night to you Miss, and you sleep well 'cause tonight you's in the safest place in this here world," he chuckled and winked.

POTUS was in the house. But I never did catch sight of him.

A month later, I found myself gazing out the west-facing window of another plane, as the light of day decreased faster and faster. We flew over irregular checkerboard patterns of colorful farmland. All seemed to sparkle after a late afternoon drizzle. The farms gradually merged into zones of small communes with rings of farmhouses, stables and assorted other outbuildings, large and small. These more rural zones gradually blended in with the densely populated *banlieues* that spread outward all around the edges of the city.

When Ted returned to his seat, I leaned over to kiss his minty-smelling mouth and whispered our secret in his ear.

"We made it. Dreams really do come true."

In that one moment, I felt triumphant, without a smidgeon of fatigue or fear; only intense anticipation. We touched down, taxied to the terminal, and disembarked the aircraft. We were whizzed through passport control with the help of the airport aide who pushed me in a wheelchair with cat and carrier in my lap. He even helped us to retrieve our inventory of baggage from the carousel. After that we sped through customs.

By the time we exited the terminal at *Charles de Gaulle* our chauffer, with his 'MITRANI' sign in hand, stood ready to escort us to his SUV. The ride into the city was very different from many such rides we'd taken into Paris over the previous thirty-five years.

35

In the past, Ted would always have spoken amiably with the driver in an astonishingly fluent French, just to loosen up his jaw muscles, facilitating the change in tongue from English. All the while, I'd look around silently as the landscape changed from the mundane to the magical. This time around was like as chalk is to cheese. We both held onto our words as tightly as we gripped each other's hands, bridging Ziggy's carrier which was arranged snuggly on the seat between us. The driver took the usual course, Autoroute A1 to the *Peripherique*. About twenty kilometers on, we exited in *St. Denis*. Driving South through the city, we arrived at *Boulevard Malesherbes* and, after crossing the 8th and 9th *arrondisements*, we finally entered the 1st. I felt like a naughty little kid who had just robbed *Cartier*, escaping apprehension by the police.

It had been little more than six months since our retirement, after nearly 40-years of engrossing-if-demanding study and practice as psychoanalysts. All was going according to Hoyle, with only that one slight delay for something as insignificant as a water leak.

Quelle Horreure!

CHAPTER 6

THE DECISION WAS MADE in December of 2014 during a four-day road-trip up to the central coast of California. We had visited this colorfully pebbled moonstone beach countless times throughout the years. Walking the shoreline, picking up shiny agates, jade, jaspers and other semi-precious stones after a storm was one of life's simple pleasures.

The room in the terrace annex of the Cavalier Inn had a private balcony over-hanging the Pacific. The hotel was located on California's Highway #1, nicely situated seaside between the small town of Cambria—with its arts and crafts, bohemian clothing, artisanal jewelry and hand-blown glass shops, as well as every caliber of restaurant one might crave—and the famous Hearst Castle on Northern end of San Simeon, where one could catch sight of a herd of zebra that had run wild there for decades.

We also cherished visiting the harems of elephant seals, hauled out on the sand just North of the Castle. December was the time of year when they began to give birth to their pups. We first discovered them when we were coming back down the coast from Carmel one Christmas many years before. As Ted drove past the shore, I thought I had seen dozens of enormous, smooth, grey rocks in the sand.

Suddenly I cried out.

"Ted. Pull over, quick!"

Ted came to a halt on the shoulder of the road. Now he too could see what I was on about. We walked to the sand to find out exactly what these strangely symmetrical forms were, and we were both overjoyed at the sight of dozens of elephant seal cows, such wondrous creatures, all in the wild and sunning on the beach. As we moved closer, we could see that a few had pups by their side.

In those days, there was nothing to come between us and these giants of the sea, except for common sense. Eventually, as their numbers reached 25,000 in this sanctuary protected from poachers, the State built a formal, raised boardwalk and viewing area just above the rookery. The intent was to protect people from the dangers of getting between an 1,800-pound cow and her pup, or between two 5,000-pound bulls waddling about, squalling loudly, and viciously vying for a female with whom to mate. To this day, San Simeon's is the only rookery of its kind in the world, open to the public all-year round.

The first evening in our room after dinner at The Sow's Ear in Cambria, we sat snuggled close together by the fireplace as it roared with warmth in our second-floor suite. We sipped a glass of wine with our sliding doors opened, watching and listening to the surf crashing on the rocks right below our terrace.

I had chosen this two-week Christmas holiday-break to end my all-too-long career as a smoker, which had begun nearly 55-years earlier as a right-of-passage in a family of smokers. All but Mother, of course. The fact that I was still smoking after all these years was evidence that psychoanalysis can't cure everything, or perhaps it proves that life's unbearables and unimaginables frequently trump science and good sense.

My abstinence followed an epiphany I'd had after social distancing had been imposed on smokers in public places, once it became an indisputable fact that secondary smoke, besides being repugnant to many non-smokers, was quite likely lethal to all. It occurred one evening as I stood on the sidewalk in front of *Spago* in Beverly Hills a chic restaurant. I had left the good company of my friends and husband, with whom I'd been enjoying a lovely evening, just to take a few hits off a cigarette. At that moment I had an out-of-body experience, one in which I saw myself as a high-class hooker in a cocktail dress, standing on the curb smoking on Canon Drive. After that night, my number of smokes began to dwindle down to four per day, and much to my surprise that hadn't been an insurmountable feat.

With the aid of a nicotine patch to help sustain my self-discipline, at least until the behavioral associations had a chance to break down over the first few months, I realized I had quit for good. I was certain that this time cigarettes were *fini* for me. I had gone 'cold turkey' several times before, but each time I'd turn to nicotine in the face of some exceptional occasion. The last of those special events was in 1995, and until the end of 2014 I'd been unable to cast off my crutch.

The phone call hadn't come as a total shock. It was a matter of when and not if my sister would bottom-out in a manner that might ensure that no one in her sphere of influence could continue to ignore or misinterpret her symptoms. The voice over the phone belonged to Jeff, Carole's eldest child. By then he was a medical doctor doing his residency in family medicine at Kaiser-Permanente in Hollywood.

There appeared to be some cultural of belief, in most health management organizations in the United States, that patients were over-diagnosed, over-medicated and over-treated. This motto came in handy in the American culture of medical-care-as-a-money-making industry, and it worked quite well so long as the insured remained well. But things could go side-ways and often did whenever a person became seriously ill.

"Aunt Judi? Mom's in the emergency room. And please don't say I told you so." Jeff's voice was shaking.

"Can you come now and collect Grandma from her apartment on your way? Mom's at Kaiser in Woodland Hills."

I agreed, even though the prospect of nearly an hour on the road with Mother was fraught with angst. I left a voicemail for Ted, still locked in his room with his next to the last patient for the day. I grabbed my keys from my desk drawer, my handbag from the closet, and dashed down the hallway and through the private exit of what was then our Beverly Hills offices. I careened down five flights of stairs to the garage, jumped into my car, and peeled out of the underground parking in our building. My tires screeched as I turned up the ramp to Linden Avenue.

The 7-Eleven was on the way to Interstate 405. I bought my first pack of cigarettes in over ten months. Seated in the car, I opened the sunroof, unwrapped the pack, and lit a 120 Capri menthol. I inhaled deeply without so much as a cough. Only then did I feel sufficiently armored for the ordeal that I knew was inevitable, encountering Mother.

It was nine months earlier, during a phone conversation with Carole that, for the first time, I had recognized that something was off.

"Would you remind me of the ingredients for your Caesar salad dressing?"

When I was thirteen, Carole had taught me to make this yummy addition to Romaine lettuce and garlicky croutons, one that she had learned from chef and restauranteur Cesare 'Caesar' Cardini, who had emigrated to California from Italy's Northern lake district in 1895, and then to Tijuana, Mexico during Prohibition in the 1920's. Cardini opened a restaurant that eventually became a favorite of Hollywood icons like Clark Gable and Carol Lombard. They could just walk a hundred or so yards across the California-Mexico border for authentic ambiance, great Mexican food, and legal booze.

Cardini moved back to Los Angeles after the WWII and patented his family's famous salad dressing in 1948, the same year my family arrived in LA. My Dad was part of a co-op that owned the Hollywood Algiers Hotel, something of a celebrity haunt on Rossmore Avenue, just behind the Wilshire Country Club in the early 1950's. It was during this nexus that Dad made Cesare's acquaintance.

Caesar salad was forever after on the menu in our kitchens.

"Sure, honey. Extra virgin olive oil, Dijon mustard, Worcestershire sauce, a raw egg yolk, lots of crushed fresh garlic, fresh squeezed lemon juice, coarsely ground pepper, grated parmesan cheese and. . . ."

Carole paused abruptly.

"A can of those little salty fishes, you know? I don't understand what's wrong with me these days," she stuttered.

"Sometimes, I think I have Alzheimer's."

Carole laughed nervously and too much. I froze.

This was not Alzheimer's. She wasn't just confabulating or creating work-arounds for forgotten names or words. I sensed that she could clearly *think* the word, but it just couldn't find its way out of her mouth. This was expressive aphasia.

She might have a left temporal lobe tumor, I thought to myself. I was no physician, but in a mandatory course in graduate school on differential diagnosis I'd been taught to make the distinction between symptoms of depression, normal pressure hydrocephalous, various brain tumors, and early Alzheimer's disease. I also learned when to treat a patient psychotherapeutically and when to refer her to a neurologist in order to rule out any organic basis for a particular symptom that, on the surface, might appear to be just a series of senior moments or the consequence of a depressive illness.

I had done a post-doctoral externship on the Alzheimer's unit at The Jewish Homes for the Aged in the valley town of Reseda. I'd committed some hundreds of hours to the taxing task of performing neuro-psych testing with possible early-stage Alzheimer's patients in order to determine eligibility for inclusion into or exclusion from a drug study sponsored by one of the pharmaceutical giants. I was charged with providing empirical evidence as a first step toward ruling out those elders whose memory deficits originated from other sources.

Lives were often saved in cases of normal pressure hydrocephalous by early detection that could be confirmed with a spinal tap. The subsequent surgical insertion of an intra-cranial shunt could return both cognitive and physical functioning to normal for many NPH patients who at first were thought to be suffering from early-stage Alzheimer's disease or some other form of dementia. It was almost miraculous. Surgery was also made less risky and brain damage kept to a minimum in cases of early detection of brain tumors confirmed

41

by MRI or CAT scans, depending on the nature of the memory loss detected through cognitive testing, a worthy cause even if a cure for Alzheimer's was never discovered.

I was finally dismissed from this plumy, pro-bono, post-doc position after being caught red-handed applying my psychotherapeutic skills between testing duties in an attempt to ameliorate the painful realizations suffered by those who had at one time been quite high functioning. They'd once had families, friends and careers, but were now relegated to fancy warehouses dedicated to the safety of the demented and the convenience of the families.

One of my favorite memories of that period was of the patient named Mary.

Mary was easy to find when it was her turn for testing because she was nearly always seated against the wall across from the nurses' station in the middle of the second floor. One day, I stopped off at the station just to say hey. Nurse Karen had apparently noticed that I was in the habit of sneaking in some psychotherapy alongside my official duties, and she asked if I would have a talk with Mary, time permitting.

"She's been complaining incessantly about constipation. But I can smell her farting as she walks down the hall. I know Mary's not constipated, but something's going on with her."

"Sure. I'll have a chat with her right now."

I was happy for the excuse to postpone my regular duties for a time. Therapy was much more rewarding than testing, even with these cognitively impaired elders, especially when testing and its resultant sense of failure made so many patients all too aware of how much of themselves they'd already lost, how their sentience, their consciousness, even their own brand of humanity was fading more and more with each passing day.

I came to find out that many of these patients had been artists, college professors, doctors, lawyers, schoolteachers, scientists and writers, and nearly all with few exceptions had spouses and had raised families of their own.

I sat down in the chair next to Mary.

Although there was no real recognition of my identity in her eyes, she said hello.

"Hello. How are you today, Mary."

"Well, to tell the truth, I have this terrible constipation."

Having learned that delusions should never be directly challenged, instead of showing Mary the error of her ways, I commiserated with her situation.

"I've heard from Nurse Karen. That must be awfully uncomfortable."

Mary nodded.

"Tell me, has your family been here to visit lately?"

"Not for a long time," she replied sadly.

"Or at least, I can't remember when they were last here."

Mary whined and whimpered plaintively and in detail for some time.

I listened.

"I don't really know why I'm here. Do you? I have such a lovely home South of the Boulevard in Woodland Hills, with a swimming pool, a beautiful garden in which I enjoy working, and a great big kitchen. I love to cook, you know, to have the whole family over to enjoy. Here I can't cook, or swim, or drive anywhere. Did you know, they keep the doors locked all the time."

Mary's lament nearly broke my heart.

"Do you know why they put me in this place, with all these strangers and nothing to do?"

Tears welled up in her eyes and rolled off her chin, first one by one, then in profuse spurts.

"You seem to be really stuck in what must feel like a terribly nasty place to be left in without the things you love at this time of your life."

"You're darn toot 'in!"

Now Mary was rageful. She protested.

"I feel stuck and helpless to get myself out of here. They both plunked me down, dumped me in this strange, cold place, my two sons. It's just plain shitty."

Mary angrily protested, all the while crying her heart out.

When she made a fist and began to pound on the wall beside her, I reached for her hand with both of mine. I held it in my lap as I looked into her stormy, sea-blue eyes for what seemed like a very long time. I could almost feel her pain and confusion, as if they were vibrating through her skin.

As the medical director walked by and shot me a disapproving glance, I knew I'd have to disconnect from Mary and soon. This wasn't her day for testing, and he knew it. With one hand, I gave Mary a Kleenex from the package I kept in my pocket for just such occasions and gently smiled at her until she let go of my other hand.

"I'll see you day after tomorrow, Mary," I said cheerfully as I got up and walked to my consulting room.

I felt so stupid. Without short term memory, I knew that time didn't have much meaning for Mary, so my words of reassurance probably weren't very helpful. Still, Mary attempted a little smile as she gave me a feeble wave goodbye with the Kleenex that I'd given her.

I was pleasantly surprised the next day, when I approached the nurses' station. Nurse Karen stopped me, a big pearly grin on her shiny sable face, her eyes wide and sparkly. She was elated about something.

"Hey Doc."

She scurried out from behind the counter at the nurses' station and grasped my hand.

"I don't know what on God's green earth you said to Mary yesterday, but after a little bit she got up from that chair and said that she felt much better. I was flabbergasted when she told me, with that sweet little smile of hers, that she didn't have constipation anymore. Then, after lunch, she announced in passing that she was going dancing as she headed off for the salon where group dance lessons are offered each afternoon."

Karen glowed, nearly knocking me off balance with her big bear hug.

I couldn't help but wonder if Mary's articulation of the shitty break she'd been handed, the life she found herself stuck in, the crap that fate had dealt her, and the spilling out of all those angry frustrations along with the pain and sadness that had previously been pent up inside was just what she'd needed at that moment. Perhaps her outbreak of temper and the tears she'd shed with me that day, once set free, had relieved her of the physical sensation of constipation.

Maybe the act of letting all that was inside out, gave Mary the space of what was left of her mind to think about taking advantage of all that her luxurious prison had to offer.

Or perhaps Mary just felt like dancing.

CHAPTER 7

MARY TAUGHT ME TO BE THANKFUL and reminded me that some people are truly dealt a bad hand. My brother-in-law Chuck, the love of my sister Carole's life, died less than two years after their 25th wedding anniversary party. The celebration took place lakeside at the Sportsman's Lodge in Studio City. It was the same spot where they'd been married. This string of man-made fish ponds, fed by natural springs, was the focal point of an Inn and restaurant in Studio City that had been a hangout for celebrities even before the city acquired its name.

These pools of fresh water, with their bridges and sandy shores, were flush with an array of rainbow trout, making a perfect Hollywood backdrop. Some of these same celebrities had also frequented my Dad's hotel, home of the Casbah Lounge where my Mother always sang on weekends.

Ever since I could remember, I'd fish for trout at that same place with my Dad. On Sundays, while Mother hibernated through much of the day, my Dad and I got up with the first rays of sunlight and drove three miles on Ventura Boulevard to the Sportmen's Lodge in Studio CIty to catch our breakfast.

During that period, Sundays with Dad were always special happenings.

We'd trek home with our catch and Dad would put on his white chef's hat and heat up a big cast iron pan. After a hearty meal of fried trout, sunny-side-up eggs, and buttered toast, he'd exchange his *toque blanche* for a *yarmulkah* and we'd get down to the business of religion.

46

Because my Dad was short of cash during my early pre-teen years, belonging to a synagogue was out of the question. Thus, he transformed himself from topnotch Chef into my private Rabbi, my master teacher. After home study, I'd join my Dad now sporting a Dodgers baseball cap in his wood-working shop in the garage. I was in charge of the sanding and painting department.

These were some of my favorite childhood memories.

Recollections of Chuck and Carole at The Sportsman's Lodge, amorously dancing to their favorite Johonny Mathis lovesongs, both at their wedding recepton and on their anniversary, were as vivid as the images that remained in my mind's eye of rainbow trout that danced on the end of my line each time my Dad and I went fishing.

Barely a year after that anniversary party, Chuck was stricken with an aggressive form of cancer. The tumor had breached its capsule and metastasized just about everywhere before it was diagnosed. Then just a medical student, my nephew Jeff stood by and watched the doctors whom he had revered as they made his father increasingly miserable with each day that they kept him alive in hospital, all for endless chemotherapy that had next to no chance of saving his life.

I sat in a chair by Chuck's bed the week before he died. He confided in me for the first time in nearly 30 years. Me, his little pear of-a sister-in-law, whom he'd gleefully teased since I was a pre-teen.

"I wish I could've just spent these last weeks at home with Carole and the boys, even if hospice were necessary," Chuck confessed.

"You know what the worst part is? The chemo fucks with your taste buds. I can't savor the chocolate chip cookies Carole still bakes for me; I can't smell or taste the Cupid's chili dogs she brings me or the Big Boy hamburgers with French-fried onion rings and the chocolate cokes I used to love. Can't taste a thing. So, what's the point?"

Chuck was filled with frustration and anger. He carped bitterly about everything he'd lost, not just his sense of taste and smell, but also the loss of the raucous sound of ball games on TV. The volume was controlled, the patient in the next bed, dying.

Chuck's black humor emerged.

"I'm a bag of bones with no hair, no sex drive, and I have little skin left to put into the game of life. Can't even hear the crowds cheering anymore."

Soon after that conversation, Chuck passed away with the aid of hospice, unconscious with morphine, at home in a hospital bed that had been set up in the center of the living room. Both of Chuck's parents had died of malignant cancers. But these didn't run in our family, any more than happy marriages. Unfortunately, Carole fit the criteria for what medicine called the "widowhood effect," when a spouse falls deathly ill within two years of the loss of their beloved, long-term husband or wife.

The Caesar salad episode, in those months after Chuck's death, was not the first time I had heard Carole struggling to get past a word that she knew but couldn't seem to enunciate.

"Anchovies," I said.

"And I don't think it's Alzheimer's. Of course, it couldn't hurt to talk to your internist. Why not ask him to send you to a neurologist for a scan, a CT or MRI?"

I was playing it safe, not wanting to scare her into a cavern of denial.

"Oh no. I'm fine, really."

She placated me, adding a hurried goodbye before hanging up the phone. I knew what she was thinking. I wasn't a real doctor, just her baby sister, ten years her junior with a degree in psychology not medicine. So why should she listen to me?

The same impediment got in the way of my repeated attempts to convince both of her sons, her friends, and anyone else who'd pretend to listen to me. But at best they all gave me lip-service and in the end, they did nothing.

Arriving at Mother's apartment house, I found her standing on the curb. She was nearly 85-years old, still a beauty, and amazingly healthy, if a bit frail. Her platinum-silver hair was as thick as ever, long and swept into an attractive chignon at the nape of her neck. She wore an expensive-if-oversized outfit of silk pants and a jacket, an old gift from one of her many wealthy former suitors. The outfit was adorned with a colorful silk *foulard*, worn to conceal her slightly wrinkled *décolleté*.

She'd opened the car door before I had the chance to jump out to help her. She seated herself beside me in my Mazda 323. Thank heavens for bucket seats. My skin crawled as she leaned in to kiss my cheek. I pulled away from her and the curb without a word, made a fast U-turn after looking both ways, and drove South on Coldwater Canyon Drive to the 101 freeway. All the time Thelma, as I had come to call her, chattered on asking what I thought Carole would want for a get-well present.

Get well? Her saccharine sentimentality left a bad taste in my mouth. Nevertheless, I made the grand error. I took her seriously and answered her in earnest.

"I think she would love to have Grandma's diamond lavaliere before she dies. The one you let her borrow on her wedding day. You never wear it anyway and she treasures it so much, not just because it's so pretty but because it's a souvenir of her marriage to Chuck."

I felt like I was petitioning her highness to no avail. She was completely incensed.

"Oh dear, no! I couldn't possibly part with that piece. She'll just have to wait until I die," Thelma proclaimed, with the exquisite sensitivity of a rhinoceros.

That did it. I completely lost my cool and raised my voice.

"She is dying, Mother. Why are you waiting?"

I began the steep ascent up the onramp to the freeway, but I couldn't let go.

"Get real! She'll die before you ever do."

I nearly jumped out of my seat as she vented her rage at me.

"God forbid, bite your tongue!"

She bellowed more nonsense and cursed me while grabbing my right arm with her long, polished, talons digging deep into my bare skin and nearly causing me to run off the ramp and down the roadside embankment.

I pushed her away in self-defense.

She bumped against the car door, screaming red-faced in an operatic pitch that any soprano would envy.

"Elder Abuse!"

I lit another cigarette as I merged onto the freeway, knowing that this would keep her at a distance and my mouth shut. Gradually, I pulled over more and more to the left side of the road until I reached the fast lane, racing all the way to the hospital.

After parking, I followed behind her through the entrance and waited for her to go up in the elevator. I thought it best that we refrain from being in close quarters alone together any time soon. When I arrived at the glassed-in waiting area, I could see Thelma kissing and hugging my eldest sister Mimi and all of the grandchildren, clustered together around her like chicks around a mother hen.

Jeff was the only one to acknowledge me. He stepped out and took my arm, leading me across to the other side of the floor. We sat close on a leatherette sofa. I knew I had to be gentle with him.

"May I ask what happened?"

Jeff was shivering. I wanted to hold him as I had when he was a baby.

"Mom was driving in an underground parking lot in the mall and ran into a block wall, full speed."

He held his head down, as if this would keep me from seeing his bloodshot eyes. He'd always been courageous and precocious, making appointments for Carole to see her gynecologist by the age of four. Crying was for small children, which Jeff had never been allowed to be.

"The ambulance rushed Mom to the emergency room. She was conscious, complaining of what sounded like blinding white headaches. They took her in for a CAT scan. They're in surgery right now."

He was shaking his head. I put both my hands on his shoulders until he looked up, tears swamping his pale blue eyes, now ringed in red.

"The last report was that the tumor's in her left temporal lobe, just like you thought. It's so large, it's pushed her corpus collosum half-way into the right hemisphere of her cranium."

I knew what came next, but it gave me no sense of satisfaction. I just waited for it.

"They think it's a glioblastoma."

"So, what can they do at this stage?"

"They'll debulk all they can, hopefully without causing further damage."

Jeff 's tears began to pour down his flushed cheeks. It's hard to see a grown man cry. I gave him a big hug, excused myself, and went outside for another smoke, without ever having been noticed or missed by anyone else there. It was really the first time I'd reckoned with the truth that life is unpredictable, and things can change in a heartbeat. But my family would never change.

I continued smoking.

It didn't really help much as I watched for four long years while Carole lingered on with ever-increasing cognitive deficits after a brief remission. The remission was followed by a steady deterioration of both her ability to communicate thoughts with words, and her capacity to coordinate physical movement with thoughts.

She joked about the irony of having stopped smoking at twenty, hanging onto her girlish figure, deprived of sweets, and most times fasting with the help of amphetamines, and using as many age-prevention products as she could find on the shelves of the drug store.

"Now, I'll never get old," she gloated.

One day, after she'd lost all cognizance of her deficits, I arranged for a taxi, equipped with a lift for her wheelchair, to drive us from her condo in Newbury Park, over the Canyon to Malibu for lunch. Since Ted and I were *habitué* at Geoffrey's, a scenic and scrumptious restaurant with a large terrace overlooking the ocean, the manager arranged a special table. It was right next to the white railing, adorned with trailing, fuchsia-colored bougainvillea, and located in a corner of the veranda where other diners wouldn't be disturbed by Carole's inability to handle utensils.

I was thankful that she had lost all self-awareness. She suffered no shame while gleefully scooping up everything with both hands, from the scallop, avocado and crabmeat entree, to the main course of steak tartare and fries, with loads of freshly baked breads that I had generously buttered for her. The finale was a dark chocolate mousse topped with heaps of whipped cream, all chosen by Carole from the menu that I quietly read to her. Throughout, the waiter discretely brought damp towels to wipe her gooey grinning face, covered with green, brown and white glop that Carole ate with the abandon and the bliss of an infant.

She seemed to be having the time of her life.

It was the last time I would see her before we flew to Israel for a conference and a stop in Paris on the way home. Carole died while we were in Tel-Aviv. In Paris, I felt her presence strongly. Always fearful of flying, but longing to visit France, I'd always felt like her proxy. She'd made do with the many photos I had brought her over the years before her death.

CHAPTER 8

IN JANUARY 2015, after our return from the Christmas break in San Simeon with a firm sense of conviction, we informed each of our patients that we'd be retiring in mid-December. We proceeded to tell our supervisees the news as well. Only after these most difficult admissions, we announced our plans to close colleagues, friends and what little family that remained in Los Angeles. We also carefully crafted a letter to the Society President and the Dean of our Institute. We made it clear that our retirement was not related to health issues.

As word got around, the responses ran from "No one does that" to "You can't be serious." The most frequent expression was "Unbelievable!" A few of our younger colleagues revealed that they'd secretly been saving for retirement. Some confided that our announcement gave them encouragement and the confidence to keep the possibility open. It seemed that others also had things they yearned to do before they were so old that they no longer could make big changes, travel far and wide, or have time to fulfill some unspoken dreams.

Eventually, the reality sank in for all. Much to our astonishment, the Society planned a retirement party in October. It took place in a private room that spanned the top of a well-known, West Hollywood restaurant. We were positively gob-smacked as a majority of our colleagues plunked down their hard-earned bucks just to celebrate our careers and our departure with champagne toasts and reminiscences that moved us, generating tears and hilarity in equal portions. Even the President, a very senior analyst whom one might say was not amongst our biggest fans, flabbergasted us by his sincere declaration, made with glass raised high.

"I can personally assure you that you will be most welcome should you decide to return in six months."

Of all people, he knew how difficult it was to emigrate to a foreign country, which he'd undertaken with his wife and children in the late 60's as a newly certified psychoanalyst from London. I suspected how much more difficult it might be to move to a country where a foreign language was spoken.

Ted and I were touched by the tributes to our work and the expressions of gratitude for our contributions that came from both students and faculty. We'd never before felt so valued in our home-town, although we had both been globally sought after since the early 90's.

Our penultimate trip abroad together was near the end of 2014. It was one of the highpoints of each of our careers. I had been asked to present a paper to what turned out to be an audience of over 250 at a conference in Paris. Ted had been invited to be that year's Anna Freud Lecturer at the University of Vienna, in Austria. Ted's lecture was sponsored by the *Wiener Psychoanalytische Vereinigung*, Sigmund Freud's own society, the oldest in the world. We were bowled over as we passed kiosks around the *Ringstrasser*, where posters featured Ted's name and the title of his paper in bold letters against the background of a golden image of Anna Freud herself.

The first and only other time we'd been in Vienna was right after we'd earned our doctoral degrees. We had only recently taken up our psychoanalytic post-doctoral studies. As candidates in training at our institute in Los Angeles, we had come to Vienna as tourists on a stu-dent's budget during the coldest December in Europe in many years.

After having our boots resoled with spikes for the icy walkways and streets, we paid our respects to the 'Father of Psychoanalysis', visiting his home at 13 Bergasse, a famous museum.

We crossed through the courtyard where Freud's children had played. We'd been told stories about the Freud family by a senior

Argentinian colleague who had been born and raised in Vienna before WWII. Her parents were members of the intelligencia and close friends with the Freuds. Our friend Lizzie had shared her vivid early memories of playing with Sophie and Anna in that courtyard. When we arrived at Freud's home, we rang the bell marked 'Prof. Dr. Freud' to gain access to the museum. It was difficult not to feel small when ringing that bell and impossible not to experience a slight thrill. In 1987, we had never dared to imagine how things would change over time, how we would change throughout the years.

Before the holidays in mid-December of 2015, we shut the doors to our practices as planned. We'd prepared the house for sale by the end of January 2016, sold it in March, and closed escrow before our departure to Paris on May 2nd. Our belongings, which would eventually be shipped overseas, had been put into storage. We were right on schedule to utilize the one-way airline tickets we'd purchased with our Air France loyalty points eleven months minus one day beforehand. We claimed our twelve-month tourist visas in the beginning of April and managed to sign, seal and deliver our lease to the one-bedroom flat on *rue du Mont Thabor* that we'd found through the internet.

Our lease was drawn up for a period of exactly six months, the amount of time we'd anticipated needing in order to locate, purchase and prepare our permanent home for a smooth *demenagement.* Our choice of this apartment, out of countless flats available for rent in Paris, was predicated primarily upon its owner's tolerance of pets, the promise of a comfy environment, and a well-situated, temporary springboard for all that lie ahead of us in our first half-year in Paris. Before we signed, our friend Marie-Claire made an inspection to verify that all was as advertised. Upon receipt of the validated lease, we were able to Google our no-longer-anonymous landlady and were surprised to realize that she had been a renowned beauty. Now in her sixties, she'd once been Yves St. Laurent's muse. He'd discovered her in the mid 1970's, and she became the first international supermodel, long before the term had even been coined. We were looking forward to meeting her one day.

We had checked off number twenty-four out of thirty-six on our long list of tasks that we needed to accomplish before moving into our new home on October 30, just one day ahead of the expiration of our lease. It was with great pride that we submitted our application for and received with much joy our French residency cards less than a year after we'd arrived in France. My Dad used to say that whenever we sincerely set our hearts and minds on something, we could make it happen.

Yet, it took more than resolve or good fortune. We had plenty of help, first in the form of the bequest that my Dad had left me when he died from a massive heart attack in 1988. He had made it possible for me to afford my psychoanalytic training, with just enough left over to make the down payment on our own first home, the condo on Greenfield Avenue.

More than twenty years afterward, when Ted's parents passed away within little more than a few years of each other, he received a legacy large enough to pay off the balance of our mortgage on the Fairburn Avenue house. Hannah's and Leon's passing also closed a very long chapter in our lives, one too lengthy and complex to maintain in a single piece, linear and unabridged in memory.

My recollections from our times with them exploring Israel, hosting them in the States, and enjoying tourism abroad together still make frequent cameo appearances in flashes and by association with so many other happenings since their passing.

CHAPTER 9

AS I NEARED THE STAIRS, I spied a two-foot-tall, towheaded toddler playing on the carpet, blocking the passage to the upper-level
seating. His mother, nearby if oblivious, grudgingly spoke to her
tot in Hebrew. I strained to avoid stepping on him, holding the rail
to mount the three short steps in the Dan Lounge at Ben-Gurion
Airport.

I sighed into a vacant chair and glanced about. The usual energetic swarm of assorted travelers seemed to buzz in all but the English
language. Unfortunately, I knew no other. With my coat and purse
I reserved the seat next to mine for Ted, still behind after signing
us in, struggling up the long narrow aisle to join me, lugging our
carry-on baggage behind him.

I noted a duffle bag in the outer passageway. A single empty glass
was on the table between the two seats I'd chosen. For a second, I
considered the possibility that the seat I'd appropriated belonged
to some naïve tourist who'd gone off to graze the sumptuous buffet
of fresh Middle-Eastern delicacies. Sure enough, when I looked up,
two ebony eyes stared down at me apologetically, brows raised, lips
murmuring a few words in Hebrew. I shrugged, smiled, and shook
my head as if to say, "Sorry, I only speak English."

The stranger shrugged his shoulders in return, gesturing toward
his bag in the aisle next to my seat, while juggling two plates in one
hand, a newspaper and a glass of white wine in the other. Flashing
my turquoise blues and a beguiling smile, I cunningly waved him off
toward the free seat behind me. With a reluctant nod, the stranger

capitulated. Putting his provisions on the table behind me, he pulled his luggage over to his side of the aisle and said, *"Shalom Aleichem."*

Safely settled in my seat, I became aware of the man seated diagonally across from me. He wore shorts that exposed a prosthetic leg. I wondered if he was a soldier who had stepped on an IED, or some reckless biker who'd 'laid it down' on the switchback road to Haifa University. Or perhaps he suffered from bone cancer, sacrificing the leg to salvage his life.

I couldn't decide if his exhibitionism was a sign of courage, an indication of unusual self-esteem, or just the mark of a sadistic nature that moved this one-legged man to display his disfigurement in a setting where other grown men wore long trousers.

Ted announced his arrival with a nibble on my neck, my favorite spot.

"Would you like to put your legs up on your bag," he asked, as he leaned over me.

"That would be nice."

I pecked him on his cheek as he turned my carry-on sideways and propped his against the side of my aisle seat.

"I'm going to see what there is to eat. Would you like anything?"

"Something sweet."

"Sweeter than me?"

His pouty lower lip always gave his sixtyish, silver-bearded face the look of a latency-age boy. As he walked away, I turned my attention once more to the man with the prosthesis as I rested my left leg on my suitcase. I'd been unashamed to ask for special services from airline companies. At sixty, my osteo-arthritic knees entitled me to a wheelchair limousine complete with a chauffeur who, with passports in hand, finagled us through bureaucratic red tape, whisked us past the ticket desk, obtained boarding cards, checked luggage, and negotiated exclusive lines on both levels of security as well as the congested passport control that had become a fact of life after 9/11.

A rapid ride in an electric cart terminated at the business lounge and, just before boarding, a wheelchair would reliably arrive to speed me to the front of the pre-boarding line and up the gangway to the door of the plane.

I caught sight of the amputee's cane. I imagined he'd tough it out on his own. For the first time, I did feel ashamed of being such a wuss. Ted returned with a plate of humus, eggplant in mayonnaise, green salad, whole wheat challah, and some fruit for himself, as well as a square of chocolate cake for me. I cooed like a nest of pigeons as he sat down beside me.

"Oh yum, thanks honey."

We were on our way to Paris from Tel-Aviv after a few grueling months that had begun with my father-in-law's phone call in March. We'd just been to Israel to be with him the previous November, but for all his good nature and lack of demandingness, it was clear that he needed some extra attention, not just the virtual kind.

The two of us skyped weekly with Papa, and he and Ted spoke on the telephone nearly every day after Mama's death. But it was clear that this time something more was vital. Papa needed real care. He was older and even more frail at ninety-five than he'd been the year before. No one in his social circle had survived with him. Ted was an only child, so off he went in April for a 10-day visit, while I stayed home to work. We had already planned another trip to Israel for the two of us in October of that year, but we both feared it might be too late. So, when Summer came around, Ted took off again in late July for another two-week visit with Papa, while I held down the fort in Los Angeles.

Just days after Ted's arrival in Tel-Aviv, Papa was rushed to the hospital with a bleeding gut. Unbeknownst to us, he'd taken a bad fall, and rather than consult an orthopedic doctor when the pain became too much to bear, he self-medicated. As a dentist, he had pre-scribing privileges, so the differential between a doctor of dentistry and any other variety was irrelevant, at least for Papa.

Three lost pints of blood later, the result of a hemorrhaging ulcer caused by the anti-inflammatory meds he'd taken in huge doses, a CAT scan revealed four fractured thoracic vertebrae that left several bundles of nerves agonizingly exposed. Considering the extent of his injuries, Papa was buoyed up by Ted's visit, which lasted longer than he'd planned.

After talking with Papa's doctor, a lovely Russian woman, there was full agreement that the hospital would do whatever was necessary to manage Papa's pain, even though his lungs and heart would eventually be impacted by the opioids. Unfortunately, only palliative treatment was indicated for such injuries with a man of Papa's age.

Sadly, the amount of morphine required to manage Papa's pain became too much for his already compromised body. It was one o'clock in the morning on the first Tuesday in September, just weeks after Ted had returned home, that a phone call came from the medical director of the hospital in Israel.

"I regret that I must inform you that your father, Dr. Leon Mitrani, died this morning of respiratory insufficiency. He looked peaceful and he did not suffer. We are so very, very sorry."

Ted put the receiver back in its cradle. He looked at me and we climbed out of bed. No words were necessary. Still half-asleep, Ted packed both our bags while I logged in online to book our flight and a room. We'd each telephoned our respective patients and supervisees to notify them of our sudden departure due to a family emergency. We cancelled sessions and quelled anxieties as best we could. It was not clear when we'd return from Israel. By seven that morning we were ready to go.

At the Renaissance Hotel, where we'd always stayed, I took a deep drag on my albuterol inhaler followed by a cigarette on the balcony overlooking the Mediterranean. This cocktail kept my much milder respiratory insufficiency in check in times of stress.

When we finally arrived at Papa's apartment, it was stuffy and dark. It looked like no one had been there for weeks. I made the mistake of throwing open the drapes and pushing the sliding doors wide apart for some fresh air. The beautiful Fall light streamed into the living room, filtered through a veil of dust particles. I began to wheeze.

"Damn!"

I dug into my purse, feeling around for my rescue inhaler.

After another couple of puffs, Ted left to prepare for the Shiva with his cousin Varda and I began the work of clearing away Papa's extensive collection of supermarket premiums, including coffee pots, kitschy Melmac dish sets, and two blenders amongst the lot, all in boxes that lined the walls of the salon.

The dining table was piled high with papers, bills, and small notes to remind Papa of things he had to do. In another pile, this one in the kitchen, I found other small notes reminding him of where he had put the reminders.

Old, battered, suitcases filled with outdated dental supplies, remainders of Papa's clinic that he'd closed five years earlier, upstaged what had been an otherwise tastefully furnished sitting room. It had been neglected, with a fine layer of dust on the furniture, and the artwork on the walls hanging all askew. The kitchen, immaculate throughout my mother-in-law's lifetime, was now coated with the sticky remains of home cooking carried on by Schula, Papa's part-time cook and housekeeper since Mama's death. A fine silt had settled on the greasy surfaces, rendering them unfit for human use.

The entire apartment needed work before the *Shiva*.

I rolled up the sleeves of my silk jacket and searched the broom closet and underneath the sink in the laundry for an apron, a mop, some rags, sponges and the like. I found a bottle of what appeared to be Windex and another that looked like an all-purpose spray cleanser. Everything was labeled in Hebrew characters, so I couldn't be sure what was what. Sniffing the contents confirmed my hunches and I began a thorough wipe-down of the appliances, cabinets, counters, and kitchen table. I washed the floors and the windows that were fogged over by humidity and grime. I mumbled to myself in dismay.

"Mama will be rolling over in her grave."

My mother-in-law, Hannah, deceased these past several years, had been a proud and elegant Sophia Loren look-alike, whose personal dignity and sense of worth relied largely upon the beauty of her home and the quality of her cuisine, which was beyond inspired, eliciting constant compliments. She'd *kvell*.

"I learned from my own mother the culinary style of the Viennese, and from Papa's mother, Sephardic stuffed vegetables and savory pastries."

The food for the *shiva* was ready-made. Hannah would be chagrined.

I sensed Papa's presence while I worked. I could almost hear his voice.

"Hannah, your *bourekahs* are much better, your cheesecake much lighter, like a feather."

Hannah feasted on this sort of praise. I suspected that it contained a very benign undercurrent of manipulation. This was nearly always Papa's dictum when dining out. At such times, Mama would glow with *nachas*.

I remembered the day I learned that I was never to intrude upon Hannah's domain. Her kitchen was sacrosanct. It was her personal altar to God, along with her meticulous hairdo, her flawless makeup, and her custom-made wardrobe, impeccably accessorized, and of course adorned by her precious jewelry, some inherited from her beloved mother and much that Papa had custom designed and commissioned just for her.

It wasn't until long after Hannah passed away that I realized that all of this perfection was compensatory. She was made to relinquish her ambition to study law in London when the war broke out in Europe, and there was also the loss of her beloved piano when the Italian's bombed Palestine.

The half of her parents' home in which her upright stood had been blown to smithereens. She also may have felt the need to offset other losses, the loss of at least one unborn child, and that of a breast to cancer when Ted was just a toddler.

Even against the background of these many disappointments and losses, she was a truly attentive, loving and caring mother who adored and was proud of her precious son. She even made me feel that I was not just an acceptable daughter-in-law, but the daughter she'd always wanted. I was moved to recite a poem for her funeral, for Papa as much as for Mama.

Annie, you're the mama we love, we see you in the sky above
We see you in the birds that fly, we see you when the moon is high
We see you in the stars that glow, and in the seas that always flows
We feel you in the warm red sun, we think of you when our day is done
We see you when the flowers bloom, we smell you in wine's good perfume
And in our morning coffee brew, and also in a yummy stew
We know you know how much we care, because you're with us everywhere.

CHAPTER 10

MY OWN MOTHER RARELY pulled the mask from her eyes until late in the afternoon. She'd drag herself out of bed only if she had to teach piano, or when called to substitute teach at one of many primary schools in the Valley. Othertimes she'd awaken before I returned from school. On these occasions, I'd usually find her in the garden, nails blackened with soil from the flowerbed she'd been weeding. Her flowers were her real children. They never spoke back and they always bloomed with minimal effort or heartache in the Southern California sunshine.

"Cookie. Get to your violin. Your homework can wait until tonight when your father comes home."

Fat chance. Daddy didn't come home for dinner very often. He was more likely be found at a table in the back of the Casa Escobar, drinking his supper to the tune of 'In a Little Spanish Town.' Frankly, I couldn't blame him. Mother's idea of cooking was a piece of calf's liver in the death-grip of a wire-grill basket, blackened bone-dry over the flame of a gas burner. This delicacy was accompanied by a wedge of wilted and suspiciously furry iceberg lettuce, smothered in store-bought blue cheese dressing from Ralph's market, often the best part of the meal.

The grease and blood from the liver dripped onto the burner during cooking, producing a long trail of smoke in the air and a dark smelly stain on the stove top. The spills from the jar of dressing pooled on the counter like viscous polka dots. Frequently, the rancid residue of Mother's so-called home cooking was enough to inspire even a ten-year-old girl to scrub down the range and to wash and put away the dishes, something Mother would never think to do. All would just be left piled up in the double sink. She never learned to use the automatic dishwasher Dad had bought for her. It stood in the kitchen, just for show.

Mother was utterly mindless about the consequences of her actions or inactions. One day when I returned from school later than ususal, she was in the kitchen serving Twinkies and milk to two of her piano students, girls just a few years older than me. They were both leaning on the cuttingboard-top of the dishwasher, chatting about Chopin when I came on the scene. The three of them didn't even look around at me. I felt like a ghost.

Mother never had sweets and milk waiting for me when I came home.

"I'll be in my room practicing my scales."

I told her what she wanted to hear, but I had the sense that I was still invisible.

On unique occasions, Mother would greet me at the front door, smiling and all dressed up, in contrast to the usual and customary,

"Wanna go for a ride with Aunt Helga?"

These were cherished episodes, when Mother as Aunt Helga was all dolled up when I returned home from school and she'd drive us over Coldwater Canyon to Blum's in Beverly Hills. There we'd sit at the counter and order their famous Coffee-esta treat, three scoops of vanilla bean ice cream in a large footed dish, topped with their crunchy toffee honeycomb candy, and drowning in oodles of hot dark fudge sauce.

As 'Aunt Helga' Mother would even play games with me while we drove to-and-fro over the Canyon lined with beautiful mansions.

"Which one do you want when you grow up and you marry a rich man?"

"That one," I'd shout out, pointing at a two-story Tudor.

Aunt Helga stopped the car so that we could get a good look. The house had beautiful windows with diamond shaped panes of beveled glass, colorful gardens with a used brick pathway leading up to the regal entrance, and a harmonious driveway from the tree-lined street, running underneath a trellis of flowering vines of *etoile violette clematis* entwined with star jasmine, all the way past the detached garage and into the back yard.

Disneyland!

As a child, these outings with Aunt Helga felt to me as if Tinker Bell had used her magic wand to transform Mother into another person. Only in my late thirties did I recognize the truth. Mother was a very ill woman who'd been physically and emotionally abused as a child, one who had survived by dissociation. 'Aunt Helga' was the name of the vessel Mother used for the safekeeping of what remained of her soul. Aunt Helga was the external physical manifestation of what remained of Mother's innate self. When I reached my late teens and left her to live with my Dad, I may have provoked the permanent oblation of Mother from her own soul. 'Aunt Helga' disappeared forever after from my life.

One day after my Bluebird meeting, Mother was uncustomarily waiting for me in her car at the time I'd usually embark on the long walk home after dark. At first I thought it might be 'Aunt Helga.' But as I came close I could see it was Mother, hair in rollers covered with a scarf and a tatty housedress.

"What've I done now," I wondered, as I hopped into her car.

"I've been thinking. Wouldn't it be nice if Pete had a companion?"

"A what? What for? I'm his companion. Do you mean another bird?"

I was scandalized by the notion.

Pete was a beautiful tourquise blue parakeet. His dark beak and eyes gave him an air of intelligence that his yellow-beaked female counterparts with their prominenent white sclera didn't possess. This was why I'd chosen him from the pet shop when Daddy took me there for my 6th birthday. We named him Pete, after Pete Grey, a baseball player with the St. Louis Browns who had lost his right arm in an accident when he was just a kid, and who batted and played outfield with his remaining left arm. He was one of Dad's heroes, and since our Pete usually stood on his perch on his left foot only, with his right leg tucked up into his chest feathers, it seemed a logical choice and a neat secret between us two.

Pete's cage stood in the family room where there was more air and light than in my tiny bedroom, shaded by the roof of the front porch.Mother had always complained of the mess Pete made. This mess consisted of a few feathers and seeds that had fallen on the floor below where Pete's cage hung like a Christmas tree ornament in the far corner of the oversized room that had served as my sister Mimi's bedroom before she left home when I was four.

I fed Pete and changed his water, and I swept up any mess he may have made before dinner every night. Mother always had something derogatory to say about anyone or anything receiving more attention than she did.

One evening I came to the dinner table with Pete perched on my shoulder. She let out a gasp. Sure that this was not quite enough to get her goat, I extended my finger for Pete to climb onto, and once dinner was served I let him jump off my finger onto the rim of my plate to share in my greens and bread.

Mother screamed.

"Judith Lee! The dining room is no place for that dirty animal."

"Look who's calling the kettle black," I thought, and with a bitter defiance I picked up my plate, parakeet and all, and sulked off to my room. Even a little bird was too much competition for Mother. I plunked down in my desk chair. I remembered the time I was followed home from school by a big yellow dog.

I was five, a lonely kindergartener and I welcomed the company of this shaggy vagrant on my usually lonely ten-block walk home. By the time I arrived at the corner of our street, I'd named him Blah-Blah. It was a perfect handle, since that's what I'd done all the way home that day, blah, blah, blah, blah, blah. I'd spoken to him as if to an imaginary friend. Trotting alongside me, tail wagging enthusiastically, tongue lolling happily; he looked up at me with a profound expression of interest throughout my soliloquy. I felt completely understood.

As Blah-Blah and I approached the palm-shaded door of the 1940's California bungalow in which we lived, my sister Carole drove up in her new '51 Chevy coupe.

"What a gorgeous dog! Where did you find him? Can we keep him? Does he have a collar? Is there a tag?"

Carole squealed her questions one after another, as she sprang from the car with a load of books in her arms, her long dark hair floating on her shoulders, her giant violet eyes fully dialated.

"Nope, no collar. Who knows what she'll say. I don't care. What do you think?"

"I think he's a Golden Retriever. Maybe she'll say yes this time. After all, he's not just some mutt."

Sis sounded confident, patting both of us on our heads as she unlocked the front door. I recalled the previous Winter when I'd brought a lost puppy in from the rain.

Mother had scowled, "We'll see."

But the next day, while I was at school, she dropped the pup off at the animal shelter, a death sentence in those days. That betrayal caused me to lose all hope.It dredged up memories of the time Dad gave me a yellow duckling for Easter.

Returning home from work early on Good Friday, Daddy scooped me up in his arms.

"Whadaya say we take a swim?"

"Oh, can we really?"

"I'll get my suit on and meet you out back," he replied as he set me down.

Daddy joined me in the backyard, wearing trunks and a straw golf hat. I dashed off ahead of him and dove into the deep end of the pool.When I surfaced, he was still standing there.

"Come on Daddy, take off your hat and jump in," I begged, and dipped back under the cool blue.

He knelt on one knee and hunched over on the coping as I popped up from underwater, directly in front of his face.

"You take it off for me," he demanded.

"Okay."

I lifted his hat off his balding head. I was about to put it on and re-submerge when I caught sight of what was underneath the hat. Perched on Daddy's shiny pate was a tiny yellow bit of fuzz with orange feet and a matching bill.

"Wanna buy a duck," Daddy asked, with his best Joe Penner impersonation, holding his cigarette in the corner of his mouth, like a cigar.

I gigled with glee as two black eyes looked at me, and with its bill opened wide, emitting a diminutive quack. I took the baby duck in my then-small hands.

"Wanna take a swim?"

I named the duckling Tim-Tam, not yet sure if it were a he or a she. On the side of the house near the clothes lines, just outside the kitchen door, together my Dad and I constructed a wood and wire pen for Tim-Tam. We swam together all Summer long, and by Fall Tim-Tam had reached his snowy white, feathered prime.

Mother seemed disinterested in our activities, which was as good as it got. I was a fish in the pool and would spend whole days there, that is when I wasn't practicing the violin or taking lessons. I always fantasized about my escape from home each time I'd descend to the bottom and touch the drain in the deep end.

I thought that there must be a better place on the other side of that drain, a parallel world where mothers are lovingly present and fathers don't periodically drown themselves in bottles of vodka camoflaged with orange juice in the morning, and whiskey in Coca Cola at night. I prayed, but no exit appeared. At least none like C.S. Lewis' armoire entrance to the magical land of *Narnia*.

One day Mother brought out my usual for lunch, a peanut butter and jelly sandwich on stale Wonderbread with a glass of milk that she had set down close to the side of the pool. I thought I could detect, through the water above my head, that her rippling shape was turning to leave.I surfaced and grabbed the sandwich.

I chewed with my elbows propped up on the coping. Tim-Tam was sunning on the grass when all at once he saw the sandwich, and waddled over for a crusty hand-out. After gulping it down, he dove into the pool. As he hit the water he defecated. Hiding in shadows on the porch, Mother took in the whole scene.

She ran to the pool, screaming at me.

"That dirty bird has to go."

Screaming and shrieking were her favorite modes of communication, both indoors and out.The next day, Dad brought the bad news.

"Nestor's place is great. Tim-Tam will love it. There are chickens and other ducks, a goat and loads of squirrels. He'll even have a fish pond to swim in. That duck will be living the life of Riley, and your mother will get off our backs."

Nester Paiva was my Dad's good friend and drinking buddy. He was Portuguese born, but famous for playing a recuring role in the TV series *Zorro*, and in many films that cast him as Mexican. He was a nice man. I'd visited his home with Dad when they played cards.

All sweet memories aside, Dad was clearly a coward. He didn't stick up for Tim-Tam or me. But how could I blame him. Mother was insufferable. Sometimes, I really wished she'd sleep forever. As for Tim-Tam, I heard years later that Nestor had become enraged when Tim-Tam had beaten his prized fighting-cock to the death, so he turned Tim-Tam into a roast duck dinner. A bad end for my good friend.

At the pet store, the only female parakeet was cobalt blue. I made a face.

"We'll take her," Mother said.

She never cared about what I wanted. She just opened her wallet and the she-bird was in the car on her way to our house. I still couldn't imagine why Mother wanted another bird. She hated the one we already had.

As she pulled the car into the driveway and shut off the engine, Mother turned toward me.

"I thought this would be the best way to tell you."

"Tell me what," I sulked.

"Pete is gone," she said, without a hint of emotion.

"Gone? What do you mean, gone?"

I already feared the answer. His wings were clipped, so he couldn't have flown away. Could he? No. It had to be worse than that.

"Well, there was this little accident. They didn't mean to do it."

She was humming and hawing the way she did when she was uneasy, those rare moments when she felt anything.

"Who's they?"

"I don't know how he got out, but he was on the floor in the kitchen when they leaned on the dishwasher while they were having their milk and cookies."

She continued with a malifluous tone.

"And . . . well, it just couldn't be helped," she stammered as she opened the car door, closing it quietly and walking up the front steps with the new bird in a small cardboard carrier, leaving me behind, still in the car, hopelessly stunned.

As wrath took over my shock, I flung open the car door on my side of the car, shot out of the seat, and slammed the door. I ran behind Mother and her new acquisition. She unlocked the front door. I rushed in after her.

"Where is Pete, what have you done with him?"

"He's in a box in your bedroom closet."

She spoke without a trace of care.

Rivulets of cold tears ran down my rageful face. The front of my blouse was soaked. Mother looked at me with a saccharine sneer.

"We can bury him if you like. It's not that bad, you'll get used to the new bird. She's very pretty, even prettier than . . ."

She was trying to weasel her way out.

"Dead. How could you? Why didn't you just tell me?"

I flew to my room, slamming that door, too. On the closet shelf I found a shoebox. I held it close, sitting on the bed for an hour before opening it. Inside was my beautiful turqouise blue-boy. He didn't look dead, just asleep, silent, still. As my tears subsided and caked on my face, I could see that Pete was flattened, each feather still in its place, like a butterfly pinned to a spreading board. I picked him up and tenderly held him in both hands. I hated Mother. The new bird went back to the pet shop.

There was no way to replace Pete. How could she believe that any other bird could ever take his place? I wanted to scream. Loved ones are never interchangeable. I knew this truth as a child, even if Mother could never get it.

CHAPTER 11

I WAS REMINDED OF THAT FIRST LOSS, and all those that followed, when Ted's Mother Hannah passed away. Ted's father was not as timid as my own. He didn't need a drink to make himself bold, controlling, intimidating, and unflinching. After Hannah's death I had some idea of what had fortified him and of how he'd survived the Nazi occupation of France.

Ted and I gingerly opened the door to a small room on our left, just inside the gates to the entrance of the cemetery. This room was provided for the next of kin so they might be able to say goodbye to their loved-one in privacy, to capture a last glance of a cherished face about to be covered forever in a linen shroud. Here one could sob, caressing a cheek or a hand for the last time.

Papa stood over Mama's head from behind, shedding tears. He held her face between his arms as he spoke softly to her in Hebrew. I'd never seen him so tender and vulnerable as he was in that moment. I was deeply touched, observing him in those last minutes with his wife of more than sixty years.

A few months after Mama's death, Papa agreed to come and stay for a month. Ted and I strongly felt that this was no time to leave him alone with his grief. We secured a round trip ticket in business class, arranged assistance for him in both airports, and made plans to be together every evening and all througout the weekends for an entire month.

Ted bought a new down comforter for the guest bed, something that would be lightweight on Papa's sensitive feet. At his age, it's not uncommon to suffer from peripheral neuropathy. We also filled the refridgerator with things we knew he'd enjoy. Ted prepared stuffed vegitables, *gedemte* chicken and stewed prunes, while I baked a chocolate cake, chocolate chip cookies, and a slow-roasted brisket to welcome him.

Papa arrived in a surprisingly cheerful mood. He was effusive about the house into which Ted and I had moved both our home and offices a few years before Hanna's death. We drove Papa straight home from the airport, gabbing all the way.

Our two-story traditional was set high up off the street. Well-manicured emerald lawns stretched practically to the front door. Used brick steps wound through two rows of brilliantly colored and fragrant roses, and the beds were edged with sturdy red and white tufts of begonia leading to the front porch. Our seventy-five year old ornamental pear tree stood like a master of hospitality, its branches outstreached to visitors in front and provided shelter for the porch and dining room from behind.

Ted parked the car at the curb, handling the luggage while I helped Papa up the steps, one by one. He was captured as he walked through the dark green front door and caught sight of the warm parquet floors, a glowing framework for lush Persian carpets in hues of brick, ivory and teal. The fireplace was adorned with an enameled wooden mantlepiece and a marble hearth, all set into a charming, traditional inglenook.

Brass sconces shed light over each end of the mantle. In between the two hung an oil painting of Piazza San Marco in Venice, with its majestic clock tower and gently lapping waters brimming with colorful gondolas, ready for hire. Displayed proudly below each lamp were two, ruby-red Gallé vases, a gift from Papa's sister, Aunt Mathy.

An elephant cast in solid bronze, a Māokōng Lǎnchē gondola carved out of red jasper stone, and several small ivory figures arranged in opposing stances were also displayed on the mantle piece. These had belonged to Mother, given to her parents by her father's wealthy employer and patroness, Julia Morascini. I loved these pieces and, since no one else in the family appreciated them, they were handed off to me when Mother died, willing me nothing but cruel words and a single dollar as a final insult. Although my eldest sister Miriam already knew the contents of Mother's will, she was able to finagle me into paying the whole bill for her burial, crying poor, when all the while she knew she would be the recipient of Mother's fortune. This was one of the many realizations that contributed to the dissolution of our relationship.

Papa entered the dining room, off the vestubule and across from the living room. With its diagonal entry and vaulted ceilings, it provided a perfect spot for the French provincial buffet that officiated gracefully over our dining table. From there, we ushered Papa through the door to the kitchen. He drew a deep breath as he set eyes on our Viking stove that stood, fit for a Pro opposite the doorway. On the wall over the range beneath the hood, was a hand-painted tile mural that Ted had designed, a French picnic of cheeses, salami, baguette, fruit and a bottle of red wine. The label on the bottle diplayed a cleverly concocted coat of arms, two bears that seemed to be playing patty-cakes, and the words *Le Chateau des Ourse, 2003*. This was our equivalent to children placing their hands in wet cement of the foundation to mark their territory.

Across from the stove was a breakfast nook covered with, of all absurd materials, bordeaux ostrich leather. Papa relaxed into one of the banquettes that flanked either side of a heavy wooden table with a smooth patina born of years of orange-oil and use. He ran his hands appreciatively over the surface, and his mouth turned upward at the corners as he nodded with pleasure.

His eyes sparkled as he looked around at the cabinets that overhung the dinette, as well as the walls on each side of the double-sink across the room, and over the counter and drawers on the wall perpendicular to the stove. Each cabinet was enclosed with beveled glass doors. Papa's smile broadened as he signaled his approval with a chef's kiss.

The upper floor of the house seemed to impress Papa the most. Seventeen-foot ceilings with wall to wall built-in book cases, large windows spanning fifteen feet from scarcely above the floors to barely below the crown moldings that surrounded the ceilings. All overlooked the garden and Ted's office building in the back yard, as well as the driveway alongside the house, where our next door neighbors' Chinese Elm provided a jade-green, shady vista.

The windows were adorned with sage draperies garlanded with crimson climbing roses and peach magnolias, topped off with matching cornices. The off-white sheers matched the ceilings and the moldings, while the walls borrowed their tint from the magnolias in the drapes.Papa regarded the second wood-burning fireplace facing the bed with more windows on either side, and the floors covered with creamy, plush, wall-to-wall carpeting.

At the top of the stairs, across the landing from the bedroom, was a sizable study with two mahogany desks and a matching library transplanted from our former offices in Beverly Hills.The windows yielded ample light and a view of the trees and flowers that bordered our lawn. A spacious master bath with separate shower and toilette and a dressing room and two huge walk-in closets completed the ensemble.

"*Mazel Tov*," Papa said.

We returned to the first floor where Ted opened the door on the right, at the foot of the stairs just across from the kitchen.

"*Abba*, this is your room."

"What do you say? This is something special, no? And there's the garden."

Papa conveyed his pleasure with his usual exclamatory question.

He reached out to touch the French doors that led to the brick patio, complete with its white French bistro table and chairs. One pull on the handle and he was bathed in a pleasant breeze, as he peered out through the brilliant flowers covering the pergola and shading the entrance to his south facing room.

Papa turned an eye toward the floor-to-ceiling bookshelves that stretched over the longest wall of his bedroom, with just enough room on one end for a small writing desk and chair with a telephone just for him, all sitting below a large sash window. It was in this library that Ted kept his serious litertaure and poetry in several languages, as well as our joint collection of cookbooks, and dozens of art exhibition catalogues. Many small and sundry souvenirs were placed between and in front of the books. I loved *chatchkas*.

"Why not get settled? The closet is here in the dressing room, and your private bathroom is just beyond. The drawers in the bedroom are all yours too."

I opened each one while Ted lifted Papa's suitcases onto the folding wooden luggage racks, one on either side of the dresser. Papa gave a look of recognition to the rattan furnishings that we'd purchased to welcome Mama and Papa to our first apartment when they came for our wedding in 1982.

The colors were cheerful and the small Persian carpets that he and Aunt Mathy had given us were scattered about the parquet floors. Their colors tied in with the gold and cherry draperies, pulled back on either side of the doors and the window.

"Make yourself comfortable, and when you're ready, come across to the kitchen for some tea and cake."

I kissed Papa on both cheeks, moist with joy. He may have had tears in his eyes, but he was smiling that sweet, lopsided way I knew so well, clearly glad to be with us, and bursting with equal portions of pride and peace of mind.

Ted sat in the kitchen while I filled the kettle with water.

"He seems in good spirits,"

"Yes, I think it's going to be a good visit."

And it was. For the most part.

Papa merrily went along with all the plans we'd made. There were Philharmonic concerts at the Disney Concert Hall on several evenings, a series of Beethoven symphonies and one concert featuring the work of Elliot Carter. Papa had never heard of Carter, one of the most respected American composers of the second half of the 20th century. Combining elements of European modernism and American ultra-modernism into a distinctive style, Carter had achieved a personal harmonic and rhythmic language of his own. Papa was encouraged and impressed by the fact that Carter was alive and still composing music, and that the work we'd heard had been written when Carter was Papa's age.

We arranged dinners and brunches with friends, both at home and in restaurants, and Papa adored our night at the Jazz Bakery. After *bouillebaisse* at the small French restaurant nextdoor, we sat in the front row of the nightclub and Papa looked up at the singer on stage, a black beauty with long russet hair and bare legs to match showing through the seductive slit in her long, sparkling gown. Papa was enraptured by her renditions of American songs from the forties.

We also visited the Getty Center. Papa insisted to see everything on exhibit. He allowed us to push him in a wheelchair for convenience, safety and speed. Ted and I both felt it was as if he had come to life for the first time in years.

"I can't believe it's been so long since I have been to an art museum. I had forgotten how wonderful it can be."

Papa sighed softly, as he stared at a beautiful Gainsborough. He constantly commented as we sat for lunch in the mountain-top restaurant, the Pacific Ocean glistening far in the distance and the emerald green hills surrounding us from behind. Heaven on earth.

"The view from this place is something unusual, the food is so wonderful."

Then, one night at home after dinner, Papa requested a movie.

"I missed so many when Hannah was alive, but I knew she could not bear the better ones. They would have been too disturbing. What about that Netflix you talked about?"

I'd already moved up several films into our queue that Papa had previously mentioned, those that were noteworthy. I was certain that Mama had refused to see any of these award winning films having to do with either World War II or the Holocaust.

I slid *The Pianist* out of its red envelope, and installed it in the DVD player. My two favorite boys made themselves comfortable in the TV room, just off of and two steps up from the living room. With interest, Papa began watching the true story of Wladyslaw Szpilman, who in the 1930's had been known as one of the most accomplished pianists in Poland, if not in all of Europe.

The film took place at the outbreak of the Second World War. Szpilman was a victim of the anti-Jewish laws imposed by the Germans. He moved from the concert halls to the Jewish Ghetto in Warsaw. Papa witnessed Szpilman suffering the tragedy of his family's deportation to a concentration camp, and his own conscription into a forced labor compound. Szpilman escaped and went into hiding, a refugee and a bystander during the Warsaw Ghetto uprising.

The film vividly portrayed Szpilman observing, as if in a rear-view mirror, images of the inhumane captures and vicious murders of his musical associates, his family and friends, while he barely evaded their fate. During these tense scenes, I looked over and noticed that Papa had grown increasingly agitated.

Unexpectedly, Papa rose up. He cried out, staggering from the room.

"I am sorry, I cannot watch this anymore."

Ted and I looked at each other, bewildered by Papa's response, suspecting that something very personal lurked behind his sudden reaction. Ted had never heard any war stories from his father. He only knew that Leon had arrived in Palestine in 1941 by ship from Trieste through the port of Alexandria Egypt to Haifa. The story had always been relayed smoothly, as if without extraordinary incident.

We were at a loss and becoming more and more concerned. Papa had closed the door to his room and wouldn't come out. The following morning, he refused to leave his room, to speak to either one of us or to eat breakfast. We decided to wait until after work before intruding into whatever it was that he was going through.

I had a cancellation and was finished seeing patients before Ted. I couldn't find any sign that Papa had been out of his room. I was worried and decided to knock gently on his door.

"Papa, please let me come in."

Silence.

"I just want to bring you some water, to see if you need anything."

"Come," he said, ever so faintly.

The room was darkened, the draperies shut tight. When I opened the door, a stream of light from the kitchen revealed Papa lying down, still and pale, his head propped up on pillows. I approached and sat on the side of his bed with a glass of water in my right hand, stroking his cheek with my left.

"Please, drink," I begged, bringing the water close to his face.

He drank like a Bedouin who'd been lost in the desert too long.

"Can you tell me what happened last night?"

After long minutes of silence, he began to speak.

"I just couldn't watch anymore. It brought back everything, all I thought I'd forgotten long ago. I know this story. Something like mine. I was a dentist in Strasbourg, in Northeastern France. On the border with Germany."

Papa spoke in fits and spurts.

"I was content. I had graduated from dental school. Had many friends. Women friends, too. Where I lived, there was a beautiful view of the Rhine. Charming rooms."

He sighed deeply and asked for another glass of water. I nodded, took the glass from his hand, and kissed him on the cheek. I was shaking as I walked across to the kitchen, returning with a pitcher of water and the refilled glass in less than three minutes.

He drank two more glasses of water before continuing his story. Only now his voice was flattened, emotionless, although tears fell from his sunken eyes, streaking his gaunt face.

"The Nazis took France in three weeks in May of 1940, and Paris right after."

"Strasbourg, all of Alsace, came under the German government by September. I knew we, all the Jews, had to get out."

Papa grasped my hand, squeezing tightly.

"Just like the movie, I could see everything. It was as if it was a reflection in a glass window, or like I was looking over my shoulder at a nightmare. They were all shot, one by one, as I ran away. All my friends, everyone I loved there, they all died"

Papa was out of breath, as if he was still running through the forests.

"But I escaped."

He spoke sadly as he sipped another glass of water.

"I had a valid visa to enter Switzerland, but everyone I loved was dead."

"I never told anyone before, can you imagine?"

I put my arms around his neck and hugged him tight. He laid his head on my breast. His dread and despondency penetrated me. The fact that he had dissociated himself from those terrible experiences, that he never told a soul was understandable. It may have been his only path to psychic survival, one that enabled him to go on. In Palestine, he was united with his family, who had preceded him by a few years.

What amazed me was that, before he had left Israel to visit us that Fall, he'd requested specific movies like *Schindler's List*, *Sophie's Choice*, *Saving Private Ryan*, *The Pianist*, all films that would most certainly stir up that past that he'd so deeply buried in his subconscious.

It was as if he'd needed to tell someone in these, the last years of his life. After long moments, looking into Papa's cavernous blue eyes, I dared make a suggestion.

"I think these are experiences you need to share with your son. Please come and join us for dinner. Teddy will be back in the house in a little while, after work. And dinner will be ready by 7:30. Will that be okay, is that enough time for you?"

Papa nodded and I kissed him again before leaving him to ready himself. He was always so proper, rarely leaving his room without showering, shaving and dressing in a clean shirt, trousers, socks and shoes, a tie and a sweater or vest. Sometimes he even put on a sport jacket. Papa was always the proud gentleman.

That night he ate well, and he did tell his story after dinner. But this version was a completely factual, detailed account of his movement from Strasbourg to Geneva, with the more amusing elements of his time in Switzerland. He talked about his move to Trieste where he was able to board an *Adriatica* ship on its last voyage, sailing from Italy to the port of Alexandria in Egypt. Finally, he retold the story of his journey and eventually dropping anchor in the Port of Haifa in what was then called Palestine, safe and under a British mandate.

Perhaps providentially, the raw and excruciating emotional details of love, loss, and the harrowing experience of survival in Nazi Occupied France, that story that I had heard in splintered excerpts, had all been deleted from Papa's conversation with his son. It was a blessing that he'd been able to re-bury these horrors. He'd been forced to flee France, and now in our retirement, we brought him back with us to France, if only in spirit.

CHAPTER 12

"HI DAD!"

Even at seventeen, I was gleeful to hear my father's voice at the end of the line.

After I'd moved out of Carole's house and into my own apartment, complements of generous Dad, he'd ceased paying child support to Mother. Being the reasonable adult that she was, she went to court.

Dad retaliated by cutting-off Mother's alimony as well, with a well founded belief that, as long as she was being supported by him, she would never re-marry although she was constantly being courted by men of significant position and wealth. Dad said that my mother, who had always been a great beauty, was also terrific in bed.

Predictably, the courts didn't agree with Dad's arguments and found for the plaintiff in the case. Since he didn't appear for the hearing, he was found in contempt, and his freedom to return to California, without winding up in jail, came to an end.

For many years, we'd all meet in Las Vegas.

"What's up Daddy?"

"Airlines are up, for one thing. Seriously, your old man misses his baby. So how 'bout I send you a ticket, and we'll do some deep sea fishing here in Miami?"

I couldn't reisist his humorous cajoling. Those wonderful memories of fishing with Dad sparkled like water in full sun. After my parents' divorce when I was eleven, exhilarating deep sea fishing off Miami Beach replaced the leisure of rainbow trout fishing in L.A.

"I'd love to. Can I bring Dennis," I asked in my most beguiling, little girl's voice.

"Who?"

"Da-a-ad, my boyfriend, Dennis Robinson," I moaned.

Without skipping a beat, my father spoke his favorite ganster threat.

"If you don't stop whining, I'll give you something to whine about, young lady."

I was contrite, the only way to move in this game.

"Sorry."

"Does he fish?"

That's when I knew I'd won him over.

As Dennis and I descended the escalator to the sidewalk at Miami International, we were smacked in the face with the equivalent of a hot steam bath. September in South Florida was unbearably humid and made me wish I could grow gills.

Dad pulled up to the curb in a brand new, sleek yellow 1966 Cadillac, and popped open the trunk, a cue for Dennis to load our luggage. I gave and received Dad's hugs and kisses as usual, but I was saddened watching the cool handshake he offered to Dennis.

My stepmother, Christine, greeted us in the lobby of the Hotel President Madison. Although it reeked of urine and old clothing, it still had a modicum of tropical colonial style. It was a retirement hotel on the beach side of Collins Avenue, sandwiched between the hip la-la Land of the Fontainebleau and Cadillac Hotels, where I'd been given complimentary admission and a black and white cabana and lounge chairs on the chic and youth-filled beaches when I used to come to Miami on weekends during the year I attended school in Pompano Beach.

"Stow your gear in your rooms," Dad said, handing each of us a key to the two rooms reserved for us.

"Let's meet in our suite after you clean up," he proposed, this time with a broad grin on his weathered face, compliments of his love of golf.

Dennis showered and put on a fresh shirt and slacks. He wanted to make a good impression. I had changed into a white sundress with pink spagetti straps and my pink belt and sandals. My long, dark hair hung down around my shoulders. I looked in the mirror, freshened my pale pink lipstick, and tweaked my cheeks to a complimentary shade of rose.

We rode the elevator to the penthouse, hand in hand.

He knocked on the door.

"Come in, door's open," Chris called out.

"Hope you've got an appetite," she said, peeking out of the kitchen.

"Always," we said in unison, as we entered her domaine.

She gave Dennis a peck on the cheek. I hugged her. Then, I silently tippy-toed over to the dining room, where Dad was already seated at the table reading the newspaper. I kissed him on his bald spot, as always, and sat next to him while Dennis took a seat across the table.

I sideled up to my father.

"I love you Daddy."

He replied in the same mocking way he had ever since I'd hit puberty.

"Cut the bullshit."

I suppose this was his way of managing his role in the complex relationship between Father and daughter. It had taken time to get over my hurt feelings, but by then it was old hat.

Chris was taking longer than usual in the kitchen.I called out to her.

"May I help?"

"No hon, I'll be there faster than a jack rabbit to a lettuce field."

I loved Christine's colorful Oklahoma colloquialisms.

Dad wasn't wasting any time.

"Rumor has it that you two are serious."

Hearing this on our first night, there could be no question that he was leading up to something ominous. Dad was clearly not happy about what he had heard, probably from my rat-sister Carole.

"And, that you two have been living together since Judi moved into that apartment in Sherman Oaks."

This was not a question. Father did not have a smile on his face. No wonder Chris was dawdling around in the kitchen. We were in deep trouble. Dennis was twenty-one and I was seventeen, a minor.

"So this is the deal, either the two of you get married when you get back to California, or Judi stays here and Dennis goes back alone. No ifs, ands, or buts."

I was clear that this was Dad's final and firm ultimatum. He had us in a corner.I was completely dependent on his financial support. And Dennis and I had been sweethearts since we were kids, thirteen and seventeen. Breaking up wasn't hard to do, it was unimaginable.

The next day, Dad was called away at the last minute to a business meeting, and Dennis and I had the time to talk over our decision on the way to and while deep sea fishing, an apt metaphor. I managed to hook a sailfish that day, and after a three hour struggle, I had the fish on deck. The struggle with that catch was nothing compared to the effort it took to ward off all the men onboard, including Dennis, who just wanted to help the poor little girl with the big mean fish at the end of her line. But no one could have guessed that the battle of girl against fish seemed a far sight easier to me than the one I had to face within myself; the one in which I was the fish on the hook.

After he learned the story of my 'catch of the day', Dad was so proud of me, he offered to take the seven foot, six inch, seventy-seven pound fish to the taxidermist. When we told him our decision, to return to L.A. and to be married by the end of the year, he offered to ship the fish there as well.

This was the strangest shot-gun wedding anyone could have imagined. Dennis was over the moon, but I was seventeen, not pregnant, and had some very sensible plans for my academic future. I wasn't sure what would become of those plans once I was married to Dennis, who was not so inclined.

By the time I woke up, I was nearing my twenty-ninth birthday.

All had begun to go dark. In the full-length mirror, I saw myself for the first time in ages, a pretty if overweight woman, hair long, bangs straight and nearly covering my eyes. I was wearing an over-sized sweatshirt turned inside-out, and my rubber boots were pulled up over a pair of too-snug stretch jeans. I looked down-at-the-heels and as scruffy as an old yellow dog as I was headed out to muck the stalls.

I wondered when I had begun to let myself go. I realized that I'd made a point to restrain my reflection in the mirror to a point above my shoulders, applying eye make-up religiously before going out to the barn to feed the horses at six every morning. I became an expert in applying cat eyes, just like Liz Taylor and my sister Carole, who like Taylor, had violet eyes. Although my eyes were blue, I used cosmetics just the way Carole had taught me, before she abandoned me for marrage when I was ten and a half, the day I first began to menstruate.

That night, I looked over at Dennis, sitting next to me on the couch, glued to the television. I suddenly and soundessly questioned everything. What happened to my classical music, poetry, and mystery novels? What happened to pre-med? When will it be my turn? I was as low as a belly-gunner on an armadillo.

"I'll be right back, honey," I said smiling.

I walked down the hallway past the kitchen to the study and slid open a drawer. I glanced over my shoulder before lifting out a catalogue that had been hidden under the bills and checkbooks as if it were porn.

The cover read, "UCLA Extension: It's Never Too Late To Learn."

"Want some coffee and dessert," I called out.

"Great," Dennis bellowed back at me.

His response bought me some time. Paging through the psychology section, I hastily completed the form I'd begun to fill out weeks before. I silently ruminated.

"This is a good start, sixteen units for the Summer. Four basics, just to see if I'm still capable of learning anything serious, and if

Dennis can tolerate the separateness. It'll work out, I'll make it work out."

I felt more sturdy as I signed my name to the form, coaxing it and a check for tuition into the already-stamped envelope. I sealed the flap and stuffed it into my handbag while the coffee dripped into the pot. I cut and plated two pieces of pecan pie, and put both plates and the two mugs on a tray. One read "I love you." The other, "I love you more." Dennis had bought them for me.

"Where are you, babycakes, I miss you," he cried out during the commercial.

"Coming right up," I clucked back, as I poured his favorite brew.

In spite of my deceit, I really did love him, but each year I had begun to feel like another stone had dropped into the glass that held my life. And with each stone, more of me sloshed out of the glass. The glass would soon be dry. Not a drop of me would be left.

The next day, I went to the post office.

A week later, Dennis brought in the mail.

"What's this, Honey?"

"Oh that, it's just . . ."

I snatched the letter from his hands, trying to cover up the UCLA return address. Right away, I thought better of it, and I charged into what seemed like a great gulf between us.

"Den sweetie, I've been wanting to speak with you about this for a while. It just never seemed like the right time, but it's important."

"Well, of course it is baby. Anything that's important to you is important to me."

He sounded sincere. I was relieved.

"You don't know how happy I am to hear you say that, because I also think this is important for both of us. You see I've decided, now that your business is stable and the ranch is under control and we even have some help, and well, you know how much I've wanted to do this ever since I was a kid . . ."

"Do what? I thought all you ever wanted since you were a kid was me," he grinned clutching me to his chest.

I tried to accept his warm lips on mine and ruffled his hair. He was a darling, a pure romantic who made love to me every day. There could never be any worry about another woman where Dennis was concerned. But he just wasn't enough for me, after all.

"Seriously, I've registered for extension classes for the Summer."

"At Moorpark College?"

"No love, at UCLA. I want to try for pre-med. It's time now, can't wait . . ."

Dennis interrupted me with a smirk, half kidding and half enraged.

"Well it will have to wait. For your next life with your next husband,"

"Very funny, but it's no joke. I start in three weeks. The beginning of June."

"The hell you do!"

I tore off my apron and threw it at his feet.

"And why not?"

" 'Cause I say so! That's why not."

He stomped off out of the room.

I went after him and he shoved me away, grabbing me back in less than a heartbeat.

If this was his way of demonstrating his control over me, I didn't appreciate it. He was scowling, eyes bulging, brows first pulled together, then arched high. He startled me when he let go of me, his fists clenched like rocks hung from the ends of his tan and muscular arms.

"Please Den, I'm serious about this. Why on earth are you so set against my going to school ?"

"Because, the next thing you know, you'll be running off with some wise-ass professor-type, that's why."

He was thoroughly convinced that what he fantasized was an inevitable fact.

"Dennis, please don't do this."

I begged with my arms outsretched to embrace him. I knew he was hurt. I had suspected all along that he would be.I tried to reassure him.

89

"I do love you, but I need to be free to pick up where I left off when we were married, not to be free of you."

It seemed to me that he was so wrrapped up in his pre-conceived notions that he couldn't comprehend anything I said or did.

"You wanna go back to your father in Miami? Well, be my guest."

Miami may have been where our marriage began, but it was not where it was going to end.

I'd been bullied one too many times.

CHAPTER 13

IT'S REMARKABLE HOW THINGS sometimes happen serendipi-
tously. What are the odds that two Jewish, 30-year-old undergrads
at UCLA would meet in a course on American History in a make-
shift classroom in the basement of an art deco-inspired Gothic-style
Methodist church in Westwood Village? Probably just as great as the
odds that our history Professor's elderly mother would die a sudden
death, late on the eve of our third class.

Ted and I happened to be sitting at neighboring desks when
the bearer of bad news, a woman who worked for the church,
entered the classroom and made the announcement. She assured
us that Professor Harris would return as early as the next week.
I turned and looked at Ted with a shy smile. I was not throwing
away my shot. I pumped myself up and performed my best Barbra
Streisand impression, complete with my own mother's Brooklyn
accent.

"Just so it won't be a total loss, how about we get a cup of coffee
in the Village?"

Ted was straightforward and encouraging.

"That would be nice."

This was the start of our romance. We walked into Westwood
Village and seated ourselves in a small coffee shop, nearly empty
in the mid-afternoon. We spoke energetically, fueled by mugs of
caffeine, refilled countless times. Ted clued me into his method
of writing a review for those mandatory tomes that neither of us had
any intention of reading. I shared my menthol cigarettes.

We discovered our mutual preference for milk in our coffee and our ardent interest in both psychoanalysis and classical music. There were also vast differences.

Ted was born in Tel-Aviv, several months after independent statehood had been declared in Israel, and during the continuing strife with invading Arab countries. He was an only child in an apartment that housed four generations of both sides of the family and his father's dental clinic. His parents had a mixed marriage. His father was *Sephardic*, his mother *Ashkenazy*.

Ted's hometown was filled with people of almost every European culture. Some had come as Zionists well before WWII. Others, more ethnically Jewish than religious or political, had fled Europe before Hitler could annihilate them. My parents were first generation Americans. Their immigrant parents had come from Romania and Russia to New York on the cusp of the 20th century. I was a baby boomer, conceived in the Fensgate Hotel on Beacon Street in Boston, the home of the then-famed steak and lobster house that featured some of the best jazz in town.

This ten-story brick hotel, in which my parents and two elder sisters Carole and Miriam had lived, was situated between the Charles River and Kenmore Square, a stone's throw from the famous Fenway baseball park. The hotel was one of three in Massachusetts owned and managed by Dad and his army-buddy and partner after WWII, during which Dad had been a flight instructor in the Army Air Corps. When my family moved to California late in the Summer of 1948, my Dad purchased a home in Sherman Oaks, a San Fernando Valley suburb of Los Angeles. I was born a 'Valley Girl' even before the moniker had been coined.

Both Ted's and my hometowns had essentially been desert villages, close to large bodies of water and occupied by influential residents; In Israel the population was noticeably populated by refugee academics, businessmen, composers, financiers, medical professionals, musicians, scholars, scientists and writers. Ted's father, a practicing dentist in Strasbourg, had fled to Palestine when Hitler invaded France. He'd met Ted's mother in Tel-Aviv where her family had immigrated just after World War I. Ted was an only child. My Dad studied law at Fordham University and Mother majored in Latin and Greek at Hunter College when they were newlyweds in New York City. Prior to World War II, my Dad became a Public Defender in Manhattan, where my sisters were born in 1936 and 1939.

The decision to move cross-country from Boston in 1948 was prompted by Mother who had announced that she was pregnant and wanted to live in a warmer climate. This suited my sisters who, as tweens, dreamed of going to Hollywood and tanning on Santa Monica beach. Once I was a little older, my sister Mimi told me about the rumors of another woman in Dad's life when they had lived in Boston.

"She was the cause of our sudden cross-country migration, and the liquidation of Dad's hotel business. He'd asked for a divorce, but when Mother announced her pregnancy in April of 1948, Dad agreed to stay on."

Anyone who could count would have known that, if Mother had already been pregnant with me eleven months before they arrived in Los Angeles, I would have been born a baby elephant. I was the bait Mother used to keep Dad on the hook.

Ted and I had each encountered Freud early in junior high school. His class had been on detention in the faculty library for some teenage misdemeanor, and Ted spent the bulk of his incarceration reading the *Interpretation of Dreams*. I had come across the same title in my neighborhood public library. However, when the right to check out the book had been denied me, due to my impressionable age, I slipped that volume of the *Standard Edition* into my backpack, along with Karen Horney's *Psychology of Women*, and quietly exited the building. All that night and for the next several nights, I read by flashlight with my head under my pillow and a mixture of wonder and juvenile incomprehension. The ensuing week, I returned the books in the same way I had taken them, quietly and without ceremony.

Ted and I savored these comic twists of fate and consoled one another in our shared sense of dismay. At the time, there was no way for non-medical, mental health professionals to train as psychoanalysts in the United States. In American psychoanalytic institutes, medical waivers as they were referred to were the stuff of myth. Training was supposedly available to all, but in the end, not considered legitimate. No certification had ever been granted to a non-medical candidate by the American Psychoanalytical Association, and therefore membership in the International Psycho-Analytical Association was denied.

I also learned that after Ted's military obligation had been fulfilled, he'd taken up a seven-year course of study in Medicine in Bologna, Italy. Why Italy? Because all Jewish mothers wanted their sons to become doctors, and at the time Israel had only one medical school, located in Jerusalem.

The University of Bologna, the oldest in the world, had one of the foremost medical schools in Europe, and was a wise and popular choice. Unfortunately, it seemed clear that the lack of real moral support from his parents, who were dead-set on his becoming an engineer or a dentist, alongside various other distractions eventuated in Ted leaving Bologna sometime during his fourth year of study. Feeling defeated, Ted emigrated to Los Angeles, where he had many good family friends to encourage him and to sponsor his residency. They opened the doors for Ted to find gainful employment teaching in a Temple school, as well as tutoring Hebrew to Westside Jewish kids preparing for their *Bar* and *Bat Mitzvahs.*

At the same time Ted enrolled in those courses in the social sciences that had not been a part of his medical curriculum in Italy, but which were compulsory if he were to obtain a degree that would qualify him for entrance into a graduate school in psychology.

I had been seriously ill and hospitalized with pyelonephritis near the end of the last semester of my senior year in high school. With one day more than the allowable absences, I was not permitted to graduate with my class. Rebellious as always, rather than to redo classes in Summer school, those in which I had already excelled in spite of illness and absences, I dropped out and obtained a General Education Degree that qualified me for university by comprehensive examination.

My impulsive first marriage was not anywhere close to my initial plan for the future. My design had originally included the study of medicine, which I had yearned for ever since my sisters had taken me to see John Huston's film *Freud: The Secret Passion*. That marriage, predicated on puppy love, had led me in an entirely different direction for over thirteen years.

Dennis had returned home from Frankfurt, Germany after three years in the Armored Division stationed next to *Checkpoint Charlie* on the American side of the Berlin Wall. My simultaneous return to California followed a year away boarding in a private college prep-school in Pompano Beach Florida in order to be closer to my Dad. Unfortunately, at the end of that year, I was not invited back in spite of my straight A's.

I had been caught teaching my dorm-mates all about birth control. These girls were mostly from conservative Southern or New England families. After each weekend or holiday break, one or more girls always failed to return to school due to unplanned pregnancies in the years before Roe v. Wade. Grown tired of losing one room-mate after another, I took it upon myself to teach sex education in the dorm, long before it was permitted let alone mandatory in any schools, particularly in the conservative South.

I resigned myself to accomplish my senior year in California, where there was a more sophisticated understanding amongst my peers about the birds and the bees, as well as a certain basic knowledge about where babies come from. When she received my request, Mother was pseudo-apologetic.

"Sorry, but I'm using what used to be your room for other purposes now."

I could guess what this really meant.

Mother was a hoarder.

In my absence, she had filled my room and every other room with all those things she couldn't bear to throw away, such as every stitch she'd ever owned, my sisters' old clothes, everything that had belonged to my father, plus all I had left behind when I'd moved out. On top of that, there were ceiling-high stacks of newspapers and magazines that she couldn't suffer parting with, and my shower was the new depository for her unwashed laundry.

Rejection was also her pay-back for my having left her before I turned sixteen to live closer to my Dad. Now, my only alternative was to move in with my sister Carole and her family in Thousand Oaks, not too far away from Taft High School in Woodland Hills. I bought a 1957 Fiat 1100 for $100 so that I could drive myself to school, but I never could be sure that it would survive the day. Luckily, Dennis, had developed his well-honed mechanical talents in the Army, and would work on it in my sister's driveway every weekend that he was home on leave. He told me that Fiat stands for 'fix it again, Tony'.

There were other breakdowns that he couldn't repair.

Carole was not so happy to have her kid sister in the spare bedroom, especially since she was pregant with her second child. On the other hand, a built-in babysister for her three-year old son and a generous stipend from our father, supposedly for my expenses, turned out to be ample compensation for having to put up with a 16-year old sex-pot who sashayed around her husband in gossamer baby-doll pajamas, while she continued to expand beyond her former Scarlett O'Hara seventeen-inch wasteline.

Unfortunately, Carole was nearing the end of her eighth month when I became ill with severe urinary tract pain and a one-hundred and six degree fever. It was pyelonephritis, a serious kidney infection. To give her full credit, she had attempted to nurse me back to health, even after I returned from the hospital, but we all knew that the hard work and the emotional and physical stress of caring for me had contributed, perhaps alongside her smoking, to the premature birth of her second son, Larry.

I must confess that I never made it easy on Carole to nurse me. In fact, I had always been a veritable monster when I was ill or on the verge of helplessness. I recollect that when I was eleven, not long after both my sisters had married, and Dad had just moved out, I returned home on the last day of school, the eve of Summer vacation, with a high fever, coming down with a mean case of the measles.

I was bedridden for eight weeks.

The day that the doctor was to give the okay for me to leave my room, I was diagnosed with walking pneumonia and sentenced back to bed behind a closed door for what turned into another full month. My only solace was that Mother visited infrequently. All I had were my books and a transister radio to keep me from losing my mind. To be honest, I was so weak, I probably had little capacity to do anything but sleep and to slurp down the bowls of dishwater that Mother called soup.

One day, Mother came into my room. All I can remember is that I was so infuriated by whatever she did or said, that I spewed four-letter words at her as if from a fire hose. Then I threw my radio, aimed straight for her head, at the precise moment when she slammed the door to my room. My beloved music was shattered into pieces. The next day, the doctor released me, just in time for the first day of the new school year. An entire Summertime lost, but not nearly forgotten.

CHAPTER 14

TED AND I WERE EACH MAKING-UP for lost time when we met. Right from the start, I sensed a certain charmed brew bubbling up between us, more like Champagne than coffee. Whatever it was, those four hours we'd spent together that first afternoon in the Village flew by like seagulls soaring over Santa Monica and left me light-headed.

Before parting, wired with adrenaline, caffeine and nicotine, and after immersing ourselves in one another's histories and interests, Ted invited me to join him for a rare concert, a performance of Bach's complete Brandenburg Concerti. The event was to take place that Thursday evening on campus at Royce Hall. I was beyond blithe in my acceptance of Ted's gentle advances.

Ted was a full head taller than I, with nearly black hair just beginning to grey at the temples. His fair, smooth complexion glowed, and his soft hazel-green eyes glistened when he gazed at me. His adorable nose and pinkish lips seemed to beg for kisses. He resembled a cross between Tyrone Power in *The Eddy Duchin Story* and Oskar Werner in *Fahrenheit 451*. He was remarkably sexy, incredibly earnest, with just a touch of tragedy in his life to impart a hint of heroism. The evening was delicious. I was dizzy with joy. I'd dated a few men since my separation from Dennis, but not one had captured me at first sight like Ted had done.

The Bach was sublime, and my escort, a prince charming. Sometime during concerto number three, Ted reached over and took my hand in his. From that moment on, he didn't let go. After the concert, we sat talking about all aspects of the performance. As the hall slowly emptied, we sauntered out of the building. The air was still warm, the beginning of Indian Summer. Ted walked me to my car and, after a shy kiss on the lips as we stood under the stars atop parking structure five, I invited him to dinner at my home for Sunday evening.

The next day, I floated into my therapy session with Diane.

"So how do I know if he's the one? I've had three other dates in the past week."

Diane sat in wait for more.

"How do I tell?

I was genuinely lost and confused.

"Can you imagine how it would be to wake up next to him every morning, to look at him across the breakfast table every day?"

Diane wasn't even Jewish, yet she answered every question with another.

"He's adorable, sexy, bright, tall, and we smoke the same brand."

Diane batted her long, curled sable eye lashes.

"How do I know? He makes my toes tingle," I said, sarcastically.

Diane just smiled her enigmatic therapist's smile.

"I think I'll wait and see how he likes my cooking on Sunday."

Just before Ted's arrival for dinner, I realized that in all our lengthy conversations, I'd neglected to tell him that I had a roommate, a gay man, formerly my psychotherapist before he'd suffered a well-planned depressive breakdown that ushered him into an early retirement.

With admirable integrity and restraint, Dr. Ron Roy had conscientiously ended his work with each of his patients over several months, without so much as a word or sign of his deterioration. Upon my request he'd referred me to his partner Diane and disappeared from my life. Or so I'd thought.

It was just before that year in therapy with Dr. Ron that I had made a clumsy attempt at suicide. During therapy my suppressed desire to go to university to study medicine and eventually psychiatry and psychoanalysis, stifled throughout a dozen years, had gradually re-emerged from the depths into full awareness.

I was further emboldened to pursue my ambitions in therapy with Diane. She was not unlike her ideal character Dominique from *The Fountainhead*; written by Diane's favorite author, Ayn Rand. I later discovered that Diane was an avid romantic and a devout libertarian, with an implacable faith in human potential. She could recognize an individual's capacity for achievement, and she encouraged me to discover my own.

When Dennis became fearful that I would meet and fall in love with some academic white knight who would sweep me up in his arms and take me away on his white horse, I had attempted to mollify his concerns.

"We already have four white horses," I joshed, a lame attempt to lighten him up.

Unfortunately, no amount of jest nor reassurance could quell Den's unshakable fears, and the jealousy and suspicion that were consuming him, as well as my patience. Unwavering in spirit in spite of sundry self-doubts that I continuously fought to push away, I maintained my determination to go full-speed ahead with my plan to attempt two Summer sessions. It was the only way I could think to test the waters of my academic ability, to make sure that my intellect hadn't entirely dried up.

The first day I attended two courses at UCLA, I returned home to find my husband gone. Dennis had packed most of his clothing and left me. This was no whim on his part. He was deadly serious. He had ridden his chestnut gelding to a friend's ranch in nearby Santa Rosa Valley, and had moved into my sister's spare room on that first day.

He hadn't even left a note.

Not long afterward, he was admitted for inpatient psychiatric treatment at Wood View Calabasas Hospital by his psychiatrist. He was having a major psychotic break and didn't utter a word to me after that for nearly two years.

Of course, I was kept in the loop about his condition by my sister. They continued to remain close. Dennis and his psychiatrist kept in touch with her, but it had been nearly a year and he was in stasis.

I told my sister to let him know that he was free to file for divorce, if and when he wanted one. I wouldn't fight him, and I would make sure that he received his half of the proceeds from the sale of the ranch, all of the equipment and vehicles, and the horses, if and when they were sold.

Surely, out of a sense of guilt, I had even offered him all else that we jointly owned, with the exception of a bedroom suite, a sectional couch, my sewing machine and a few small pieces from our equine art collection. Less than a year after Dennis had abandoned me, I was doing very well at UCLA. I'd arranged the sale of our Arabian horse farm, once a part of Joel McCrea's Ranch in the North end of the Conejo Valley. I had offers on all of the mares from the owners of some of the best studs in the country, but I decided to lease them first rather than to sell them, as I was still uncertain that I was ready to give up all that Dennis and I had worked for during most of our marriage, especially all of my beloved horses. They had been the realization of a childhood dream. Such dreams and wishes are rarely outgrown. They may evolve and take on unexpected form, but they never completely vanish. For me, the dream had to do with my passion for all things equine.

When I was six, there was the pony-man, a fellow with a cart drawn by a huge Percheron horse. In tow behind the cart, was a string of at least ten Shetland and Welsh ponies, blacks and bays, dapples and greys. A ride on the back of one of the ponies through the neighborhood was a nickel, and I saved my twenty-five-cent allowance each week to make sure I had enough for a ride or two.

The remainder of the quarter was spent on Nestle's Crunch candy bars. Not only did I love chocolate, but inside each wrapper was a chance to win a pony, which I filled in and sent by mail religiously. One day I received a letter.

Dear Judi Lee, it is our pleasure at Nestle's to inform you that you have won your very own Shetland pony. Please send a letter from your parents to the address below, permitting us to arrange for delivery of *your pony. If you are unable to receive your award, we will be happy to send as a substitute, a check in the amount of $100. Congratulations!*

My mind was going at a gallop as I waited for Mother to return from her shopping. Up the street, just a block away, was an enormous, grassy field where an orange orchard had recently been cleared away. I envisioned tethering my pony to a stake in the middle of this green meadow, bringing him carrots and grain, picking out his hooves, and taking him for a ride every day.

I drew a number of pictures of what I had imagined as a golden dappled palomino with a thick, cream-colored mane and tail that I'd brush before and after each ride. By the time Mother returned, I had written a story to go with the drawings and had bound the pages with yarn in a felt-covered book. I had already named my pony Trigger, the same as Roy Roger's palomino. When I heard Mother's car drive into the garage, I ran to the kitchen door to open it for her.

She came inside and after I told her the whole story, she said, "That's nice."

She then went about her tasks, non plussed by what was an event of a lifetime for me. Daddy sat me down that evening, looked through the book I had made, and smiled. He lovingly put his arms around me, blue eyes twinkling, cheeks red with the effects of the alcohol, and he patiently explained why my plan wouldn't work.

"The field was cleared by a contractor who plans to build houses there, and we really can't afford a place to board a pony," he said, regretfully.

My parents accepted the $100 check, and I was left with a deep hole in my heart that lasted throughout the rest of my childhood and into adulthood. It swelled up from a yearning for a pony into a craving for a full-sized horse of my own. I never expected that fourteen years later, that childhood desire would find fulfillment, patching the hole in my heart until it was once again ripped open a decade later, in an attempt to fulfill yet another juvenile desire.

After midwifing and selling that year's crop of foals, along with the custom built three-horse trailer, two pickup trucks and the Kubota tractor, I found a buyer for the ranch, and I placed it securely in a short escrow. I quickly began my search for a nice used car to get me to and from campus, no matter where I ended up living.

An ad in the L.A. times offered a three-year old BMW at a price I could easily afford if I sold my Oldsmobile diesel sedan. I called the number listed in the ad and made an appointment for 2PM the next day as suggested on the answering machine. I enjoyed the ride through the hilly, green, bohemian terrain of Lake Malibu, a ritzy, rustic residential retreat for mostly Hollywood types, just off Kanan Road in Agoura. I made it up the precarious driveway off Paiute Road and came to a stop on a plateau just barely wide enough to turn my big car around in front of the carport attached to a sprawling ranch-style home surrounded by oak trees, overlooking the lake on one side and the community swimming pool on the other.

A bearded man, in his mid-forties with a slight-if-muscular build, opened the door. He was a real hippy-type with grey blue eyes and faded blue jeans, fashionable tennis shoes and a tight white tee shirt, worn neatly tucked in and displaying his six-pack abs. Immediately, his mouth broadened into a grin. I suddenly recognized who this stranger was. He recognized me too and offered a warm hug.

"Hi, Doctor Ron. So, it's your BMW."

"But it's not for you, Judi. It's a real lemon.

"Oh?"

That's why it was for sale.

"But since you drove all this way, come in and have some coffee or tea."

A bit stunned, I followed Ron inside. The house was all redwood with double hung sash windows, each with true dividing lights separated by wooden strips and partitioning each window into several glass panes. The herringbone parquet floors were buffed to a satin shimmer, the sunlight streaming in from all sides made the whole room glow. All of a sudden, a young and frisky Doberman Pinscher leapt through the screen that had been detached from the bottom and one side of its wooden door frame, clearly for doggy accessibility. Ron knelt down, vigorously hugging and petting the enormous, excited pup until it finally calmed down.

"This is Rommel."

Rommel's docked tail wagged his bottom receptively, and he licked my hands as I reached out to caress his head. We took our coffee outdoors to a large redwood table with benches on either side and adorned with clay pots of what I later found out was marijuana. Ron asked me to tell him all about me. When he'd left his practice, I'd been tending horses and working as a real estate agent, peddling farms and avocado orchards, mainly as tax shelters for the wealthy or retired in Ventura County.

"I'm back to school now, majoring in psycho-bio."

Ron was more than enthused and full of questions, both about me and Dennis. I told him about our separation. Brotherly advice followed, something Ron had abstained from as Dr. Roy. I asked what his life had been like since we had last met, and it was then that he told me about his breakdown and subsequent hospitalization. I almost wished I hadn't asked. Like me, he was separated from his spouse. But this is where our stories diverged in the extreme.

"All my life or nearly all, from age six, I knew I was much more interested in boys and men than in girls or women. In New Hampshire, where I grew up on a farm with my older sister, my younger brother, and our parents, I was spotted right away by a group of older homosexual men. They lured me with kindness into their circle and educated me in the ways of a proper buggery. They referred to each other by women's names and would lovingly call each other bitches. They labelled each other as butches or queens and I learned all the mannerisms of my secret family, the one in which I felt I truly belonged."

Ron smiled.

Now I was curious. He had always seemed so ordinary, so masculine.

"What about your biological family?"

"I was close to my older sister, who had been onto me almost before I knew anything of my proclivities. But I resented my big-bear of a little-brother, and I held my mother in contempt for failing to intervene on my behalf when my sadistic, sociopath of a father called me a sissy and tortured me. He tried to make a man of me by setting me down on the dirt in the barnyard, forcing me to watch as he murdered new-born kittens by pitching them at a very large boulder."

Ron's chin trembled and his nose reddened, as tears formed at the outer margins and glazed over the surfaces of his grey-blue eyes before having the chance to fall.

"I left them as soon as I was out of high school. I went as far away as I could and landed in pre-med and then in med-school at UCLA. I had many loves in L.A. and Frisco and finally settled down after my psychiatric residency with a famous hairdresser I'd met at a party. I showered Alan with lavish gifts and invited him to live with me in my home, half-way between his salon in Encino and my work at UCLA in Westwood. Later, I joined the private group practice with Hamlin and Diane in Thousand Oaks."

"So, was Alan the one?"

"No. We broke-up after a couple of years. He was young and promiscuous, and I was old-fashioned and serious and wanted a long-term relationship. But we remained friends and he introduced me to a woman. She was beautiful, bright and young, if uneducated. There was something about her, or maybe it was the marijuana. In any case, I fell madly in love with her and the sex was something I had never imagined with a woman. I loved her and I thought that she loved me too. So, she moved in."

I was stunned silent. Who would have guessed?

"Then, she stole all my cash and ran up huge bills on my credit cards. Nevertheless, I still married her, thinking that it was just her insecurity, but it soon became clear that she was a drug addict."

Ron admitted this, with his head down and between his hands.

"Amphetamines, cocaine, morphine, pot, tranquilizers, anything she could get her hands on. She nearly ruined me financially, and then one day, she was just gone. Just like that."

Since I too knew something about abandonment, I felt for him.

"I've filed for divorce, it's in process. Thank God, she's not fighting it because I gave her a generous settlement. More than any court would have imposed."

"You still care for her," I hazarded a guess.

"Yes. Very much so. She's the love of my life. And most likely a major contributing factor in my breakdown."

From that day on, Ron and I became the best of friends. I realized, shortly after our reunion, that I had to get going and find a place to live with my Australian shepherd Delilah and my tabby cat Tiger Lilly. Ron offered to rent me half the house for a song. The place was perfect. I would still have the country atmosphere but was closer to school, and I really needed not just a roommate, but a mentor and companion.

The in-suite bath was an old-fashioned-pink-tiled dream, and the large wood-paneled bedroom with tall open-beamed ceilings accommodated my Paul Bunyan king-sized, maple wood four-poster bed, complete with its enormous dresser and its tall hutch on top. The twin lamp tables on either side of the bed also provided drawers for storage, and when the lid was closed on the maple cabinet that housed my sewing machine, it made a perfect desk with ample drawers down one side for paper, pens, pencils, a stapler and other necessary items for my studies.

The wall of windows, looking out onto the woods and the flowering vines made everything feel cheerful and homey. Ron even installed a phone line for me with a separate number all my own. Because I hadn't dated since the sixties, I didn't have a clue about being single in the eighties. So, Ron began my social education. He took me dancing on the weekends at gay bars, so that I could become acclimated to the times, without feeling threatened. I would chauffeur us in my brand-new BMW, just in case he chose to go home with someone afterward.

106

When I'd return home from school in the late evenings during the week, he'd have tuna-salad sandwiches and freshly baked cookies waiting for me on the kitchen table. I'm not exaggerating when I say that he was the best mother I'd ever had. The best big sister too. Although Mimi and Carole had instructed me in the arts of cooking and sewing, Ron taught me how to flirt and how to be safe while having conversations with men at straight hangouts.

"No dancing. Just talking over a single glass of wine and be sure to go home alone at least until you've got your bearings."

One of the best things about our friendship, we weren't competition for each other. Just best buddies. He introduced me to his former lover, who cut my big-hair into a new, chic, shag style. I lost all the weight I'd gained since I was seventeen, and I became buff by swimming the icy waters of the huge unheated community pool across the street from our house, even in Winter in below freezing temperatures.

Every morning at six, I'd pull on my tank suit as I got out of bed, and Ron would hand me a cup of coffee as I walked out the door with a big terry towel, my eyes half closed. When I returned, wrapped in the towel, he'd have breakfast ready and we'd talk about his date or my adventures at school or at O'Hannigan's, a straight bar where I'd stop on my way home on Thursday nights, flirting innocently with men who struck up conversations with me.

My life felt fulfilling, uncomplicated, safe and serene, like living in grandmother's house in the woods with no wolves.

And I felt pretty again.

And then, I met Ted.

CHAPTER 15

WHAT TED HAD FAILED TO TELL ME when I invited him for dinner was that his least favorite food was steak. I wanted to kick myself for not having inquired. Luckily, in spite of my awkward and potentially disastrous omission, Ted actually seemed to enjoy meeting and chatting with my roommate, who was on his way out to go dancing. He had brought a lovely *Borolo* wine, the best choice for my rare filet mignon, grilled to perfection and accompanied by Lyonnaise potatoes and my irresistible Caesar salad. The meal was topped off with a home-baked chocolate cake, and Ted relished all.

Clearly it's true that the way to man's heart is through his stomach. Unlike on our first date, Ted's goodnight kiss at the door was anything but shy. Once I could collect myself from his magnetic embrace long enough to utter a few words, I asked a very forward question with my arms still around his neck and his around my waist.

"Are you sure you have to go home?"

He shook his head no and kissed me deeply, again and again, as I stood on tingling tippy toes. I took his hand and led him into my room. We ended by spending that night and nearly every night thereafter together, either at his apartment in West Hollywood or at my place in Malibu Lake. As for my housemate Ron, he and Ted became fast friends over time and Ted became accustomed to Tiger and DeeDee, who slept with us at the end of the bed and had adored him from that first sleepover.

During the December school break, Ted and I planned our first trip together. The entire month of December was free, and Ron agreed to mind the pets while we were gone. This trip was to be my introduction to Ted's parents. I abided by Diane's recommendation to travel with him in order to ascertain if it would be wise for us to consider cohabitation.

Our visit to the Holy Land to meet Ted's parents and cousins, aunts and uncles and assorted friends of the family would be followed by a four-day stopover in Paris, where many of Ted's French paternal relatives lived. By the time we left for Israel, Ted had proposed marriage, which happened in the most unexpected, unique and utterly romantic way.

I had made appointments at my dentist in Thousand Oaks for the two of us. One of my mares had just given birth on the previous night, and we had planned to visit Dr. Fineman on our way to the Gainey Arabian Stud Farm in Santa Ynez to see my mare and her newborn foal. While at Fineman's office in separate rooms, he asked each of us the same question.

"When's the wedding date?"

Caught off guard, we had each admitted that we weren't yet engaged.

"So, what are you waiting for," Fineman inquired.

I wanted to say that it was none of his business. but being a blatant busybody and a hopeless matchmaker is a congenital-if-benevolent quality in most Jews. After we left his office, we shared our common experiences with the good doctor.

He's right, what are we waiting for, I silently wondered.

At first, we were both hushed as we drove down the freeway. After just a few minutes we simultaneously burst out in peals of laughter. We talked and reveled in classical music on the radio. I snuggled close to Ted while he drove his Chrysler Cordoba sedan with the bench seat, his right arm around my waist and my left hand hanging seductively where it had no business being when he was behind the wheel of a moving vehicle. By the time we reached Santa Barbara, we were both more than just in the mood for love.

Turning onto the snaky San Marcos Pass, reveling in the ardent strains of Rachmaninoff, we dropped down into the Santa Ynez Valley at Lake Cachuma. Spontaneously, Ted pulled over onto the shoulder of the road across from the lake and kissed me passionately.

He spoke the three magic words.

"Come with me."

We exited the car, and he pulled a blanket from the trunk with one hand. With the other hand he held mine, and we walked down the embankment to a spot between two coastal live oak trees. The ground, surrounded by dashes of wild currents and gooseberries, was made soft and clean with freshly fallen foliage. He spread the blanket and we made uninhibited love within nature's sanctuary.

Afterward, Ted proposed to me.

Ron happily accepted Ted's invitation to be best man at our wedding when it became clear that being my matron of honor was out of the question. Diane had already been promised that title, since she and I had become fast friends after the end of my therapy. The decision to terminate had been made mutually during one session when we were both laughing.

"Sometimes I think we'd have more fun doing lunch than sitting here giggling in my office. Especially since you seem to feel that you're on the right track now."

I agreed and we set a date for the ending, just before Ted and I left for Israel and France. I was somewhat apprehensive. I 'd never really left the States before, unless you can count a family trip to the Canadian side of Niagara Falls that I was way too young to remember, or a Summer vacation in Mexico City at the age of thirteen with my recently divorced mother who found pleasure in using me for bait in order to procure male attention. Not a good experience, a version of *Suddenly Last Summer*.

Now at nearly thirty-one, I was utterly unprepared for the experience of being an outlander, although initially feeling beyond excited by the prospect of a cross-Atlantic voyage with the man of my dreams. Paris clinched the deal. Our stay in Israel was all but a blur of people, receptions, and dinner tables in Ted's parents' and his Aunt Mathy's homes. The conversations were a towering babble of countless foreign languages exchanged between dinner guests, from Hebrew to French, Italian to Yiddish, Bulgarian to German, and even Ladino, an ancient dialect of Spanish spoken by the Jews in Spain before their expulsion, along with the Moors, by Ferdinand and Isabella in 1492.

There was also an occasional question addressed directly to me in English, usually from someone with a smile, inquiring about when I was going to learn Hebrew.

Ted was a *weisenheimer*.

"As soon as she has finished her studies in Mandarin Chinese."

Ted's parents, Hannah and Leon, approved of me even though I didn't speak anything but English. Perhaps to put me at ease, they even recounted an adorable tale of their first meeting, and the fact that to begin with, the only language they had in common was English.

After a tearful goodbye, with countless hugs and kisses exchanged at the airport in Israel as well as an astonishing security procedure that could make a girl blush, Ted and I were off to France. In Paris we were greeted by his cousins Cathy and Jean, who settled us into a spare studio apartment belonging to Cathy's parents, Uncle Henri and Aunt Joya.

"Dinner is at eight on the *7éme étage*."

Jean was smiling as he handed Ted the keys. He was born in France of Greek parents and had been educated in London. Thankfully, he spoke excellent English. Our studio apartment was small and sweet, facing a lovely garden court, but I was utterly stunned that evening as we entered the home of Henri and Joya. Their double *sejour* had four pairs of stately French doors, each pair opening onto its own ornate, black wrought-iron balcony. The way close-up and breathtaking view of the *Tour Eiffel* absolutely dumbfounded me.

Their spacious dining table in the adjacent *salle manger* was set with the most exquisite antique porcelain dinnerware, all arranged quite formally upon a centuries-old lace tablecloth with silver place settings, each with countless pieces whose utility I could only imagine. Two elegant sterling candelabras circa 1800 stood in the center of the table.

Aunt Joya was an elegant woman in her sixties. She wore her long black hair in a chignon that agreed with her black silk sheath. She sat at the head of the table, across from her husband Henri, presiding over his carving of the *Canard à l'Orange*, with all the trimmings. Everyone conversed in French, a spellbinding, musical language. Ted brushed his lips against my ear, as he translated every word throughout the conversations between older and younger generations, an even dozen guests in all.

After dinner cousin Jacqueline's English-speaking husband Jean-Paul joined us on the balcony for a cigarette. I felt I could reach out and touch the tower. He pointed out innumerable illuminated monuments. The farthest away to the North was the *Sacré-Cœur* atop *Montmartre*. It glowed an eye-catching immaculate white, appearing deceptively nearby.

There were so many other notable landmarks that I couldn't keep track of them all. I was in a deafening state of awe; Jean-Paul's words of description escaped his lips and flew straight in one of my ears, dissipating at the neuronal level *sans* connection. All sparkled before my eyes in the crisp wintery air. Nearly every tree and building were decorated for *Noël*.

After dinner, coffee was served in the living room in tiny cups, no cream. It tasted bitter, but when in France, follow the herd. Afterward, Jean and Cathy offered to take us for a ride around the city. We gleefully accepted their invitation. Our jet-lag was hardly noticeable. It was late in the evening and the traffic was light. Snow had just begun to fall softly in playful flurries created by the gentlest of breezes.

I was dizzy with the sights as we rounded the *Arche de Triumph* and crossed the River Seine on the luxurious *Pont Alexander III*. We navigated back and forth across the river over various other bridges until well past midnight, driving by several monument we'd seen from the Alcalay's balcony just an hour before.

Back in our studio apartment, after our *magical mystery tour*, Ted and I made love and talked until four in the morning, falling asleep to Jacques Brel as he sang *Ne Me Quitte Pas* on the radio. I was crazy about this man and his family. Ted was already an essential part of my life. At the same time, I felt uncomfortably like an infant in the presence of all of these refined strangers, unable to understand anyone around me, and completely incapable of making myself understood. Worst of all, I was utterly dependent upon one single person, whom I had known for just four fleeting months.

All of this might not have happened if it weren't for Dr. Fineman, who chose to undertake far more than his professional duties. Was this a dream come true or a nightmare? Was this going to be yet another and more subtle version of my first shotgun wedding? If things didn't work out, could I sue Fineman for mal-practice?

Upon returning to Los Angeles, there wasn't a dissenting word from anyone when Ted and I announced our engagement. I felt upheld in my decision to take this man to be my second husband, for better or for worse. Thirty-four years later in Paris, the driver of the SUV bid us *au revoir*, as Élie began our fifty-cent tour of our provisional residence. I was in a semi-state of shock. We'd actually pulled it off. For the first time, we didn't have return tickets to the States. We were taking up permanent residence in the most beautiful place in the world.

CHAPTER 16

"I'M SORRY. Beatrice could not be here to greet you because it was getting late and she was to leave on holiday. So, I offered to take her place. She will be absent until Tuesday next," Élie explained.

We learned that Beatrice was the personal assistant to our landlady, Kirat. But who was Élie?

"I've taken the liberty of picking up a few things I thought you might need. I was certain you would not wish to go out tonight."

Amongst the items Élie had thought we might need was a plastic kitty-litter box, a bag of litter, and three pouches of moist cat food. He'd brought us a variety of cheeses wrapped in white paper and labeled from the local *fromagerie*, a bag of mixed greens, a package of sliced prosciutto from *la boucherie*, a half-dozen brown eggs from a French chicken, and a bottle of *Veuve Clicquot* Champagne, which happened to be Ted's favorite.

There were also two zero cokes, a carton of orange juice, and a plastic bottle of milk. Topping off his list was a quarter-kilo of butter, and a tiny pot of raspberry confiture to accompany the fresh baguette and the four croissants for our morning breakfast. On the table was a basket of fresh fruit, and a good bottle of *Malbec Bordeaux* wine the color of rubies.

Quel service!

While Élie and Ted talked copy machine, electrical outlets, operating instructions for the washer and dryer, stereo, scanner, thermostats, TV's, and both internet and cable TV passwords, I discretely opened Ziggy's 'luggage'. The taped-up box contained his hooded *toilette*, organic scent-free hypo-allergenic litter to ward off his asthma, K/D kibble to coddle his sensitive kidneys, and his electric water fountain complete with a converter-adaptor plug. I'd set up everything *trés propre*, his food and water in the kitchen, the cat-box just over the threshold of the door into the bathroom, and Ziggy's toys sprinkled like breadcrumbs between the two spaces.

Only then in the kitchen did I unzip Ziggy's carrier. He gingerly stepped out of his safehouse. He had seen and smelled every one of his belongings. As anticipated, he first made a beeline for his litter-box. Thoroughly relieved, Ziggy rapidly turned back to the kitchen, lapped up *beaucoup d'eau* from his fountain, munched his special food with zest, and proceeded with the most essential task, reconnoitering the entire apartment until he found just the right place with the softest couch in which to curl up for the night.

I relaxed once Ziggy's purring and snoring resumed its familiar and soothing signal. All was well. He had rapidly made himself at home. He had made the journey with flying colors with all systems operating. If only we could adapt as easily. My feet and ankles were quite swollen. After the chaos of our initial arrival, my eyes gradually began to scan the details of the scene. The apartment was almost exactly as represented. The living room had two cream colored, overstuffed couches with two ottomans to match. A coffee table in between was adorned with a vase of fresh flowers.

A large black marble table and six lacquered wooden chairs furnished the dining area. Assorted carved and artfully painted *Qing Dynasty* occasional tables and chests were usefully placed, here and there. Ornate ceramic vases, lamps and jars, ashtrays, bowls and statuettes decorated the tables and filled in the spaces between the books in the built-in bookshelves that ran across one wall. The radiators had been discretely encased behind filigreed doors.

A simple black lacquered headboard and frame supported a king-sized bed that felt comfortable, and there was a large matching armoire on one wall, and two squat, black chests of drawers placed below the windows that would light up this surprisingly large boudoir.

A black enameled buffet and hutch provided ample storage on the wall in the *cuisine* across from the kitchen cabinets, dishwasher, sink and stove. There was also a small breakfast table with four chairs situated in front of another pair of tall windows.

The fact that the room was painted a ghastly shade of mustard, and the brick red tile floor was cracked in more than a few places, was a minor shortcoming. The kitchen was not decorated to our taste, but it was quite roomy, well outfitted and utilitarian.

The remainder of the apartment was painted in shades of cream, soft dusty rose or sage green and adorned by copies of Italianate religious oil paintings, each framed in fake gold leaf. The ceilings were eggshell white, and the draperies and sheers matched each ensemble and complimented the décor in both color and pattern. Large Indian and Chinese carpets added warmth to all but the kitchen and bathroom, drawing attention away from the parquet floors which, although clean and shiny, were badly in need of restoration. The creaking sounds they made as I walked barefooted added percussive accents to the energetic atmosphere that seeped in through the windows that opened onto our street full of cafes, restaurants and bars, often open late into night. The apartment had seen better days, but it was still beautiful in my eyes. The area was alluring and sandwiched between some eye-popping historic sites.

I returned my attention to the happenings inside the apartment. Élie was still in conversation with Ted in the living room, in French, of course. I noticed that our benefactor's hair was a bit shaggy, in contrast to the appearance of his trendy designer suit and the mandatory silk scarf worn by French men and women in cool weather. Élie was a patrician figure with a slight hint of a foreign accent beneath the formal British English in which he spoke with me. Ted's well-groomed silvery hair and his rosy complexion contrasted with the casual black travel vest and jeans that he'd worn on our long trip. His eloquent and literary pronunciation of the native tongue in our new city distinguished him from his partner in conversation. My husband, as always, made me proud.

As I wandered from room to room, what I saw was, without a doubt, a weary version of the apartment pictured in the photos on the internet. Nevertheless, I was not disappointed in the least. The three of us had made it to Paris, the apartment promised to be comfortable, Ziggy had given his sign of approval, and this was all that really mattered to me.

At the door, Élie turned.

"I suppose tomorrow morning, you will want to unpack and to get settled in a bit. However, if you wish I will check in with you by phone just to see if there is anything you need, any problem with the flat, if that will not create undue pressure. Around eleven in the morning?"

We both nodded in agreement, said *bonne soirée* to our new patron, and closed the door in a fog. I pinched myself. Hard.

After a light supper with some much-needed wine, we opened up our luggage in the large spare room, contiguous to the vestibule at the entrance and adjacent to the double *sejour*. Our bedroom was next door and in line with the long and surprisingly well-equipped bathroom, which was just as it had appeared in the photos. The flat was convenient for two people and one cat and could even accommodate a guest in the spare room. Fully appointed if slightly tatty around the edges, in Los Angeles it would be called shabby chic.

We finally fell into our comfy bed around one in the morning and slept soundly until nine. When we woke up, we cuddled a bit with Ziggy, who was un-customarily squeezed in between the two of us, purring. After breakfast, we finished unpacking and decided to postpone the three appointments I'd made to see apartments that day before we had left the States. These had been arranged in keeping with my initial good intentions to hit the ground running, which proved to be an entirely unrealistic goal.

Instead, we organized the apartment with Ziggy tracking us here and there between catnaps. We discovered oodles of space for everything. There were roomy wardrobes for clothing and shoes, a large linen closet filled with clean towels, extra sheets, tablecloths and *serviettes*, and secret storage places wedged in between walls that would serve as out of sight depositories for our emptied luggage.

I answered the phone when Élie called as promised, eleven on the dot. He asked if we needed anything.

"There are a couple of things. There seems to be a leak under the kitchen sink. I found some water in a pot I pulled out this morning to make breakfast, and I felt the pipe above. It was moist. You might want to call a plumber before it gets any worse. Also, the landline handsets don't seem to hold a charge. We could use some batteries if available."

"No worries. I can be there in a few minutes. We live practically next door."

"That's great," I chirped.

A few minutes later, we heard the doorbell.

I opened the door and there was Élie, dressed in yet another elite Italian *costume*, this one, a silver-grey silken Glenn check pattern with a matching waistcoat.

He pecked me on both cheeks, *les bises* as they call it in France, and he went straightaway to the telephones. Once he'd replaced the batteries, Élie headed for the kitchen with a certain fervor, both in his action and in his voice.

"Now let us see about that leak."

"At least let me get a towel for you to lie on."

Élie cheerfully replied, just before plunging his head under the sink.

"No trouble, I assure you."

"Okay."

I was amazed when Élie emerged from the cabinet three minutes later declaring victory.

"That should do. *Alors,* would you like me to show you two around the *quartier*, is there anything you need?"

Ted and I glanced at each other and pronounced "yes, *merci*" with enthusiasm.

"In that case, let's meet outside in an hour. Will that give you enough time?"

"*C'est parfait.*"

Ted grinned as he walked Élie to the door.

"Can you believe that?"

"What? Fixing the plumbing in a bazillion euro designer suit, or offering to be our guide to the neighborhood?"

Ted planted a wonderful wet kiss on my mouth.

"Both, Dear."

In an hour, Élie was waiting for us outside the front door of the building.

"*Bonjour*," Ted said.

"*Bonjour. Alors*, we must begin with what you need!"

We needed to mail our OFII forms. These were the all-important forms that had to be filed by mail within 72-hours of our arrival to the French Office of Immigration and Integration. This act would begin the process of or transition from tourists to immigrants on the way toward acquiring legal residency, the *Titre de Sejour*.

"*D'accord, La Poste* is very near here. I will gladly show you the way."

Élie strolled off at a long-legged pace. We followed on the narrow sidewalks that rarely had space for two abreast, let alone three. We entered the spacious *Place Vendome* where we stopped while Élie spoke.

"As you may know, this column was the most important symbol of Paris throughout the 19th century, upon which each government attempted to leave its mark. Its checkered history was that of 19th-century France itself. In the first half of the century, a decree ordered the erection of a column dedicated to the heroes of each department in France. The obelisk, originally was meant to be decorated with 108 friezes, one for each department, was topped off with a statue of Charlemagne. In 1805, one day after the battle of Austerlitz, it was proposed that the column be dedicated to the *Grande Armée* of Napoleon."

It suddenly seemed that our guide was taking his duties very seriously, continuing his tour in a way we had never expected.

"This was constructed by melting down 1,200 artillery pieces, seized from the Russians and the Austrians and was cast in bronze on an eight-hundred and thirty-foot *bas* relief frieze, representing that memorable military campaign."

I remembered reading somewhere that a team of sculptors had been commissioned to execute the frieze, which was forty-two meters tall and was topped off with a statue of the Emperor Napoleon in Roman dress. Apparently, that statue of Napoleon had been taken down by the Allies in 1814 and was replaced sometime during the Restoration by a flag bearing the *fleur de lys*. Under the July Monarchy, the flag was replaced with a statue depicting Napoleon as a 'Little Corporal', until the original statue was finally hoisted back atop the column, and the 'Little Corporal' was sent to reside in *Les Invalide*, where Napoleon had been laid to rest in grand fashion under its golden dome, the tallest one in Paris.

Élie added a coda.

"Although it was dismantled during the Commune at the instigation of Gustave Courbet, the Vendôme column was restored once again in 1873,"

Ted inserted a few words, demonstrating his literary bent.

"And Balzac was quoted to have said that the city of Paris has a great mast, made entirely of bronze, with sculpted Victories and Napoleon as its lookout".

Up until that moment, I'd never had any serious investment whatsoever in the subject of history. My previous disinterest was about to be forever replaced with pure fascination. Now we'd be living in history.

We turned onto the *Boulevard des Capucines* where we found the *Bureau de La Poste* within a stone's throw of the *Palais Garnier* where Ted and I, along with Diane and her husband, had attended the Nutcracker Ballet on Christmas day of 1982, during our honeymoon. It was a Christmas day I would never forget.

Élie took us inside *La Poste* and instructed us in the use of the French machines. He even weighed each envelope for us and stamped them accordingly.

"Now we shall go to the *Monoprix*, the supermarket in this

neighborhood on the *Boulevard d'Opera*. You will need to buy some things, as do I."

Once again, Élie took the reins in hand. After demonstrating the ins and outs of shopping the sales, which were mostly the items stacked at the ends of each aisle, he took us to a special counter where he helped us apply for a loyalty card. Next, he showed us to a podium at the back of the store, where a man stood ready to swipe our loyalty cards and to accept our shopping carts for processing. No waiting to check out, and delivery was *gratuit!* I thought we were in heaven when we left, hands free, confident that between one to three hours later, our groceries would arrive at our apartment. Only then would the deliveryman request payment by check or credit card. No tipping allowed.

These were all things about which we had previously known absolutely nothing, in spite of the many years that we'd stayed in Paris for weeks and sometimes even a month at a time. Living in Paris, we were about to discover was, for better or worse, nothing like being a tourist in Paris.

We had just enough time for a *café*, before walking back to the apartment. We coincidentally sat on the sidewalk terrace of the same restaurant where we had dined in an elegant upstairs room on Christmas day after the ballet on our honeymoon trip. Neither of us recalled reading the part of the lease that stated that the apartment came with a thoughtful and astute escort.

"Kirat tells me that you are looking for a flat, a permanent residence."

"Yes, we begin our hunt tomorrow," Ted answered.

"And what precisely are you hunting for, what are your expectations?"

"We'll need two bedrooms, at least 100 square meters, a cook's kitchen with an eating area. At least one and a half baths, preferably an older building with classical moldings and high ceilings, maybe a balcony or a terrace, a good street, and of course a basement. Oh, and a formal dining room, too," I added to my lengthy list.

"We like to entertain. And air conditioning," Ted spoke emphatically.

Élie repeated Ted's last words, a touch of concern in his voice.

"In France we call it *climatisation*. *Bon*, you must be careful not to stir up too much envy in your co-proprietors if you have air conditioning installed. Some people have never gotten over the revolution."

Élie was half smiling.

"It may not be wise to give anyone a clue to your comparative wealth. Some of my ancestors lost their heads over this matter."

He no longer was smiling.

"*Addition*," Ted signaled out waiter, squiggling with thumb and forefinger in mid-air.

My thoughts wandered off on the word envy. I had the unfortunate opportunity to learn all about that term all too early in my career. I discovered that it was not only an essential psychoanalytic concept, dealt with at great length in our study of the works of Melanie Klein and her followers in London, but it was also an experience to be reckoned with throughout my career.

On the evening when I presented my graduation paper to the psychoanalytic society and was awarded my certification, it was duly noted by the Chair of the committee who introduced me that the paper I was about to read had been accepted for publication by *The International Journal of the Psycho-Analysis*.

After that publication and others were released from 1991 onward, I was told by several friends that I had become the topic of envious slights by many of my senior colleagues, none of whom had been published in that prestigious journal, and not for lack of trying. One elder female colleague, who always joined with the senior male analysts in couch canyon for lunch, gave me full warning that nearly all they could talk about were my papers, published with regularity, one year after another. These conversations were apparently laced with derogatory comments about the 'fictional quality' of my clinical work.

I'd been advised early on that sticks and stones can break my bones, but words can never harm me. Sadly, I had to learn the hard way that this was untrue within the analytic community. I not only felt terribly bruised, but if I had not become so well-known as a result of the continuing publication of my work, my career would have ended before it even had a chance to begin, and we wouldn't be here in Paris.

For many years, none of the referrals sent my way came from local sources. And by association, Ted also eventually became a target of falsehoods spread in bad faith. I had hoped that retirement, and our relative anonymity, might put an end to such painful encounters.

Ted paid the check and left two euro on the table.

"*Bon*," Élie said, staring at Ted's head while we began to walk home.

"You will no doubt be needing someone to cut your hair in the weeks ahead. Allow me introduce you to my *coiffeur*."

Élie motioned us to turn left rather than right toward our building. We followed him half-way down the block into a *petit*, up-scale salon called *Le Sens du Cheveu*, where we were greeted by Eric. He was the owner of the salon and Élie's personal stylist. They exchanged *les bises*, as is the friendly French custom with men as well as with women.

The salon was softly lit, with a fresh floral arrangement in demure shades of soft pink, sea green and ecru to salute Eric's clients. The atmosphere was unusually tranquil. A resonant refrain of a Bach solo cello sonata pulsed the air, pure perfection in both humidity and temperature. Cell phones were expected to be silenced. It stood in stark contrast to the beauty salons in Beverly Hills, where scads of stylists frenetically flitted about to the tune of loud rock and heavy metal music. Some shouted "chemicals, chemicals," and all gossiped about movie stars who'd recently undergone major make-overs.

At Eric's, a woman in the process of having her hair cut, wordlessly implied that Eric also styled women's hair. Ted and I both took his card upon leaving, promising to call for our first appointments soon.

"Is there anything else I can help you with," Élie asked, a few meters away from our building,

"Well, I have a problem. My navy blazer was mistakenly swept up by the movers in their enthusiasm while packing our home for storage in Los Angeles, and of course I packed only the ties that went with that blazer, nothing for the brown sport coat that I also brought to hold me through this next six months," Ted explained.

"As it happens, my youngest cousin, Philippe, is having a big celebration Friday afternoon to mark his success in passing the Bar. It's taking place at the *Cerce des l'Union Interallée*. His father is a member. I'm certain I'll need a tie in order to attend. Can you recommend a nearby shop where I can purchase one?"

Élie chuckled, and with a bow he opened a door just two steps on, herding us into the small but fashionable men's boutique on the ground floor of our building. Inside was a tall, lanky and jovial fellow with a stylish mustache. He was on his feet instantly, greeting Élie with an enthusiastic bonjour, and introducing himself to us.

"I am Christophe, how may I help you?"

The three of us looked around until Ted found exactly the right tie: a lovely woolen woven model that seemed to fit the bill precisely. After the tie was carefully wrapped and paid for, and the usual mannerly *merci, je vous en prie and avec plasir* had been exchanged, we said *à bientôt* and were good to go.

Arriving at our port, Élie turned, with an emphatic statement.

"Now, you be sure to tell me if you need anything else. We are just two doors down."

He handed Ted his card, we thanked him for the lovely and helpful afternoon, and went up to our apartment, Ted by wooden staircase, me in the mechanical coffin.

"He's really thoughtful," I said as we passed through our doorway.

"We should've asked him if he would join us for dinner one evening or perhaps for lunch. I wonder who he is. I mean, what his connection is with Madame Young. Perhaps he's her boy toy," I added impishly.

"I don't think so."

Ted looked quite serious as he examined Élie's card and spoke with reverence.

"He must be her partner. The card says that he is Élie *Marquis de Dampierre.*"

The card also listed several email addresses in Athens, Bangkok, Bombay, Hong Kong, London, New York and a mobile number in Paris. He surely got around. I was amused.

"No kidding, the *Marquis* fixed our plumbing?"

Inside the apartment, I took out my cell phone to Google the *Marquis.* Strewn all over the society pages was our landlady, Kirat Bhinder-Young and her escort, Élie Marquis de Dampierre.

"Evidently, our plumber is a very special Frenchman."

Élie had been so kindly, generous and unassuming, with the exception of his handsome wardrobe. We were bowled over. From the long history we'd read of the Dampierre family, it became clear that many of his ancestors had indeed lost their heads over the revolution, just as he'd indicated.

As for his *dame,* Kirat, not only had she been discovered by Yves Saint Laurent, but she'd also been a favorite of *Karl Lagerfeld, Oscar de Laurentis, Valentino, Versace,* and *Chanel.* She'd been a nineteen-year-old fashion student when she landed her first gig with *YSL,* one that any model would give her eyeteeth for, and quite possibly would even have thrown in her lash extensions, for good measure. In retirement, her exclusive and exotic jewelry designs were clearly sought after by affluent women all over the world.

This couple were true celebrities, jetsetters and socialites.

CHAPTER 17

TED AND I WERE BLESSED WITH a few good friends. Lana, a gregarious and slightly younger blond born in Riga, visited Paris the previous Fall after traveling to Latvia to see her elderly mother. She was caring and curious enough to pass by the apartment, to explore the quarter, and to find the farmer's market nearest our apartment. She reported that the *Marché du St. Honoré*, open from 2-8 on Wednesdays and 8-2 on Saturdays, was an easy 10-minute walk from our place. We'd have plenty of time to visit this Parisian institution later that afternoon.

We checked in with Ziggy to make sure he didn't feel abandoned and I rang up the various realtors called *Immobiliére* with whom I had connected by email over the past year. I wanted to confirm our Thursday appointments to visit five apartments. I had organized these *rendez-vous* two weeks before leaving the States, so I was dismayed to hear one agent after another exclaiming *desolé*, sorry. Our previously confirmed appointments would have to be re-scheduled. With the two holidays, nearly all sellers and agents were out of Paris through Tuesday as Monday was the celebration of VE-Day, the anniversary of Europe's declaration of victory, that had ended WWII.

Holidays in France tended to blend into one another, creating frequent vacations that Americans could only dream of. Now I was beginning to understand when Ted described the Italians as a people who work between a strike and a holiday. France and Italy were very close in this respect as well as geographically.

In our endeavor to begin flat-hunting, we found only one exception to this rule. Eduard, aka, ambitious, tall, dark, handsome and young, was an assistant to one *immobilier* and offered to show us an apartment we'd previewed online. The owner of the property, also out of town, had left a set of keys with the guardians of the building, who were remaining in Paris for the holidays.

I had mixed emotions about the good news. This one flat, above all others, had looked extremely attractive in each of the twenty-five photos displayed in color on the website. We both had gawked at it with high hopes for weeks before we left L.A., although we were fairly certain it would be sold before our arrival in Paris. Either that, or it couldn't be quite as lovely, well-located and well-priced as it had appeared to be on the internet.

In case it was still available, there was also some reluctance on our part to visit it on day one, before we had seen any others. If it appeared to be the right flat for us, we would dread the uncertainty that would go with making an offer on the one and only apartment we'd seen. There was also the alternate fear that we might lose out if we failed to make an offer on the spot. Our French friends and relatives had warned us that, in spite of the recession and perhaps because of the reduced prices and mortgage interest rates, good apartments were rarely on the market for very long, especially those in move-in condition, which was a must for us.

We had assiduously avoided considering any ad that mentioned the words *à rénover.* Having to renovate an apartment could be costly and time consuming. We'd been advised that the *devis*, the French term for estimate, could explode with the discovery of unforeseen problems, not a rarity in these very old buildings. Additional alterations and items not anticipated or thought of at first, and therefore not stipulated in the original estimate, could add *beaucoup* bucks to the budget.

Furthermore, the time for completion of any renovation was likely to extend far beyond what was promised by the contractor, and about that there wasn't much to be done. Go take them to court, as Ted would say.

Eduard spoke very good English.

"I can pick you up outside your place on rue du Mont Thabor tomorrow at 17h, if you wish."

With restrained appreciation, we replied in the affirmative.

Feeling more positive and relaxed after a brief nap with Ziggy, we left the apartment and walked past the *Place Vendôme* that afternoon on our way to the *Marché*. There we bought fresh fish, fruit, vegetables, bread and, of course cheeses, both French and Italian. We had found the vendors beyond friendly and later, the selection and taste of all that we purchased was absolutely scrumptious.

Unlike L.A. where fruits and vegetables looked beautiful, but often had the flavor and texture of a potato, here the perfume of the produce wafting through the marketplace promised that everything would be as delicious as it appeared.

Nonetheless, I'd ask one vendor, "Is this *sucré*?"

He happily replied by offering a slice of the peach or melon or anything else I wanted to try, just to see for myself. Smart businessman, or perhaps this was just the custom.

The Italian stall, run by a husband and wife and their daughter, were thrilled by Ted's proficiency in their language. They had wonderful goodies, homemade pasta dishes, cheeses and cold cuts galore, and specialties we could only have found in one place, Bay Cities Imports in Santa Monica, a pricy shop relatively far from our home in Los Angeles with long lines at the counter and check-out stand.

The fellow who ran the *Périgord* poultry stall was a very pleasant and patient man who had everything from duck breast to foie gras of duck or goose, to fresh rabbit, pheasant, quail, four varieties of chicken and free-range brown eggs, as well as anything else you could imagine in the poultry department. He was proud to show us photos of his farm to attest to the fact that all poultry were free-range and humanely nurtured.

There were two separate *poissonerie* with so many varieties of fish and seafood, we were kept busy with our *Reverso* translators trying to convert the French names to English. Much to our surprise, some of the mongers were ready with their own translations, an altogether heartening experience for me, a clumsy *Américaine*.

All along the *Place du Marché St. Honoré*, across from the variety of open market stalls, were cafés one after another. Large terraces were filled with local people cheerfully twittering like magpies and enjoying their attractively plated and appetizing *repas* and sipping their beer, café and wine.

Memories of paintings by artists, from Cézanne and Renoir to Van Gogh, suddenly came to life here in this vibrant area of everyday Parisian life. I had seen this before on our many visits to Paris, but this was the first time I realized that we could actually step into the painting and live *la vie en rose*.

With our purchases carefully packed into the black vinyl shopping cart that Kirat had thoughtfully left in the apartment for our use, we made our way back to *Mont Thabor* to cook, to eat and to cuddle up for the night with our cat. From the moment we'd arrived back from our shopping trip, Ziggy happily sashayed around our feet, just to remind us that it was time for tuna, his special evening treat.

The combined scent of cigarette smoke and fresh baked pizza, along with the soft sounds of the friendly conversation and jolity drifted up through our living room windows from *Le Cosy* down below. I snuggled up to Ted and pulled the blanket over my shoulder.

"We're not in Kansas anymore, Toto," I said, kissing him *bon nuit*.

We woke up late Thursday morning, experiencing a somewhat delayed jetlag, and we finally finished unpacking. We'd encountered even more secret closets between walls in which to stow away the box that had carried all of Ziggy's belongings, plus our rain boots and cold weather coats. Coffee and breakfast, a cheese omelet, toasty croissants and fresh fruit, tasted like it was straight out of the *Jardin d'Edin*.

"In Paris, every meal is a French meal."

I was tickled by the thought.

I'd expected that Eduard would pick us up in his car. However, I was taken by surprise when he introduced himself and lead the way by foot to the apartment on *rue Vignon*. It was an easy ten-minute walk from *rue du Mont Thabor*. Apparently, we were staying in that part of the 1ˢᵗ *Arrondisement* where, just around the corner and across the *Boulevard Madeleine* three blocks away, was the 9th, and two blocks further right across the street from the six-story freestone house that we had come to see, was the beginning of the 8th, an elegant *quartier* not far from *Le Palais Élysée*, the home of Emmanuel Jean-Michel Frédéric Macron, The President of France.

In other words, this small, unadorned building that we had come to see was right in the middle of the center of the historic and monumental right bank of Paris. Entering through the dark green and badly battered porte-cochère, we caught sight of the flower-filled courtyard beyond, lined with potted Azaleas, Camellias, Geraniums and various climbing vines, with and without flowers, all well cared for. Someone had a green thumb.

We rode up to the second floor in a relatively new and attractive glass elevator that easily made room for two plus people at a time. Next to the elevator was a spiral stone and wood staircase with a runner of *café' au lait* carpeting. Eduard climbed the stairs to meet us in front of the flat on the 2éme étage. The double-door entrance to the apartment was the only one on the second floor, what the French call an *appartement unique*. There were two lovely brass wall sconces on either side and a tulip shaped lamp that hung in the center over the doors. On the wall to the left, there was a small door. It was sealed off and humorously bedecked by a sign that read *Entrée Des Artistes*.

Eduard unlocked the main door. We walked inside, our open mouths took on the shape of ovals, our eyes were like saucers. To the right end of the vestibule was a pair of French windows that ran from eighteen inches above the floor to one foot below the 19th century moldings that framed the sixteen-foot-tall ceilings. There was a warm wooden, twelve-light double-door entrance straight ahead, leading into the formal dining room.

On the left end of the vestibule was a second set of double doors entering the living room or salon. With two sets of French windows, the *salon* qualified as a double *sejour*, extra-large. The vestibule was ample enough to qualify as a formal entryway, something Ted had always longed to have.

The interior doors were also in pairs, made from that very same warm wood that matched the relatively new parquet floors. The doors each had twelve lights, twelve beveled glass panes per door. They were clearly new, not the original floor to ceiling doors one might see in an apartment this age. This first visit was and always will be a dreamlike experience for me, burned into memory like a brand on a cow. I felt like I belonged to this place.

Moo!

The apartment was large by Parisienne standards, so much so that I nearly got lost. It was the kind of lost that one doesn't mind being. The layout was perfect, a renovation made by the owners just seventeen years before. The kitchen had been moved to the front of the apartment with a roomy *dinatoire* on its end nearest the windows that overlooked the *rue*.

The master bedroom with its full bath, dressing room, separate toilette and laundry room had all been relocated to the back of the apartment off the courtyard. In between front and back was a large second bedroom, another roomy full bath with a *toilette* and space enough for dressing that fulfilled much more than our previously scaled down expectations.

That first time through, I was dazzled to the point of blindness to many features. Experience had taught me that the good, the bad, and the as yet uncategorisable elements of the property would no doubt become clear only after an offer was made and the deal was closed. I had learned that I should never embark on decorating even in imagination until I've lived in a place for at least a year, when I've become fully aware of how we use it, how it functions.

After we walked through the apartment several times, we went back downstairs and met the guardians in the courtyard, a lovely Portuguese couple with cats. We were also introduced to the neighbor on the ground floor off the court. Christophe, who spoke English, was a professional freelance photographer and his partner Sandrine was the manager of the Mephisto shoe store on the ground floor of the next building North. The couple had two colorful and talkative scarlet macaw parrots, one African grey, two sweet kitties, and two large dogs.

Another couple, Monique and Daniel, came downstairs to greet us. They were older and lived on the first floor, directly below the apartment that we were considering. They owned a very well-known restaurant, *Le Roi du Pot de Feu,* which they had turned over to their daughter when they retired. This well-known institution of French comfort food had been in continuous operation for over sixty years and was just down the end of the rue near the post office. In conformity with French tradition, this retired couple also had homes in St. Tropez in the South and in Deauville to the North.

We said *au'revoir* and *bon aprés midi* and walked up and down the street with Eduard. At the North end, the rue merged into another, larger, two-way street called *rue Tronchet.* This street quickly crossed *Boulevard Haussmann,* arriving at the two grand department stores.

The Church of the Madeleine stood majestically by in the square around the corner from the rue Vignon to the right. She reigned with *grandeur* over the entire neighborhood. *Place Madeleine* was filled with upscale, small, specialized eateries and delicatessens where one could buy caviar, crab and lobster, the best macarons. Construction of the *Grande Fauchon Hotel* and *Restaurant* was under way in the Southwestern corner of the Place, and the *Café* and *Restaurant Pushkin* had just opened on the Southeast.

I couldn't stop thinking about the apartment. It was everything I had thought it would be and more. One-hundred-and-fifty square meters, a dozen double French windows, lofty ceilings with antique crown moldings, a different pattern adorning each room. Classy ceiling roses surrounded the base of each chandelier, one in the center of every room including in the kitchen, that had been remodeled with warm faux wood cabinets and counters that matched the real wood doors, and a built-in buffet and hutch occupied the wall alongside the generous breakfast room, bright and airy thanks to the French windows.

The bathrooms, like the vestibule, kitchen and laundry room, each had elegant stone floors in a diamond heritage pattern. The remainder of the floors had been recently refitted with warm, luminous wood parquet. The *piéce de resistance,* the master bedroom. was much more than large enough for our traditional mahogany King-sized suite of furniture, the one that all of our friends and relations, both in Paris and in the States, had admonished us not to ship to Paris.

"You'll never be able to afford an apartment in Paris with a bedroom that will accommodate that furniture."

Counter to all previous predictions, this *chambre des maître* was not only generously proportioned, but was also filled with light that streamed in from the quiet courtyard below. The second bedroom, unlike others we'd seen online, was a generous square, large enough to house my desk and Ted's secretaire, the large three-piece bookcase from my old office, a big screen TV, and our comfortable, if incredibly ugly, overstuffed recliner loveseat. Even with all that, there would still be ample space left over in the center of the floor for our portable, queen-sized, guest-bed to plug in and inflate, another handy feature when guests came to stay.

The formal dining room, previously used as a dance studio by the owner's wife, offered plenty of room for our dining table, even with all three of its leaves inserted, eight chairs or more if needed, our French provincial buffet and hutch, and the extra silk-damask couch that had been in our library on Fairburn. We'd brought it, just in case. It would be a perfect fit for the wall under the 19th century, stained glass window that faced the *courette*, a small internal courtyard that would most certainly allow for additional cross ventilation and access to some of the major plumbing that serviced the apartments on this side of the building.

The living room had a lovely, Calcutta granite-marble woodburning fireplace and hearth, and four great windows faced the rue. All appeared resplendent, in spite of the owner's mostly modern furnishings, unlike our classical French and Italianate décor.

"Uh-oh," I thought silently.

"I've already moved into this apartment."

I wondered what would happen if Ted had discretely done the same.

The apartment was unique. It was not just the fact that it stood alone on the second floor, but it was all these characteristics that made it feel more like a house than an apartment.

Ted and I looked at each other and cringed.

Now I was certain. We were both infatuated.

Ted asked Eduard for a favor.

"Do you think we could come back to see the apartment again after dark tonight?"

We knew that this was a significant request, as it was the beginning of May and it didn't get dark until ten. On top of that, was the holiday.

"I think so but let me just check with the guardian."

We sat waiting in the courtyard on a green wooden bench, surrounded by ivy geraniums. Ted took a photo of me with the flowering vines in the background. Eduard returned with good news. The guardian had generously agreed to re-open the apartment for us at 22h. That gave us three hours to walk the neighborhood.

"Are you sure you want to wait with us"

"It's okay, I have nothing else to do. But perhaps you would like to have time to yourselves, to think and talk, perhaps have dinner," Eduard politely suggested.

We thanked Eduard for his thoughtfulness and agreed to meet at the café across the street from the apartment before ten. After he left us, we ambled up the rue, this time looking into store windows and peeking inside restaurants all the way to the corner of Haussmann, where we could get another glimpse of Le Printemps' gold-trimmed bronze dome, its green patina highlighted by the sun as it began to set a bit lower in the western skies.

We walked in the opposite direction, window shopping on the alternate side of *rue Tronchet,* all the way back to the *Place Madeleine.* We climbed the many steps up the front of the church. At the top, we turned and gazed out over the broad cobblestoned *rue Royal* to the *Place Concorde,* past the obelisk and beyond to the *Palais Bourbon,* that housed the French National Assembly and architecturally appeared to mirror the style of *The Madeleine.* Behind that, we could see the gilded dome of *Les Invalides.*

What Los Angeles had lacked in architectural design Paris had double in spades.

This was quite a 'hood' for a retirement home.

We walked back to rue Vignon and sat at a table on the small terrasse of the café-bistro across the street. Its name was boldly printed on its red and white striped canopy. The waiter was friendly and spoke Italian and English as well as French. We enjoyed our dinner of rare *entrecote* and *frites* with *haricots verts* and a good *Bordeaux,* waiting for time to pass and looking up at the apartment as the chandeliers were lit, one by one.

We were becoming excited. Too excited.

"Let's write a list of the haves and have-nots," I petitioned.

It was no use. The haves outweighed the have-nots, three to one.

Ted held up the napkin, imprinted with the name of the café.

"Select Vignon, it must be a sign."

We kissed and Ted wrote the date, May 5th, 2016, on the napkin. He folded it in half neatly and slid it into his shirt pocket. He bought red roses from the street vendor, while the waiter ran up next door to borrow a vase in which to place them on our small, wrought iron table.

I cried.

Ted beamed.

We both knew we had found 'the one'.

CHAPTER 18

REWINDING OUR HISTORY, in a moment I recalled all the other times we'd chosen a home together. We weren't yet married, but we had decided to begin our life together in an apartment that was all ours, not Ted's nor mine. Located a block from Beverly Hills, the building was a small and freshly renovated quadra-plex. Both our cat and dog were permitted, and we felt secure with a five-year lease.

We chose the unit with windows facing Cashio Street, two floors, two bedrooms, a modest living room, a separate dining room, one bath upstairs and a kitchen and laundry room with a wooden porch outside the back door. We had a garage for one car and the large driveway accommodated cars a turn-about. Originally built in the 1920's, it was brought up to date with fixtures and appliances that were first rate.

We both came away with the impression that the fireplace, with its classic mantlepiece, was burning wood in the firebox during our preview. It was only after we signed the lease, that we realized we'd seen a mirage, an electric heater with red and gold aluminum foil streamers billowing upward simulating flames, our first lesson in the potency and power of wishful thinking. We'd seen exactly what we had wished to see.

That said, we loved the locale. Tiger Lilly was pleased with the huge Sycamore tree that stood within jumping range from the upstairs second bedroom window, and we took our walks every evening together, the four of us including Tiger and our Aussie, DeeDee at heel and off leash.

To the astonishment of the neighbors, we formed a close and orderly formation as we walked up and down Beverly drive, side by side and all in a row.

"Is that your cat, too," people asked in awe.

We both radiated pride.

Our first Saturday breakfast in the dining room, looking out the window at the bright tree-lined street, we suddenly realized that we were living in the heart of an orthodox Jewish neighborhood. Ted thought he had escaped these reminders of something in Israel he was allergic to, especially the men in the black fur hats with their *peyots* and long beards, along with their wives, some in *babushkas*, others wearing wigs walking three paces behind their husbands. Like me, Ted was an ethnic Jew, but the politics in Israel associated with the orthodox parties made this neighborhood, for him, what a right-wing Republican neighborhood would be for me.

Ouch!

The orthodox couple in the apartment next to us had a ten-year old daughter. One day when I was at home cleaning house and preparing supper after school, she rang the bell and smiled up at me when I opened the door.

"Hi there."

"My name is Alice."

"Hi, Alice. I'm Judi. What can I do for you today?"

Alice was a bashful girl about nine-years old with long blond hair.

"I live next door, and I wondered if I could come over sometime and watch *Little House on the Prairie*."

"Sure, come on in."

I began to tune in what was clearly her favorite show, weekdays at four.

"Your TV's not working?"

"No, that's not the problem. My parents won't allow me to watch because it's about a Christian family, even though I told them that Michael Landon was Jewish."

137

Ted's beef with the orthodox mentality suddenly became even more clear.

Whenever I was home before four o'clock, Alice knocked on the door and sat on my couch, captivated by these stories that all American kids loved to read, and many Americans of all ages loved to watch. This wouldn't be the last time I was astonished by the kind of Jews I'd never been exposed to in my mostly secular life.

The event that impressed me the most during this period was the festival of *Sukkot*, that lasted seven days in late September or early in October, celebrating the first harvest after the Exodus from Egypt with the construction of a small hut called a *sukkah*, customarily thatched with palm leaves, and under which most meals were eaten.

During the run-up to that holiday, our neighbor asked for permission to use the rear of the driveway for a space to build the *sukkah*. All tenants happily agreed, but the Rabbi apparently had the last word. He also had to grant permission. When the *sukkah* was completed the family graciously invited us to dine with them under the Palm leaves on a weeknight.

Ted agreed, but when the hour arrived, he hadn't yet returned from the clinic. This had been anticipated and announced beforehand, but Alice knocked on our back door exactly on time.

"We're about to go to the *sukkah*."

Her mother, Mathilda, followed close behind her.

"I hope it's still OK that Ted is running a bit late."

"That's fine, you can come anyway, and when he arrives, he'll join us. Would you like to wash your hands?"

I was confused, no end. What did she have in mind? I replied politely.

"No thanks, I've already washed up."

I stepped out and turned to lock our back door when Mathilda took me by the hand straight into her own kitchen, which was situated at a 90-degree angle from ours, off the shared redwood porch.

She placed my hands over a large ceramic bowl, poured warm water over them and said a little Hebrew prayer, after which she handed me an embroidered dish towel with which to dry myself. By this time, I'd caught on. This was a holiday ritual, not just a question of hygiene.

I was ushered out to the *sukkah* by Alice, who motioned to me to slide in on one of the benches. Her father, Moshe, sat across from me with Alice next to him. Mathilda sat down on the other side of her daughter. I felt a strange discomfort, not just because Ted was so delayed, but because these three were looking at each other, making hand motions as if playing a game of charades, not uttering a sound. I wondered if this was yet another holiday ritual. After several minutes, it had become just a bit too strange. No one seemed to understand the miming of either of the other two. I was at a loss. In fact, it all seemed rather psychotic, and I was growing a bit more than frightened, hoping that Ted would come to the rescue.

All at once, Mathilda's eyes lit up as if a switch had flipped on under her brown wig. She jumped from her seat at the table, scampered up the steps into her kitchen, and emerged with something large wrapped in another beautifully hand-decorated cloth.

It was a scrumptious braided *challah* bread, still warm from the oven. Mathilde placed it in the middle of the table and Moshe finally spoke, starting with the familiar *Baruch atah Adonai Elohenue*, his hands levitating over the bread. I recognized Moshe's chant as the beginning of just about every Hebrew prayer.

That was it, now I could settle down.

They weren't able speak a word until the bread appeared and the prayer over the *challah* had been spoken, but Mathilda had forgotten her beautifully braided egg bread, most likely distracted in her state of concern about the traditional hand washing.

Just as it all started to make sense, Ted appeared.

Hallelujah.

Our second apartment, into which we moved not long after our wedding, was also a rental that we occupied while still in graduate school. We were lucky to have found it when, with short notice, we were informed that the Cashio building had been sold and was being torn down, along with the building adjacent to it, and the two lots were scheduled for the construction of one, large, modern high-rise with a swimming pool.

We were too green at the time to realize that we could have extracted from our landlords a sum equal to the amount of our full five-year lease, plus moving expenses as our other three neighbors had done. In our panic, we weren't thinking clearly. Without much time to waste, we located a downstairs unit in a 1930's duplex owned by an old Jewish man and his wife. The apartment had some nice features to speak for it, in spite of its location, which was farther East. But the rooms were larger, the living room had a big bay window with a view of the garden and the green lawn rolling down a gentle knoll to the sidewalk. There was no garage, but we had unrestricted parking on the street and there was not one sign of orthodoxy.

The master bedroom had just enough room for our furnishings and the second bedroom accommodated both of our desks on opposing walls. This was a godsend, since much of our time at home was spent writing our doctoral dissertations, well into the wee hours of each night.

This apartment had the feel of a cottage and was, all in all, a good experience for us in spite of the grumpy old landlord, who constantly poked his nose into our business, and who never came through on any promise made. Still, it was home to us for five years with only one misadventure.

The gardener, who came every Wednesday afternoon parked his truck in front of the building, windows rolled down. One day in our third year, our cat Tiger Lilly didn't return home when we did. She didn't appear at suppertime either. This was unusual for her as she was a creature of comfort and habit and chose to do her hunting and roaming while we were away at work or at school.

When bedtime arrived, I was in a frenzy. I opened the front door and walk out to the path along the side of the house, calling out her name and "here, kitty, kitty" until I was hoarse. But no Tiger. Even

140

DeeDee was distraught, going back and forth from the bay window to the front door to keep a lookout for her companion.

Tiger had lived with me at the ranch and had survived bobcats, coyotes, hawks and owls. She had been abandoned when she was so small that when I sent her to the vet to be spayed, he called me on the telephone to confirm the procedure. It turned out that that at three pounds, Tiger was full grown and over a year old, apparently having been spayed before she came to live with us. When I moved to Malibu lake, she adapted to Rommel, a strange dog who would chase her just for the fun of it, and she'd made a rapid adjustment when I moved with Ted to the city in both our first and second apartments.

Now she was suddenly lost.

All during that first night, I lie awake, going out in my robe and slippers to look for my tiny girl every hour, but still no Tiger. She was such a clever cat, looking first in one direction and then the other before crossing a street. How could anything happen to her? The next morning over coffee Ted and I fretted.

"I wonder if she curled up in the gardener's back seat and didn't wake up before he drove away to God-knows where. Do you think she can possibly find her way home?"

Ted was consoling, helpful, and kind.

"I don't know, but I can make some posters and nail them up all over the neighborhood, in case someone sees or hears her."

The signs he made displayed a Xerox photo and a description of Tiger Lilly's meow, her diminutive three-and-one-half pound size, both our phone numbers, and our address. The landlord was away for the week, so there was no way to get the gardener's phone number in order to inquire about which route he'd taken after he left here.

Three days went by and we still called out for her, walking the neighborhood endlessly with DeeDee. We received calls from several people as far away as La Cienega Boulevard, a good mile East. All were convinced that they'd seen and heard a very small, grey tabby cat, walking westward in our direction. They described her as tired and drawn, but not accepting any offers of food, shelter or water. Could this be our lass attempting to come home?

On the third night after her disappearance, I awoke to a very weak mew at the front door, and I ran barefoot to open it up. There she was, so thin and wan, happy for me to pick her up and hold her in my warm arms, and still purring. Ted and DeeDee were right beside me as soon as they heard the door close. We sat on the floor with Tiger on her mat in the kitchen as she drank water and warm milk, little by little over what seemed like a long stretch of time.

She ate a bit of tuna and nibbled at her favorite kibble, with little strength for chewing either one for very long. DeeDee stretched out beside her, and when Tiger had finished eating and drinking as much as she could, she curled up against her big fluffy friend and finally went to sleep, once again in the safety of her own home. How Tiger Lilly had found her way back to us was the stuff of children's story books, a Collie named Lassie or a War Horse, but we'd never heard stories of a cat finding its way home through heavy city traffic over a long distance. Tiger went on to live a long life after that, unlike our DeeDee who passed away at age fifteen, leaving the three of us brokenhearted the year before our next move.

Tiger made it with us to our first condominium on the top floor of a four-story building, just Southwest of UCLA. Living in a penthouse left no opportunity for Tiger to continue her in-and-out lifestyle, but in her older years, she enjoyed the safety and serenity of her garden of boxed geraniums edging the curved front balcony where she loved to lie on a cushioned chair and watch the birds fly by. When her time came we humanely had her euthanized before she could suffer from the kidney failure that almost always ends a cat's life. She was twenty.

A year after we put our Tiger down, we found a small, five-year old, female tuxedo cat at the Sunday adoption center in the local pet store. She had belonged to an old woman who just passed away, and the family didn't want her. We took her in spite of an obvious depression, characterized by hiding and pouting, growling and hissing, and scratching and spitting whenever we tried to stroke her or to pick her up and cuddle her.

She was simply a beautiful tyrant, with short and thick black and white fur like mink, a long fluffy tail, gleaming golden eyes like garnets set on black velvet, and a perfectly balanced conformation. We just wanted to snuggle her close to console her, but at first, she'd have none of it or us. Her habit of hiding took to extremes, and one day we couldn't find her anywhere. Finally, after an exhaustive search, I happened to glance at the guestroom bed. I could just barely detect a rumple in the middle, under the quilted spread. There she was. She had in-squished herself between the knitted blanket and the cotton quilt in such a stealthy way that she was nearly undetectable. This was how she earned her new name, Squishy.

It took a year, but Squishy finally became our little laptop cat, jumping up onto our knees as soon as either one of us was seated anywhere in the apartment. She slept on Ted's chest at night and curled up with us for nearly fourteen years of our lives together. She even managed to survive the 1994 earthquake by hiding under an overturned rocking chair.

As for our condo, when we first saw it, it had nothing to speak for itself except a spectacular view of the twin towers in Century City, the Hollywood sign on the hills many miles Eastward and all the way South from there to downtown, which looked like an emerald city from our vantage point. Right from the beginning, we began making plans to turn this new-if-boxy space into something classical, classy and convenient.

We visited our dear friend Ruth-Ellen on her deathbed at the end of her long struggle with a benign tumor that had grown behind her eye and suddenly turned malignant. Before her death, she handed down to us the name and number of her excellent cabinet maker, Larry Polmier.

In that period, within two years after the earthquake of '94 had destroyed nearly everything inside our home, Larry and Ted worked out and executed a design that included double crown moldings throughout the apartment, arched curios that fit neatly into the useless niches on each side of the sliding glass door to the balcony, and arched cornices above the dining room windows that mirrored the large arched window above the sliding glass doors the curios. He even made a similar cornice that topped the louvered doors separating the dining room from the kitchen.

The bar that divided the kitchen from the den, which was a room that no one believed we'd ever find any use for, formed the top of a brace of beautifully arched bookcases, constructed all across the wall below. The windows on the other full wall, where we'd planned to place a loveseat for watching television were also decked out with the same arched cornices.

What had appeared at first glance to be a useless crook in the room became the perfect spot for an L-shaped desk with drawers that slid open as if they were greased, and below several more arched bookcases built in above the desk, providing storage for more books and framing a small window that was converted into a hatch that opened over my work area for a bit of breeze. It was perfect for me. To top off a dream come true, around the ceiling of the sitting area Larry installed an earthquake-proof plate rail for knick-knacks and paperback books.

To complete the innovative form and convenient function of this all-purpose room, Larry built a beautiful console with even more arched bookcases, a drop down desktop for Ted, decked out with useful cubbies inside, six lockable file cabinets below, and bookshelves surrounded by more archways set into the concave wall next to the louvered accordion doors that hid the side by side washer and dryer. Larry also made a tambour door that put our large television out of sight when it was not in use and slid in above the TV when it was. The ensemble looked as if it had always been there.

As for the Master bedroom, like all the other rooms, it was covered wall to wall with a dense cream-colored carpet. I gathered swag valences on my sewing machine. They were made out of fabric that matched our sheets and comforter. These were decorative toppings for the full-length sheers I'd sewn to cover the windows without blocking the light from the North. I had also trimmed the vanilla-colored terry towels in the master bath to match.

All of the woodwork and ceilings throughout had been painted an off-white swiss coffee satin latex, and the walls were dressed up with a toned-down shade of Goldengate, a warm honey color that ran throughout the apartment accentuating its 100-foot-long flow. The back door off the master bedroom opened onto a large terrace with a view of the not so far-off Pacific Ocean. We adorned the terrace with wooden wine barrels filed with hybrid tea roses of all colors. Ted stealthily installed a narrow water pipe that ran from underneath the master bath sink, tucked in between the baseboard and the carpeting behind the bed, and popped out through a tiny hole made in the exterior wall. Outside, the pipe was fitted with a faucet and hose bib for watering the roses. There were so many blooms at any given time, that the house was decorated with fragrant blossoms nearly all year long and in each and every room.

All seemed flawless and I was certain that we'd never move from this home that we loved so much, finally furnished to our liking, with windows on three sides, a single neighbor across the hall, no one above us to disturb our peace. Most importantly, it was located just two miles directly in line with our Beverly Hills offices.

Just as all seemed perfect, out of the blue Ted sat me down one day after work and broke the news to me, with a rueful look on his reddened face.

"I'm having a midlife crisis. I've been going out with someone almost every day for the past three months."

My thoughts raced. How could it be so? How could I be so blind not to notice his absences, his dissatisfaction with me, and with our life together? Of course. We had staggered our times between patients in order to allow privacy in the shared waiting room and exit hall. This meant that we might often go for hours without seeing each other, even though we shared the suite.

I began to weep. What had I done wrong? Why didn't he love me anymore?

"It's not another woman," Ted declared, after what seemed to me like an eternity.

Another man, I thought in disbelief. I turned away, not wanting him to see my tears. Ted put his arms around me from behind and spoke gently in my ear.

"Don't worry, I don't want a new wife, I just want to buy a house."

I turned around, relieved.

"I've been going out with a real estate broker, looking at houses."

He was laughing at me. I wanted to punch him, but instead, I threw my arms around his neck, joyful if confused.

"You what? What for?"

It felt like Mother was back again, wanting to buy me another parakeet.

"It's time to renew our lease on the offices. The rate is ridiculously high. Our rent will be $4,000 per month with the new contract going up by 5% each year. It's a waste, a giveaway to the landlord."

Ted was right, damn it. I didn't want to leave our perfect home, but it was idiotic to spend so much on an office when we could put that money to good use in a property that would yield appreciation for our future. If only we could find a house that would support both our living and office needs.

"So, have you found anything?"

Ted told me all about his search. He'd seen fifty homes and none of them were even close to ideal, neither in location nor in floorplan. That evening we were going to a friend's home for dinner and, as one would expect, the story of Ted's midlife crisis came up and was the source of much levity for all at the table.

"Why not get Michael to take you house hunting," Jerry asked.

We hadn't even thought of Michael. He was with an upscale brokerage firm, one we believed was out of our league and location. Within a few minutes, Michael was collecting an earful of our wants and must-haves. He let us know that, between our restricted budget and the required location, a home with a layout that could accom-modate both our personal and professional privacy without much remodeling, and in the kind of neighborhood we wanted, was not going to be an easy find.

The next day, Ted went out with Michael for a test drive to look at three homes that would, if nothing else, provide Michael with a good sense of what we were and weren't looking for. I stayed home, utterly ambivalent. I didn't want to move, but the project made sense. It was a mature move to make, but I felt like a baby.

I can't say I was unhappy when Ted returned home, describing all that he'd seen, seeming even less convinced that we could ever find something that met our criteria. The must-haves alone made up a daunting list. Just when we were ready to give up on Ted's pipe-dream, Michael called.

"Hi Guys. There's this new listing that won't be shown to the bro-kers until Tuesday's open house, and I have an appointment for us to see it first thing Monday morning with my partner Sandy, who's friendly with the listing agent. How about ten in the morning?"

"Where is it?"

"Twenty-fifty Fairburn Avenue."

Michael's enthusiasm was palpable, full of the zest typical of his endearing, hypo-manic and seductive personality. We knew that we had to be cautious. It was clear that he could sell snow-cones to Eskimos, even in Wintertime.

He already had us going.

We walked to the Boulevard for Sushi at Masu and afterward we shared a thought. Why not go look at it from the outside in the dark. That might give us some idea, a preview for tomorrow. After dinner, we walked holding hands across Missouri and up Prosser Avenues. As we arrived at the corner, we stood facing the house at 2050 Fairburn, directly across the street. I audibly gasped for breath with excitement.

Talk about curb appeal, the house was out of this world. It was a very tall, two-story white traditional-style residence, with a dark green front door and shutters, and white, wood-trimmed window-sills and white edging on the steeply gabled, hip and valley shake shingled roof. The house was perched high up on a knoll with a brick pathway of three short flights wending its way up to a covered front porch from the sidewalk. In front of the porch stood a fine-looking ornamental pear tree.

Malibu lights lit each side of the brick pathway lined with rose bushes, as well as the flowering Gazania beds bordering the driveway along the right boundary of the property and ending at craftsman-style, white wooden gates that lead to the garden behind.

We stood and stared for some time. Then we walked home to Greenfield.

I could barely sleep all night. We were on our way over to Fairburn by 9:30. Michael and Sandy were sitting in a car, parked out front. When we knocked on the rear window, they jumped.

We were early.

Michael introduced us to Sandy, the business head of the partnership and a former bank vice-president. The four of us made our way single file up the steps of the rose-lined brick path, even more impressive in the light of day. What we saw from the entry throughout the first floor, had us tied up in a state that I can only describe as pure unadulterated marvel.

On top of this, that sly Michael had managed to save the best for last. He knew that there was a big surprise upstairs, awaiting us. It was a cavernous, sunny master suite, with tall sash windows overlooking a small but promising garden that needed some work, a detached garage that had already been converted into an office building, two huge trees, and mature azaleas and camellias. A pergola below the upstairs study and off the library downstairs covered the brick patio. It was laced with baby pink climbing roses and lavender wisteria vines in summer splendor.

We were ensnared, in spite of the awareness that there would have to be a major renovation completed between October 1st, 2003 and the 1st of January 2004.

And then, there was the oversized mortgage that scared me half to death.

All these memories wended their way through my mind in that instant, as we sat in the Café Select Vignon. The clock approached 22h. It was May 5th, 2016. I became anxious and thought, here we go again.

I relaxed as I realized that there would be no mortgage this time around. We had come armed with the proceeds of the sale of Fairburn Avenue. I felt safe and secure and we were in Paris, the most beautiful place in the world.

CHAPTER 19

EDUARD SHOWED UP IN TIME to share a dark chocolate and salted caramel tarte and a petit café. Ted paid the check, our agent accompanied us to the apartment, all lit up. We walked throughout the rooms, together and separately, studying each one over and over again. We thanked the guardians for their courtesy and patience, walked back across the rue, and with wordless looks we sat at a table on the terrace of the Select Vignon and instructed Eduard to write a full price offer. His hand shook as he fumbled in his pocket for a pen.

Crazy Americans!

When I sold real estate in the seventies, I had an enormous jar of chocolate M&M's on my desk. The label read, *Buyer's Remorse Pills*. I would always prescribe them for my clients after they had signed their offer.

"You may find that you're anxious, and you might even suffer a little insomnia tonight. So, when you start to feel uneasy about taking such a big step, chew 2-4 of these and swallow before bedtime,"

When I said this, my clients roared with laughter, and they'd each take a handful of the sweets away with them. The psychology worked. They'd been forewarned, so they were sure that the feelings were universal, nothing untoward. Many would retell the tales of their giggles of relief on that first night as they munched away on M&M's in bed. But there were no such creative sales techniques, nor any cutting-edge skills involving empathy or good humor in France. Only *politesse et formalité.*

It was a rocky night for us, one filled with a mélange of elation and trepidation. We chattered away in bed and were up and down all night. I longed for a smoke, the first time since I'd quit, eighteen months before. When the sun came out, we went for a long walk in the park after breakfast with our cell phones lying in wait for a call to relieve our anxiety, one way or another.

At noon, Eduard rang to tell us that the owner had accepted our offer. There had been another full price offer submitted earlier that same day. Luckily, those buyers were Chinese and were seeking financing, while our offer was all cash with a request for the briefest period of time for the sale to be culminated.

It was a done deal.

"So, your nutty friends are about to be the proud owners of 16 rue Vignon, 2nd floor, in the 9th," I blabbed to our closest friend JoAnn in L.A. on Skype, who was arriving in about a month.

She had hoped to be a part of our flat hunt, right behind Lana who had arranged to come right away to provide a steadying force for both of us. I recognized a sharp contrast between our elated mood and the sudden sadness when I remembered that it was Holocaust Memorial Day, which oddly enough coincided with the Ascension of Christ.

Even so, I felt like we had ascended into heaven. JoAnn celebrated with me.

"Do you realize that we've actually ascended from the bureaucratic hell we've been through, just to get here."

"Hold on. This is just the beginning," Ted said soberly and within earshot of JoAnn.

"By the way, I think I found out where the bubbles go when you pop the cork on a bottle of champagne. They float into the atmosphere of the city, and each time you inhale you feel ten years younger and a little giddy."

JoAnn shared my laughter. I felt as high as a French flag on the fourteenth of July.

Ted, as usual, carried out his solemn duty as the sensible, skeptic-in-chief of the family. All the same, I must admit that there was a critical moment, underscored by a particular event early on in our French home-buyers' experience. It woke me up to some inconvenient truths I had naively failed to make allowance for. To put it succinctly, Paris was not Los Angeles. Here began the first of many culture shocks. In France I didn't have the license, I didn't have the legal knowledge, and I didn't have the language. I was helpless.

And these were only some of the countless inconvenient truths yet to come. Still, they didn't sully the truth as beauty or beauty as truth of being and living in the most beautiful place in the world. We were in a mythical city of romance, the same one that had borne witness to much of the history our personal love story.

Paris was, and always would be, the city that became the vessel that held and preserved our lifelong dreams. The guiding beam of light at the top of the Tour Eiffel always seemed, more and more, to be pointing the way to our one-of-a-kind second chance at life as we neared retirement age. After all, it was with mindboggling ease that we'd found this dream home on the third day of that new life. Nevertheless, we soon discovered that we could not begin the process leading to the legal transfer of title until the seller, Monsieur Coulont, a retired ambassador to two different African countries, would return from his home in *Saint-Tropez*.

We also learned that his return was a date to be determined. Fortunately, at Ted's request, Eduard agreed to arrange for us to bring our family to see the apartment over the weekend. Jean, Cathy, Philippe and Jacqueline all appeared to inspect the premises. Jean suggested we use the family *notaire* for the transaction. I thought it would be less complicated if we shared the seller's *notaire*, whose office was right up the rue. He spoke perfect English and had already prepared all the necessary documents to expedite the sale process. Not surprisingly, my judgement was overridden by those who spoke French, including Ted.

Here I was in Paris, once more feeling like a newborn with little to say that really mattered to anyone. With that realization, my defenses against fear and frustration began to kick in. Ted and his family all talked rapidly, their comments peppered with words like *alors, bon, bien sûr, mais* and *peut-être* in a tone of voice that fluctuated between admonishment and apprehension, with a sprinkle of enthusiasm, optimism, and some smiles here and there.

I walked alone around the apartment, this time sitting on each chair, couch or bed, enjoying the various views of each room. In my days selling and buying real estate in California as a licensed professional, I was accustomed to certain rules and regulations of the selling and buying real estate that apparently were non-existent here in France.

The ambiguity of the terms and timing of the purchase, the absence of any official legal documents signed by both parties were, right off the bat, incomprehensible and quite maddening for me. How could I call foul if I didn't know where the lines were drawn on playing field and what the players even looked like?

The postponement of the beginning of the whole procedure filled me with unnecessary suspicion. The old adage "When in Rome . . ." came to mind. I would just have to trust that this was the way it was in this new country in which we had chosen to live out the rest of our lives. We could go with the flow or fight an everlasting uphill battle.

Of course, there's always a sunny side to every cloud of doubt. When Lana arrived, the delays afforded us at least a month's freedom to be tourists in our new hometown. We enjoyed the art exhibitions and buskers in the streets, the shopping and theatre, now with supertitles, the concerts and opera, and even some sightseeing outside of Paris with Lana and JoAnn after her, and special times with French friends while awaiting the return of our seller, Monsieur Coulont.

Even with all the distractions, the nonchalance in legal transactions was uncomfortably unimaginable. I'd sold real property for a living for ten years in a state that had a very far reaching, orderly and rigorous process of exchanging cash for title to begin within 48 hours, with both parties signing and initialing mountains of paperwork, and a deposit paid by the buyer, all just to legitimize the offer to purchase a property.

In California, this process is administered by a licensed officer of the State who is responsible for engaging a Title Company to research the history of transfers of title to the property and to gather information on any existing liens, a matter of public record.

The escrow officer also guided the buyer to a licensed inspector who examined and certified all aspects of the property, immobile and mobile. If the resulting report revealed any problematic areas in need of repair or replacement, down to the last screw, the cost was usually covered by the seller through a reduction in the selling price.

As a Notary Public, the escrow officer verified the identities of each party to the transaction, established quite simply by each person's State issued driver's license, which was considered to be sufficient verification of identity. With a competent escrow officer everything was friendly, neat, simple and, in the case of a cash sale, it could easily be a *fait accompli* within thirty days.

In our case, although we'd been given Eduard's word that our offer had been accepted, we only had that word of the *Immobilier's* assistant to sustain our faith until sometime in June when we could have our first meeting with the owner and his notaire, the *Immobilier* and Eduard, all at the office of our family's *notaire*, most inconveniently located for all, way across town in the 15th.

Additionally, unlike the seller's *notaire*, who spoke my language and would have saved us both time and money, the *notaire* that our cousins had insisted upon with the best of intentions spoke French, *c'est tout*. She explained that the obligatory ten days, during which we had the right to back out of the deal, would begin only after this first meeting.

"Can't we waive these ten days, in the spirit of moving things along?"

"Mais, non. Parce-que ce période est imposé par l'État," Madame la *Maîtresse* explained, Ted translated.

This was only the beginning of a slow drip of paperwork.

The final end-date wasn't a certainty until all was nearly at a close. Unfortunately, there was much to be said and done in our case.

Even though Ted spoke fluent French, the whole procedure had to be conducted both languages, and the law required that we hire a State appointed translator, who turned out to be a very lovely youngish woman from Croatia, for whom neither French nor English was a first language. Subsequently, there were long and unnecessary hours of me helping her with her English and Ted augmenting her French, which amounted to additional Euro in our debit column.

I didn't have the right to waive the use of a translator, even though my trusted husband of over three decades both comprehended and spoke French and English, and my trust in him as my proxy and translator was made crystal clear to all. He even had my general power of attorney. I felt like I was considered to be the weaker sex in France, needing protection so much so that this safeguard was absolutely inflexible, although it was explained that the law was created in order to protect those refugees and immigrants with non-existent or poor French.

We also discovered that there were no provisions for community property in France without a pre- or, in our case, a post-nuptial agreement. Of course, the fact that the French *notaire* was a lawyer was convenient, even though this amounted to further paperwork and, as one might guess, more translations and expenses.

We were fortunate that the history of the apartment, the size of a large old-fashioned phone book, and the inspection report, a title search, the contract between the coproprietors and the syndic (also known as the co-owners and the building manager), and between the co-proprietors and the guardian, along with the minutes from the last three annual meetings were all available, thanks to the seller's *notaire*.

Even so, when there are two *notaires*, one for each of the two parties, there is only a single fee that, like the paperwork, is split between the two. This policy alone would be very un-American.

As *L'Acte de Vente* must be kept in the office of the notaire for one-hundred years, after which it is stored by the state, I'm certain that there's no such thing as joint custody between *notaires*. French

Property law had a few additional surprises, not all of them unpleasant. Since the notaire separates the immovable property from the moveable and fees paid to the *Immobilier*, all of which have all been included in the total sales price, the result is a reduction in the base upon which property taxes are computed and may result in a reduction in or even exemption from wealth taxes for the buyer and the seller.

As there was no such thing as a standardized form, like that which exists in California, each transaction called for a reinvention of the wheel. Finally, the *notaire* required all parties to the contract to prove their identities and marital status with birth certificates, marriage certificates, divorce certificates and certificates of name changes, passports and identity cards, all of which were relevant to our transaction. This amounts to so much red tape that, had I known earlier, I would have invested a good portion of our retirement account in shares of Office Depot.

It was not until after we'd moved into the apartment that we would discover that, although the pre-sale inspection was more than adequate for such things as the presence or absence of asphalt, lead, fungus, termites and mold in the building as well as in the apartment itself, and it attested to the condition and age of the roof, plumbing and electricity, the operating condition of the so-called moveable property was not a part of such an inspection, other than to verify the presence of these objects in the apartment.

There are often other surprises in life, and some of them are even more unpleasant than expected, having nothing to do with bureaucracy. I can only be thankful that *Darty*, a huge appliance store situated underneath the *Madeleine*, is only a three-minute walk away, this because we were soon to realize that, our movables were more like disposables in need of replacement, one by one.

One week before we were to sign the final papers, I became immobile, literally.

CHAPTER 20

BESIDES LANA AND JOANN, we had several other visitors from the States during the period before the closing ceremonies on our apartment. We enjoyed escorting everyone around Paris, mostly on foot, to see all of our favorite bridges, monuments, museums, *parcs*, *passages*, restaurants and assorted noteworthy scenes.

We'd average five to six miles by foot every day, seven to ten kilometers, and my knees showed no sign of the bone-on-bone arthritic pain I'd suffered in the last years of my working life. I lost weight, no matter what I ate, and the spring in my step was back again until it wasn't.

Friday afternoon in early July, the temperature was unbearably hot at 38°C.

I had planned to stay indoors in front of a fan, but I just couldn't say no to a former patient who was in Paris and had invited me for a *café* around the corner on *rue Rivoli*. I was just stepping down into the street from the next to the last curb, no more than twenty meters away from our meeting place, when I felt a searing pain that left me barely able to hobble on one foot.

I dropped into my chair where my former patient was already seated.

"Hi. What happened?"

"I think I just broke my foot."

I was half joking.

"Really?"

"Just kidding."

I was mortified.

At the time, I genuinely believed that I had spoken in jest. I hadn't tripped, fallen, twisted or anything else noteworthy. I'd simply taken one ordinary step down from the curb into the rue. Not having ever broken any bones in my life, I had no idea what it should feel like. I only knew that whatever this was, it was as if a bull elephant had stomped on me. Apparently, that was the stomp that broke this analyst's foot.

All the same, we drank wine and talked and laughed for over two hours. With no weight on my foot, nothing hurt. I was truly caught off guard when, by the time she had to go, I realized that I couldn't put any weight on that foot at all, without the sense that a thousand daggers were penetrating it from all sides.

I looked down.

Through the straps of my proper orthopedic sandal, I could see that the foot and ankle were swollen beyond recognition, the size and shape of a small watermelon. Of course, I tried to make light of it, waving goodbye as this dear woman who had been my patient headed out to take the metro. But as soon as she was out of sight and I rose up, I could barely lurch forward on my other foot from pillar to pillar. I was sure, from the stares and murmurs of passers-by, that I looked like an old drunken, grey-haired lady.

By the time I reached the corner, I could go no further.

Hanging onto a handy construction barricade for dear life, I called home.

"Teddy," I cried into my cellphone.

"Help! I can't walk."

"What happened?"

"I think I've fractured my foot."

In less than ten minutes, my darling hero was by my side. He helped me walk back to our apartment, left arm around my waist while my right arm hung on his shoulder. At the building, we squeezed into the electric coffin together.

I dared not let go of him.

Once in the apartment, Ted let me down gently on one of the sofas in the living room. He placed a pillow on the coffee table, cautiously removed my sandal, elevated my foot onto the pillow, and carefully placed a frozen gel-pack on both the ankle and the injured foot. He gave me a handful of Ibuprofen for the discomfort and inflammation.

The pain radiated up my leg like a molten rod, but after a while, I was numb. Ted called a physician friend who advised him to contact *SOS Paris Médecins*. We were approaching evening, but SOS promised a doctor would arrive in 2-3 hours. I called our 90-year-old friend Marie-Claire, who offered to come over *tout de suite*. She had crutches, a cane and a wheelchair, all in the trunk of her small SUV. Marie-Claire was always ready for anything. She even offered to stay to help with communications in case of need.

When the doctor arrived, I was relieved to hear that he spoke excellent English. He wanted to know all the details of what had happened. Only after our long exchange did this kind young physician examine me. He spoke with the three of us at great length.

The room was in agreement as to the diagnosis; a fatigue fracture of the fifth metatarsal bone in my right foot was the likely suspect. It was only a matter of an x-ray confirmation in order to determine the extent of the fracture and the subsequent treatment. The Doctor ordered me to keep ice on my foot and ankle, which were both still blown up like balloons and he also stipulated that I keep my right leg elevated higher than my heart.

Doctor Kind, as I dubbed him, issued an *ordinance* for me, a prescription for real pain meds and another for the radiologist along with a letter of referral. He advised me not to go to a hospital until Monday morning as I would just be waiting there for endless hours over the weekend. He also reassured me that waiting would not cause more harm, so long as I followed *doctor's orders*.

His charge was a mere fifty-euros for a two-hour consultation. His home visit was my first introduction to the wonders of the French medical system. I only wish I could say it was my last.

Our cousins suggested a good hospital on their side of town. We said thanks and consulted the internet. I easily located a hospital close to home, one that specialized in orthopedics and was equipped with both X-ray and MRI machines. This was necessary as we had been forewarned that sometimes this kind of fracture fails to show up on an X-ray, only on a scan.

As instructed by the hospital receptionist over the phone, we arrived without an appointment, and to our astonishment I was immediately taken by wheelchair into radiology. They detected a nasty but incomplete fracture that showed itself with flying colors on X-ray. I was wheeled into an examining and treatment room, where a nice youngish female doctor, who spoke only French, explained to Ted that a plaster cast was required for this injury. When Ted translated her pronouncement into English, I became hysterical, attempting to explain through Ted that I had very serious osteo-arthritis in both my knees, as well as a stenosis in my lower back. I offered my lay opinion that carrying around a heavy plaster cast on my foot would be counter-indicated. I thought that a heavy plas-ter cast would most certainly leave me more disabled than I was currently, even after the bone had healed.

The doctor turned a bright shade of red.

She was flustered and excused herself, most probably to consult with her superior, an elderly doctor with a long beard and a *yar-mulka,* whom we had seen just outside the door talking with other docs and looking at X-rays. Dr. Coquette, as I silently nicknamed her, had been gone for a mere five minutes, after which she returned with nurse *Ratched*—straight out of the classic film *One Flew Over the Cuckoo's Nest*—and explained in French that this was the only treatment available for my fracture.

With Ted's help, I was able to understand every word she had uttered. I insisted that this treatment would commence only over my dead American body. After listening to what Ted said in his French translation of my sentiments, Dr. Coquette said that she found me to be *trés stupide et peu coopératif.* Simply translated, this meant that

160

I was a 'very silly and uncooperative patient' and, as if anything I said was to be immediately written off as pure rubbish, she and nurse *Ratched* proceeded to prepare me for the application of a plaster cast, pulling a knitted tube over my foot and leg, clear up to and over the top of my kneecap.

For me, that was the last straw.

"No way!"

I swung my legs off the table, hopping over to the wheelchair. I plunked myself down and cried out, "Home James." Ted whisked me away in the wheelchair while I called for an Uber. My poor husband was understandably exasperated with me, his tone a mix of concern and ire.

"So, just what do you intend to do now?"

"I'm going home to find another doctor, one who'll listen to me and whom I can understand."

"So, we're flying back to the States?"

"No, I don't ever intend to return to the States, nor am I giving up on living in a country where I can't speak the language. That unreasonable I am not."

I knew, from my experience with Doctor Kind from *SOS Paris Médecins*, that English-speaking French doctors did indeed exist in Paris. Furthermore, my intuition told me that there must be another less archaic treatment for an elderly woman with a broken foot and arthritic joints.

Back at home base, foot elevated with plenty of ice to go around, and the assistance of my trusty laptop, I found just what I was seeking. It was not a hospital, but an up-scale, modern, private orthopedic clinic, with sports medicine docs, surgeons and kinesiologists as well as every imaginable kind of specialty for each part of the human skeletal system. Not only was it a state-of-the-art clinic, but the doctors spoke English, and it was quite near our home.

When I called, I was given an appointment for a time on that same day after hours with Doctor Xavier Deloin, an orthopedic surgeon who specialized in feet. When Ted helped me out of the Uber I turned and looked toward the North on *rue Lafitte*. No more than two blocks away, I could see the beautiful Renaissance revival *l'Eglise de Trinité,'* and as if sitting right on top of it like a trio of white bowler hats, the three brilliant travertine marble domes of the *Sacre Coeur de Montmartre*, so massive they looked like they were a short hobble straight ahead, rather than two kilometers uphill.

Dr. Deloin had a charming smile and a mild manner. He looked like a cross between the French cellist Gautier Capuçon, and American actor Kevin Spacey. He listened attentively with an animated expression in response to all I said, including the fact that since walking nearly six miles per day on the streets of Paris for the last two months, my arthritic pain had been greatly relieved. He even paid attention as I voiced my fear that carrying the weight of a plaster cast up over my knee would worsen the arthritis in both knees and my lower back.

I shed buckets of tears, more out of frustration than from my physical pain.

"Before moving to Paris, I was seeing a Doctor of Kinesiology for physiotherapy and had extractions of fluids and injections of in my knees of this, that, and the other thing for nearly nine years. There wasn't a day that went by when I didn't have to ice them for at least twenty minutes at a time so I could sleep at night. Paris has been my miracle cure. Walking has actually made all that treatment and therapy unnecessary."

The good doctor, whom I would now and always secretly refer to as Dr. Charming, agreed that walking and not sitting is one of the best activities for arthritic knees.

"*Bon*, when you lead the kind of life you led in Los Angeles, going from your chair in your consulting room to your car in order to drive everywhere you need to go, as one must do in that city, your bones are not accustomed to regenerating so rapidly as they need to do here in Paris where one is walking and climbing stairs every day with much frequency."

I was really beginning to like him.

"I approve of your decision to refuse the treatment offered in the hospital. Of course, you do not need a plaster cast. It would be inappropriate for a patient with your history."

Only after our long conversation, Dr. Charming gently yet thoroughly examined my right foot and made comparisons with the left foot as well, which left Ted thoroughly impressed. He also helped me to understand that when I had walked many miles in the past, sometimes for weeks or even a month, I could manage quite safely. But walking for a prolonged period of time, like the two months since I had moved to France, there was increased stress and far less down time to recuperate.

"*Voici*, a stress fracture. *Alors*, this is what you need."

As he spoke, he reached toward a small rolling table, seizing a length of wide *Elastoplast* tape, and gingerly wrapping it from the inside of my arch, across the top, and over and under the broken portion of the outer edge of my right foot.

It was a real miracle. My pain was immediately relieved. Dr. Charming had earned a new nickname. Dr. *Saint Charming* also gave me an ordinance for an air-cast. Whatever that was, it sounded lighter than plaster. I was told that the pharmacist could show me how to apply it and he instructed me to wear it day and night. I was to wrap my leg in plastic when showering, and keep my foot elevated and iced, with few exceptions, for the next six weeks.

Dr. Saint Charming scheduled me for another x-ray with the house radiologist, followed by a second consultation with him in six weeks. Before I could click my heels together and repeat, *there's no place like home* three times, I was back in another Uber headed for our last stop. I found the air-cast at a pharmacy close by. It was made of two curved and elongated plates of durable plastic, held together on either side of my ankle and down to the bottom of my heel with a system of interlinking Velcro straps. A cloth band joined both sides running underneath my heel. The whole apparatus weighed all of three ounces and it magically functioned to keep my foot and ankle stationary, so that the tiny metatarsal bone could knit itself together, once again.

I'd need crutches or a wheelchair for some time in order to keep any weight from impinging on the fractured foot, but the scheme seemed clever and doable. The only insoluble problem was that I wouldn't be able to attend the signing for the apartment on July 19, because my foot was still too swollen and had to remain elevated.

Sadly, for both of us, Ted was on his own for so many things. This was the first time in our marriage that he had no wing-woman, no second opinion, no handy partner. I was fearful that I would only become more and more of a burden on him. I also felt left out, lonely, and bored much of the time Ted was preoccupied with meetings with the architect and the contractor, working out the details for preparing the walls, painting, and building extra cabinets for the laundry room and kitchen.

I was feeling as useless as a third wheel with a flat tire. I didn't know what to do with or by myself, until suddenly out of the blue I had an epiphany. Something obvious. Just because I had a broken foot didn't mean I was a lame brain. I could talk to myself, the only person around that would listen to me, or I could come to grips with the fact that this was the ideal time to check out *Craig's List* for a French tutor. Maybe I could find one who would come to the apartment to give me lessons while I slowly recovered my mobility.

I interviewed two young men on the same day. The first candidate was from, of all places, Los Angeles. He'd been living in France for ten years and his language skills were admirable. Unfortunately, he spoke like most twenty-something Parisians, swallowing his words, dropping endings and creating contractions wherever convenient. I was concerned that even if I learned what he knew, it would do me no good in my circles. He tried to sell me on the notion that learning 'street-talk' is more important than grammar. Hearing this, I thanked him for his time and said, *"Au revoir."*

An hour later, my next victim arrived. Nicolas Thomas was Parisian by birth. He was in his mid-thirties, married to a woman of

Portuguese descent. They had two children, a boy seven and a girl two, and a little *Bichon Frisé* puppy. In that first meeting, I already learned something. In French, as a rule, one does not pronounce the last or sometimes even the last few letters of a word or name. This applied to Nicolas' name, which sounded much more French when the 's' was dropped from both his *prénom* and *nom*. Nicolas was already a step up from 'Mr. Street Talk.'

As I enquired into Nicolas' technique and philosophy of teaching his native tongue, I had a firm sense of a disciplined instructor who loved his language and, although he spoke English, was not about to let me push him around. This was a serious professor. Grammar was a must, and reading, writing and speaking true French were all part and parcel of the goal. He described many techniques that he had found helpful to use, and he appeared not only ready but excited to take on an educated professional of my advanced age. My sense was that he found these factors to be a plus.

I wasn't so sure.

That very same afternoon, we set a schedule for a five-day per week, two-hour per day intensive course of study. This sounded strangely more intense than analysis. I had hoped that this regime would get me on my way to speaking French and would occupy my mind constructively during what I thought might become an otherwise dreadfully boring six-week convalescence.

This expectation turned out to be an impossible dream.

CHAPTER 21

ONE GREAT CAUSE FOR CONCERN, both for me and everyone I knew, were the difficulties I had encountered right from the beginning of my attempt to be introduced to the French language, let alone to master it. Most days my broken foot was the only thing that kept me from stomping out of the room to escape the exasperation and humiliation that plagued me. Since I couldn't run away from Nicolas, I'd burst into tears, which made everything worse.

I had earned a bachelor's degree in psychology in three years, a Masters in two, a Doctorate—including a 375-page, clinical dissertation—in less than three, while at the same time beginning my post-doctoral training in psychoanalysis. I had excelled with honors in every subject, but I was failing this one miserably.

Everything got in my way. My high expectations, my mouth and its way of forming words, and four years of studying Spanish,≥ which I'd thought was long forgotten, but that always appeared on my shoulder as a miniature Sancho Ponza, constantly elbowing his way into the pronunciation of many French words, urging me to pronounce the "e" at the end of every word where it existed.

"Tu n'as prononcé pas la dernière voyelle," Nicolas admonished me *ad nauseum.*

Unfortunately, my biggest impediment was my mother-tongue. I was like an Eliza Doolittle, having been taught English by Henry Higgins and afterward, having to drop all but her parasol in order to learn French with Jean-Pierre Rousselot.

"If you want to learn French, you must forget your English. If you won't give it up, you will never speak French!"

Nicolas' ultimatums and warnings would cause my heart to bleed like nothing else in recent memory. I could hardly bear it. How could I just drop the language I'd worked so hard to polish throughout my career? I suspected that I'd never attain the equivalent vocabulary in this impossible dialect. Shaw was right when he wrote, "The French don't care what they do actually, as long as they pronounce it properly."

My mouth, teeth and palate were all set in their ways as I rapidly approached the age of seventy. There were so many rules and so many exceptions to those rules, along with a multiplicity of exceptions to the exceptions that my head was not swimming but drowning. I wasn't even beginning to learn the present tense in two essential verbs, *avoir* to have and *être* to be, along with a few of the verbs that accompanied them in the *passé composée*. To add insult to injury, the constant pronunciation of *oo*'s, *ou*'s, and *eu*'s, so plenteous in French, was rapidly wrinkling my upper lip that had been surprisingly smooth and youthful until my daily attempts at French *phonetique*. Just making the barest of distinctions between those three sounds boggled my mind and made my lipstick bleed.

Each day became another assault on my vanity, on every conceivable intellectual and physiological front. It was Ted who helped me to find the bright side of things. He told me a secret.

"The English language takes at least a third of its vocabulary from the French."

I kept telling myself, "When in doubt, just Frenchify an English word."

For example, the English word "exemplification" is the same word in French, but it is pronounced ex-em-pli-fi-ca-si-on, with a nasal "n" at the end. This was encouraging because it worked one-third of the time.

I was elated.

Perhaps one of the worst things about learning French was that fact that I had always loved the sound of the language. But whenever I opened my mouth, it was as if I was spitting not just knives but meat-cleavers that continuously butchered the language I adored. I wanted so very much to speak, to communicate with my new countrymen and friends, and most of all with my beloved husband who spoke this language of love like no other.

Unexpectedly, and much to my dismay, Ted refused to speak French to or with me. When we were courting, he'd read French poetry to me and then translate the lines with patience. Now, when I asked him to speak French with me, he'd say *"Ce n'est pas normale."*

I'd come back with a loud *"Je ne comprends pas"* in utter bewilderment.

I remembered that when Ted had moved to Italy to attend University, he said that he had purposely moved in with Italian strangers. In order to facilitate his use of the Italian language, he refrained from hanging out with the Israelis who were plentiful on campus.

So, what was I to do? Move in with a Frenchman who spoke no English?

I was such an irksome student that, several times, Nicolas actually threatened to quit. Those were reminiscent of my having been expelled from school in my teens, but this time it was for good reason.

Still, I worked daily and diligently, performing laudably on my homework, that consisted mainly of reading and writing French. In contrast, each and every time Nicolas would ask me even the simplest question in French, I'd react like a deer in the headlights. I froze and became deaf and dumb.

My anxiety was as high as the Tour Eiffel. I felt as is if my comprehension and expressive abilities had taken a nosedive from the antennae at the top. Each day, Nicolas rang the doorbell, I'd hobble over on my crutches to open the door, cringing before he even uttered one word.

"*Comment ça va, Judith*," Nicolas asked cheerily.

"*Bien, merci.*"

So far so good. And yet I was sure that I must have sounded rude, as I could never think of anything to say after that opening salvo. No *Et comment va tu* or anything else for that matter. The poor man would optimistically begin the lesson the same way every time. Two versions of the same, simple question were employed in an attempt to start a conversation.

Qu'avez-vous fait hier soir or *Ce que vous avez fait pendant le week-end*. Both questions left me bare, without a thread of comprehension to cover up the fact that I lacked even one iota of courage, just to simply say *Je ne comprends pas* because I truly didn't understand a word. Asking what I had done last night or over the weekend was such a no-brainer that I could have taken a guess, but it was as if I'd lost my mind at the very beginning each *séance*, a source of shame that led to chronic and intractable inhibition.

I simply was unable to express myself in French.

Meanwhile, my friends would say *courage* whenever I confessed my failures when queried. I wondered if this was some crazy, guilt-induced identification with my dead sister Carole. She'd seen the film *The Last Time I Saw Paris* in 1955. The film starred her idol Elizabeth Taylor, so she decided to learn French in school. She did well, with top grades for four years in Junior High and High School. Yearning to visit Paris, albeit too terrified to set foot on an airplane, it seemed ironic when her cancer eventually rendered her unable to enjoy the simplest conversation, in any language.

Was I here, usurping her dream? Was this my comeuppance?

Unfortunately, thinking about the unconscious why of things only added oil to the fire during this period of my physical and mental letdown while the reality took precedence. Ted had to consummate the purchase of the property on rue Vignon without me. This final act also required a legal procedure that would enable us to share ownership of the apartment, while still another would provide for a mutual tax-free inheritance if either one of us happened to pre-decease the other. This was one of the few times I missed Los Angeles, land of community property.

As my skeletal recovery dragged on, Ted toiled supervising the scraping, patching, painting, carpentry crews, day after day. He was so sweet and always remembered to bring me photos so that I could see the progress being accomplished. In the meantime, I attempted to make myself useful by tracking down our belongings from Los Angeles, which were due to arrive in the port of *Le Havre* by ship on September 1ˢᵗ, reaching Paris by truck before the 15ᵗʰ.

Curiously, both the name of the ship, *The Meteor,* and our container's tracking number, which was printed on the bill of lading, failed to match the location and date of arrival, and the shipping company was as slippery as an eel each time I'd inquire by phone or email.

"But of course, Madame, the *Meteor* is the correct ship, and it is definitely scheduled to arrive in the port of *Le Havre* in France."

The agent for the shipping and storage company insisted that this was the correct information, even though the GPS tracer that I unearthed on the internet showed that the *Meteor* had landed in Rotterdam and was already on its way back from whence it had come. I was flabbergasted and flummoxed, shouting all the four-letter words without thinking once I had put down the receiver. Fortunately, no one was around to hear me shrieking like a shrew, just like my mother.

The possibility that we might have lost all of our belongings was unthinkable.

Sleeplessness took over for several nights until I recalled that our friend Leo in Utrecht was very well-connected and respected as a former executive with Holland America. He pulled some strings with the authorities at the Dutch port, and our suspicions were confirmed. The container with everything we owned had indeed disembarked in Rotterdam. Leo was also able to confirm that the container had then been taken by road to Le Havre, and from there was scheduled to be on its way to Paris.

Nonetheless, we held our breath until we had the date and time of arrival. A miracle was happening. One more item checked off our list. To my astonishment, with all that occurred between Ted's working day and night, readying the apartment, my tumultuous French lessons, and the kafuffle over the whereabouts of our belongings, the six weeks of this torture passed like a high-speed TGV and we were on the way to see Doctor Charming. My dream, finally being able to stand on my own two feet again, was indeed sweet. I had obeyed his orders to the letter, and I hoped that the X-rays would verify my compliance.

Much to my horror, when the radiologist, whom I had dubbed Professor X, came out from behind his protective barrier, he asked, *"Rappelez-moi, depuis combien de temps?"*

Even I understood that he wanted to know how long it had been since the fracture first occurred.

"Six *semaines et un jour*, six weeks and one day."

Professor X scratched his head, which meant the same thing in any language.

He uttered the dreaded words, *"Pas très bien."*

I knew that *pas mal* meant 'not bad', which is 'pretty good' in English. But I must have looked baffled, because Professor X showed me the film. I was blown away. Even I could see that the break looked just as prominent as when I had first arrived at the clinic over six weeks ago.

"Madame Mitrani," the nurse called.

I said *merci* and lurched over to Dr. Charming's room on my crutches, films in hand. As I made my wobbly entrance he commented.

"Bonjour and congratulations on how well you are progressing on your crutches."

That should have been my first clue.

He shook Ted's hand and motioned for me to sit on the examining table.

Dr. Charming examined the X-rays, comparing the new and the old. Without a word, he gently removed the cast and the bandage and examined my foot with care, and said matter-of-factly, "Not much change."

He was as always euphemistic and gave me that handsome smile.

"This is to be expected. It may take many months to heal completely."

"How many," I asked, dolefully.

"We'll see in two more months how it is progressing. Until then, you must continue to stay off the foot. It is a little, little bone, the most fragile and the most difficult to heal. But the good news is that there is no swelling, so you can try using a wheelchair. Go out and enjoy yourself a little."

He gave me another ordinance for a wheelchair, more tape, pain meds and yet another set of X-rays to have ready just before our next meeting. The appointments were arranged, compliments of his motherly secretary. She didn't speak a word of English and was enamored with Ted and his French, I was merely an object of pity, lame and linguistically challenged.

I was crushed.

CHAPTER 22

HELPLESSNESS AT ANY AGE is a rough go. My broken foot was not my first encounter with being functionally disabled and as dumb as a post, the main features of helplessness in infancy. My first experience in memory had etched an indelible mark on my psyche. With this latest version, I experienced something akin to a painful debriding of scar tissue that left me feeling as raw as steak tartare, but not nearly as appetizing. It was nothing so romantic as *déjà vu*, but a similar feeling.

Before my first birthday, when I'd just begun to walk, some pediatrician—quite possibly the great grandfather of Doctor Coquette, the one who had planned to put my leg in a plaster cast—decided that I would need to sleep with my feet laced up in tiny, hard leather shoes connected by an unyielding two-foot-long metal rod. This apparatus was an unintended instrument of torture for a baby who was just discovering her capacity for locomotion and the wholly underestimated luxury of being able to turn over at will. This device was meant to straighten out my little feet, which had a tendency to curve inward that some refer to as *pigeon toes*.

What was not understood at that time was that this is a frequent occurrence in babies, one that often tends to work itself out as a child walks and grows. Applying braces that kept me immobile, especially during the hours when I was all alone, was a trendy fix if not too bright. Such was life in the age of paleo-psychology, when the idea that the mental and emotional damage from a cure may far outweigh any physical dividends.

Mother's fears of my deformity were assuaged, but I was left during naps and through the night feeling much more vulnerable than would normally be the case if I had been allowed to control my own bodily movements. I always believed that this was the beginning of my low self-esteem, the sense of my own ineptitude and the discouragement of my own convictions.

As for the icing on the cake, because I was at an age when verbal communication was just beginning to emerge, my limited vocabulary left me helpless to communicate my plight to anyone. Even years later, I still find it difficult to express my concerns with anything other than tears or rage. This can be annoying to other people, even to a loving spouse. After all, I wasn't an infant anymore. How could I complain about how much time I was left alone at *rue du Mont Thabor* while Ted bravely soldiered on, working out difficult and frustrating details all on his own in order to prepare to move us into our new home.

Nevertheless, sometimes one sees a light at the end of a tunnel.

The light showed itself just days before our 40-foot high-top container arrived. Ted had asked Michael, the young man who worked for us at *Mont Thabor*, if he had some buddies who could help with the post-construction clean-up of all the debris, the windows, bathrooms, laundry-room and kitchen, essentially all the gunk that had accumulated.

The light took the form of Jeffrey, one of those young Filipino men. Jeff was a true cut above the rest of them. He was not only artistically talented, bright, and kind but he also had gained a fair amount of experience in construction as well as a short period studying architecture before he'd left the Philippines.

Most importantly, Jeff was honest and sincere with an even disposition, a wry sense of humor, a wonderful smile and he simply adored *Sir Ted*. As for Ted, his heart was captured immediately. Ted found it easy to work with Jeff, and this young man was trained to work with the elderly and was always there to administer an effective massage when Ted had overexerted himself.

Jeff was also the little brother Ted had always wanted. *Quel bromance!*

The day the shipment was to arrive, four men showed up at *rue Vignon* by six in the morning. As each car vacated a spot on our side of the street, a box was put in its parking spot as a place marker. By the time the truck pulled up, there were ten slots in a row all reserved for its monumental appearance with enough extra space to navigate offloading all our goods. Two more men came with the truck and they all began to wheel boxes and furniture down the ramp and into the building.

When I arrived, there were so many boxes crowding the sidewalk, encroaching on the courtyard, and crammed into the elevator room, that I could hardly get by on my crutches. The nosey neighbors were out in full force. They all seemed to be deliberating in French about whether or not we could get all of this into one apartment. I wondered if they were wagering.

When I reached the second floor, our apartment was already stacked with cartons of all sizes and items of all shapes, wrapped in heavy corrugated cardboard and overlaid with copious amount of bubble wrap. With my crutches and no place to sit, I decided that as usual, I was just in the way. I kissed Ted goodbye and called an Uber to take me back to wait with Ziggy. Ted phoned after all the wrappings were carted off and our furniture was basically in place. I heard the unmistakable proclamation of relief in his voice.

"The whole 40-foot container was filled to the gills with packing materials when the movers left. There is very little damage, we're lucky. Do you want to come over and see?"

"Are you sure you're not too tired and hungry. It's five o'clock."

"Well, if you don't mind, I could come back and clean up and you might reserve a table at *l'Ardoise* for dinner."

"How about seven?"

As much as I wanted to see the apartment, I knew this was the best way to celebrate Ted's triumph. The table wouldn't be difficult to book at that hour and the restaurant was just next door, quiet and subdued with yummy French cuisine. We had dined there so many times, with friends or just the two of us, that the owner knew us as *habitués*, rendering service *trés gentil*.

We ate, laughed with a sense of liberation and relief, and cuddled up early, sleeping like logs with Ziggy purring and snoring at our feet. After breakfast, we met Jeffrey at rue Vignon. Our friend Laurence, just around the corner on *rue Tronchet*, came to advise. With a slight rearrangement of furniture, everything was ready for the trimmings. The art, our books and many decorative items could now be put in place. Our clothing begged to be sorted by season in order to determine what would remain in the apartment and what was essential for storing, along with our luggage, in the two stone *caves* that composed our basement, two stories below ground.

There were weeks of work ahead.

Jeff not only helped enthusiastically, but he also shared ideas and intuitions with Ted. Much to my amazement, Ted found Jeff's suggestions of great assistance rather than as a burden or intrusion. Hanging art had been a team effort, where Ted and I would decide together what went where, and Ted would measure everything meticulously before driving a single museum quality nail into a wall. On the rare occasions that I'd Uber over, I found Jeff executing this task with ease and in harmony with Ted. He had a good eye for design and before we knew it, the apartment was completely adorned and organized.

We made our move exactly one day before the expiration of our lease on *Mont Thabor*. Ted preceded me on foot to rue Vignon, while I settled up with Élie, who did the walk through and arranged for the return of our cleaning deposit to be transferred to our French bank.

"Just remember," Élie said as he helped Ziggy and me into the Uber.

"If you ever need anything, call me and I'll do whatever I can."

We exchanged *les bises* and I said, *"Merci beaucoup."*

After arranging myself in the back seat with Ziggy in his carrier on my lap, I waved goodbye to Élie and to 26 *rue du Mont Thabor*. I'd always have fond memories of that place, our *pied à terre,* our first foothold in Paris.

As we drove away, I called Ted.

"I'm on my way. I'll call when we're on Vignon, okay?"

"Of course, we'll be downstairs waiting. *A tout à l'heure.*"

As Ted rolled Ziggy and me out of the elevator and through the front doors, I all but exploded with ecstasy. It was the first time I'd been in our home since everything was in place. I burst out, absolutely elated.

"It's uncanny."

Ted hugged and kissed me and took me, one by one, through every room. I only had to use one crutch on my right side while I held onto him, my left arm entwined in his right, just to be safe.

Although our belongings were not arranged in exactly the same way, nor were they stationed in the same rooms as they'd been in Los Angeles, each item appeared as though it had always lived right where it was. This was the first move I'd made where I'd felt at home from the start, the only place in memory that was just as I'd dreamed it could be.

As we sat in the living room in our red velvet barrel chairs and let Ziggy out of his carrier, Ted pointed out that our largest Persian carpet, the one meant for the *sejour,* just barely fit to the millimeter between the edge of the hearth of the fireplace and the molding above the parquet, directly across the length of the room, the wall with the library.

It had to be providence; we'd arrived at our destination.

The sheers and even the draperies left to us by the former owners, with their faint floral figures in subtle shades of old brick red and jade green against a pale, antique gold-colored ground, were as if custom made for our furnishings. All were in harmony, and even our throw pillows and chairs were complementary in color. The walls were very close to the same honey-hue we'd custom blended for our Greenfield condo. The elaborate *dentil* crown moldings, decorative door and cabinet dado, like all of the ceilings, were painted off-white, matching the sheers and causing the high ceilings to appear even loftier and the soft color of the walls to pop.

The building had been erected in 1880. Coincidentally, years ago we'd discovered our beautiful French Louis XV-style antique buffet and hutch to complement our French dining room suite, which was made in South Carolina by Scott, before China put the American furniture makers out of business. "Louis" had somehow found his way from France to Santa Monica, hidden in a dusty store house behind a gas station off Lincoln Boulevard. He was gorgeous but thirsty.

Ted lovingly applied orange oil to his surfaces daily, until his majestic brandy luster was fully restored. I'd always promised that I would take him back home to France one day. His elaborate *cartouche,* top and center of the hutch, fit nicely beneath the ceilings in our *Salle à Manger.* He also happened to have been crafted in 1880.

Soon after our offer on *rue Vignon* had been accepted, we realized that we'd need more space than the two libraries shipped from our house in the States for our books, one for each of the two bedrooms. We were prompted to visit the famous flea market, *Les Puces de Saint-Ouen,* where we discovered an elegant *bibliothéque* with beveled-glass doors, one that fit as if it was made to occupy the wall where it would stand in the living-room, directly across from the fireplace. This piece was fashioned out of *Palissandre* wood from Brazil. With its deep, dark, rich and radiant sheen, its strength and distinctive grain, this wood had become a perfect medium for French luthiers making violins and other stringed instruments. Our old 'new' library had also been created in 1880. It was beginning to look as if we and our furnishings had been predestined to reside together in this place forever.

Even Ziggy was at ease, happy to be home with all of his own things. He padded about the flat, sniffing his recognition and approval of all that was familiar, and climbing atop all that was new, claiming that terrain as well. The first few weeks, especially at bedtime, Ted and I wended our way from room to room, as if sleepwalking, admiring our Parisian abode, with the Malcolm Liepke watercolor with its somber scene of couples drinking in intimate conversation in a public bar that hung over our liquor cabinet, the large autographed Pablo Picasso lithograph of his first wife Helga, our three Altman landscapes of parks in Paris, London and New York that brought out the blue, green and golden-yellow striped draperies in the entrance of the apartment. Sitting for a long while in the dining room, we were in awe at the resemblance of a painting of a stained-glass window onto a courtyard painted in oil by Ted's cousin Varda, and that we had placed on the right side of its twin, the stained-glass window opening onto the room onto the courette. On the opposite side of the courette window was a duo of hand painted watercolors from and of Venice that hung next to the niche that was the perfect spot to display our Burano glass sculpture, designed by d'Chirico with his signature etched in the hand-blown glass by the artist who had executed the piece for him. With my head on Ted's shoulder, I sang 'Over the Rainbow' with a scratchy voice; 'the dream that we dared to dream' really had come true.

We lived in the most beautiful place in the world.

CHAPTER 23

NATURALLY, JEFF AGREED TO STAY ON as our helper, coming twice per week, cleaning where we couldn't reach, handling the heavy lifting and the ironing, repairing this and that as necessary, and carting things from the apartment down to our basement. Not too long before our move we had begun to feel our age, when we discovered that it was quite a feat for either of us to maneuver up and down the too-narrow, steep stone staircases, two floors below ground level. Jeff was dubbed our *chevalier* in tee-shirt. Nevertheless, Jeffrey called Ted "Sir" and me "Madame" long after our relationship evolved into something more than any of us could have foreseen.

In December, just six short weeks after we had moved into our home, I had to travel to London to present a paper for which I had just been awarded a prize. As I still suffered from my injury, which had yet to completely heal, Ted agreed to come with me, while Jeff took up temporary residence in our home to serve *Prince Siegfried* and to provide company for him in our absence, especially overnight. Jeff loved staying at our place and adored Ziggy who returned his sentiments wholeheartedly.

I still needed my forearm crutches, but all train stations provided wheelchairs and I could count on the museums we'd be visiting for one as well. London by *Chunnel* from Paris was only a bit more than a wild two-hour train ride, mostly in the dark. We checked into the Swiss Cottage Hotel, our home away from home during our month-long first trip to London in 1984, an experience that truly altered the course of my life and both our professional careers.

JUDITH L. MITRANI

We'd come for the Summer of '84 to attend a week-long psycho-analytic conference and to spend three weeks sightseeing with Ted's parents. We stayed in the quaint, white clapboard, two story Swiss Cottage Hotel. The heat wave that year lasted the whole first week and of course, there was no air conditioning. But we were younger, and more heat resistant than we were to become later on in life.

I was excited about the conference, especially the day when Frances Tustin, a prominent child analyst, who had been a pioneer in the treatment of autism at the Tavistock Clinic, would speak and discuss clinical material. I'd first encountered her work when I was an undergraduate at UCLA.

I was an 'older' student, and thus was interested in taking more challenging courses than just the usual required curriculum. One course I'd never forget was taught by Professor Ende, a visiting lecturer on loan from the department of literature of the California Institute of Technology in Pasadena. Dr. Ende was not only a lit professor, but he was a psychoanalyst as well. The course he presented was titled "The Language of Suicide in Literature." It was divided in half between readings by and discussions of important literary figures who had either committed suicide themselves, or who had written stories in which characters had suicided, writers like Sylvia Plath, Virginia Woolf, Ernest Hemmingway, Anne Sexton, and Edgar Allen Poe.

The other half of the readings constituted an intensive study of the relevant works of several British psychoanalysts, including Frances Tustin. The works of these post-Freudian London psycho-analysts provided a lens through which I would more deeply come to understand the nature of suicidality. Most significantly, Professor Ende's course was to be my introduction to the work of Frances Tustin.

A few years later in graduate school, simultaneously completing my doctoral studies in psychology and beginning my psychoanalytic training, I was fortunate to be able to take up a more thorough-going study of Tustin's work in a seminar on psychosis and autism.

Her ideas merged with my own intuition and became one of the cornerstones of my dissertation on psycho-somatic elements in the development of bronchial asthma.

Ted and I attended that conference in '84. It featured four well-published analysts, including Tustin. Each spoke for a full day and commented on clinical cases presented by some of the participants, including Ted. For me, hearing Tustin in person with her lilting voice, her gentle but firm tone, and her vivacious physicality full of bodily gestures that captured her own corporeal sense of the emotional experiences of the patients she treated and discussed was the high point. Most impressive was her authentic character, which moved me deeply and personally. One could say I had a crush.

Throughout the remainder of our stay in London with my in-laws, visiting castles and monuments and museums, I felt an intense yearning to see Mrs. Tustin again before we left England to return to the States. On the penultimate day of our trip, I asked Ted if he would mind if I arranged a visit to see Mrs. Tustin. He was pleased with my idea, so I called the Tavistock and naively asked how I might contact her. I was given a phone number that I assumed was her office number. But when I called, she answered the phone in that lovely and lively way I would come to know well.

"Frances Tustin, here!"

I introduced myself and told her that we'd just attended the London conference. I asked bashfully if she might allow us to take her for tea before we returned to the States. However, to my dismay, she said that she rarely left her home, which was one hour by train outside of London. My heart fell and broke into pieces on the floor. I feared I'd never see her again.

Then, much to my surprise, she continued.

"But, if you will take the train to Amersham, I can fetch you with my car and we can spend the day together."

I was over the moon!

I wrote down all the directions she gave me, and excitedly told Ted the news. We left early the next morning and arrived at the little train stop in that small and quaint town of Amersham where we spied Frances lingering alongside an old white compact car, seated on her shooting stick.

She drove us to her cottage, just outside of the village, slipping the clutch all the way. If it had been anyone else I might have cringed. I was convinced that I was fantasizing the whole scene when she pulled the car into a circular driveway bordered with pink and blue hydrangeas and many lovely rosebushes in all colors and in full bloom. It was a true English garden.

Her husband, Arnold, stepped out of the flower bed with his pruning shears and a basket full of blossoms. He was handsome with a ruddy complexion, slim and quite tall with a stately posture at an age when others might have been bent. We were surprised to learn a bit later that he was almost completely blind.

Inside their home, filled with cozy overstuffed sofas and chairs with old English rose flowered chintz upholstery, Arnold offered us tea and cakes and we learned about each other over many hours. Arnold also recited several of his humorous limericks, mainly about various figures in Psychoanalysis whom he had known well and would tease mercilessly with his witty verses. We learned that he had been a renowned electrical engineer and quite the renaissance man, also well known in the areas of control theory, economics and biology.

"I developed new methods for gyroscopic stabilization and further applied servo-mechanisms to tanks and naval guns before the war, and I was once the Chair of the Department of Electrical Engineering at The University of Birmingham."

Frances piped up like a woodlark.

"I like to say that Arnold was given the electric chair in Birmingham."

We all laughed, and I drank more tea than I'd ever had in my life.

After a while, Frances suggested that we drive over to a lovely place in town called Ambers of Amersham. She confessed to being quite a fashionista, loving all things pink and purple.

"Ambers is the favorite boutique of the ladies in waiting to the queen you know, and mine as well."

Ambers was located, along with its quaint Tea room, inside a 16th century Tudor home that was built on an 11th century silk mill, whose crystal blue waters still ran giggling through the rooms of the building, as if it were haunted by charming tenants of years gone by. We were greeted by the owners, an elegant elderly woman named Carla and her bachelor son, Alistair. They were clearly fond of Mrs. Tustin and treated us all to an assortment of delicious sandwiches and sweets, and more wonderful cream teas. Ted even managed to elicit the colorful history of their establishment and how they'd come to own it.

They specialized in Italian silk clothing, mostly women's but men's as well, and would put aside anything in pink or purple in Mrs. Tustin's size until she could come by at sale time to try them on. When left on our own, just the three of us, we conversed endlessly with Frances about our work.

A young teenage boy with pleading eyes came over to our table and stood politely until addressed.

"Excuse me, are you psychoanalysts? May I please just sit with you and listen?"

Mrs. Tustin replied, in her cheery Northern dialect. She tittered and insisted we weren't so special.

"Of course, you may sit with us, but you know we're just barmy people treating barmy people."

This was the Frances Tustin I remember best, upbeat, unsentimental, genuinely humble, with arms wide for all who wished to learn. From that day on, we were to become fast friends. I'd call her weekly and she'd write at least twice per week. I can still recall jumping for joy each time I would catch sight of one of those blue Aerograms from across the Atlantic popping out of the mailbox.

She'd read and vetted my papers, all of which were published with rare requests for revision, thanks to her protective and sensitive counsel. My phone calls to her were often made in the middle of my night when I couldn't sleep. A hard-to-reach patient, my difficult analyst, or a question about something I was writing were all met with a big dose of empathy, stories of patients she herself had lost sleep over, or her own analysis with Dr. Bion, a giant in the field, who had lived in Los Angeles for the last eleven years of his life and had quite an impact on all three of us. Frances used to tease me, reminding me that I had been the one to take Dr. Bion away from her.

Sometimes there was a request for Ted to have a look at something she was writing, before it was sent off for publication. What a compliment!

When I called, it was always late morning for her. She'd be sitting up in bed writing. I could imagine her in her knitted pink and purple woolen bed jacket, a pot of tea covered in a hand-knitted cozy, and a cup and saucer beside her bed.

"I know just how you feel, Ducky. If only Dr. Bion had been a bit easier on me, I would have been such an amiable and good patient."

I was thoroughly consoled, and we'd laugh at the folly of it all. Afterwards, I could always find my way back to sleep or sometimes I'd return to my writing, and the world seemed right again. In secret, I called her 'Granny Franny'; She was my fairy godmother, my mentor, and my clinical and theoretical advisor, all rolled into one small person. She was, by far, one of the most significant souls in my life.

Ted and I took several trips to see Frances over the next ten years, but the last time, in October of 1994, I had to go it alone to say good-bye. Arnold had died at the age of ninety-five in January of that year and Frances, who was not yet 81, had attempted to prepare me the first time we spoke on the telephone after Arnold's death.

"It's like two old trees, whose lives and roots are so intertwined, that when one dies the other is not far behind. That is how it might be, Ducky."

The call I had been anticipating came at the end of September from Arnold's nephew, Graham Tustin. He conveyed a solemn pronouncement.

"If you want to see her, you must come straight away. Frances is dying."

I informed my patients of an urgent personal matter, and that I would be away from Thursday the 6th through Monday the 10th of October in 1994. I packed a small duffle bag with a couple of sweaters, an extra pair of jeans, a nighty and slippers, and various under things. Squashed into my bag with the rest were many small gifts and cards from all those in Los Angeles for whom she had also been an important influence.

The rough ride in the very back of the plane was harrowing and unbearably long, followed by what seemed to be a more protracted than usual train ride that made a stop in the small town in Buckinghamshire, not far from Amersham, where Frances was being cared for in a nursing home called Rayner's. She was gleeful when I told her that I was hopping a plane to be with her for a few days.

"The people here at Rayner's think you must be quite daft to come all this way from Los Angeles, just for a few days. They're convinced that one such as yourself cannot possibly be allowed out on the streets. Happily, this means that you will be taking all of your meals with me at Rayner's."

Frances laughed as she told me what to expect. She certainly didn't sound like someone who was dying. It was incredible that, even as ill as she was, she was still full of good humor and life. All the way, I was both excited at the thought of being with her once again, and terrified that she might die before my arrival. I was picked up at the train station by the owner of the bed-and-breakfast where I'd arranged to stay, supposedly within walking distance of the nursing home.

When I got into my room, I picked up the phone and called Rayner's.

"Oh yes, Dr. Mitrani," a cheery voice responded.

"Mrs. Tustin is eagerly awaiting you. She is in the sitting room, so I'll pass the telephone to her."

However, instead of Frances' voice, there was a deep, foreboding and foreign declaration from what sounded like a large woman with a complex accent.

"Frances can't possibly see you today. She is entertaining me and my group of young therapists from Buenos Aires, whom I have brought along to a conference at the Tavistock. And the afternoon will be taken up by a meeting she has with her accountant. I suggest you try to call her tomorrow."

After her thoughtless command, she hung up the phone without so much as a salutation, before I could lodge a complaint.

I was absolutely devastated. How could life, my life, change so rapidly? I refused to believe what I'd heard. I cried my eyes out in the shower. I washed off the road dust, dried myself with a huge terry towel, pulled myself together, changed into clean clothes, and applied fresh make-up to camouflage my red eyes and nose. I walked myself down the path, through the meadows, and along country shrubbery, emerging like a hedgehog two miles later through a gate that led me from a cow pasture to the front door of Rayner's, in spite of the nay-saying of this unfriendly interloper.

My spirits were lifted up by one of the nurses who met me at the front door with a heartfelt greeting. She even knew my name. She knew I belonged there. I began to relax.

"You've had a very long journey, my dear. I'll show you to Mrs. Tustin's room, just follow me. I know she can't wait to see you."

I shut my eyes and held my breath as I opened the door to the room.

There was Frances, sitting propped up in a club chair, her tiny feet resting on a cushioned stool. An enormous East Indian woman sat across from her. This visitor was dressed in traditional Indian garb, surrounded by eight or nine younger women, all sitting on the floor and on top of the bed, occupying all but a small padded square ottoman next to the door, which I later discovered was a commode, better known in the States as a porta-potty.

I quickly dropped down onto this low hassock. I was crushed by my initial impression; Frances had not recognized me. A deeply entombed childhood memory sprung into mind, in what was literally a second before a glint of recognition came into those huge blue eyes of hers, now sunken in a tiny, wizened face. She was far from the Frances with the plump and jolly Mrs. Santa Claus cheeks that I remembered.

This twinkle in her eyes was followed by arms that opened to me, beckoning me over, as she swept off the pile of papers that occupied the dressing table chair next to hers so that I might sit by her side.

"Come here my dear one."

I flew into the space in her nest that she had enlarged, just for me. We'd both changed in the two years since we'd last been together. She was now so small and frail, her tiny hand in mine. I'd put on weight since the last time we'd visited, and had much more hair, now long and greying. In spite of all the ways I'd changed, she had remembered me after all.

With a scant few minutes for introductions, she politely dispersed the crowd of visitors from South America, who'd apparently had worn out their welcome. I finally recognized the queen of the group, Kamala, whom Frances had put on the list of contacts she'd sent me over the years.

"Well, my dear, you've come just in time. Saved me from this idolizing gaggle of girls from Argentina. Please tell me, how was your flight?"

As always, she was most interested in the other. Our time together went all too quickly. I'd left L.A. on Thursday, arriving Friday. Monday was not far off, and our time was peppered by visits from other analysts stopping in from London to pay homage. A youngish Tavistock trained psychotherapist, who was very close to Frances, had been helpful to her, taking notes as Frances dictated, trying to put her thoughts on paper for a new article on autism for *Nature Magazine*. I knew this must be Maria Pozzi, another name I recalled from Frances' list.

The list had been mailed to me, bit by bit, in case I wanted to meet others she was close with. I called the list "The Sisters in Frances."

Maria and I immediately hit it off and cooked up a scheme to dress Frances up in her pinks and purples, to drive her in Maria's old and extremely small Mini Minor *Cinquecento* car to say farewell to her little cottage, just one day before the sale closed. The accountant had assured Frances that she could live to be at least one-hundred on the money she had received from the sale of the bungalow and the small pension that Victoria Hamilton had collected from all who knew and loved Frances around the world. Vickie had a list too. I didn't feel so alone.

After we visited the cottage and Maria clipped some of the remaining flowers for Frances from her garden and bunded them in foil, we drove to Amber's so that Frances might say hello to her old friends, Carla and Alistair. Carla, who had recently suffered a stroke, was much older than Frances. However, with her son's loving care, she'd recovered well and was happily showing off her new mahogany cane with its hand-etched sterling silver *pommeau rond*. We took photos all around the table as souvenirs.

Frances was so very happy and grateful to us for helping her to overcome her fear of leaving the safety of the nursing home. She even giggled about her fantasy that she had been the one to help her mother overcome her own fears of leaving the house during the Great War, when Frances was just a bit of a girl.

On my last morning before taking the train back to the airport, it was just us two, alone. I wheeled her into the garden at Rayner's and parked her under the trees by a pond. She loved the peacefulness of the garden, where colorful flowers were also saying their goodbyes in mid-Fall. I pulled up a chair and held her hands in mine. She stroked my hair and looked into my eyes through her thick lenses.

"You are my lovey ducks. You'll come again next year, when I'm much better, after all the treatment is over. And by then I will have my own small apartment right over there."

She was as optimistic as ever, gesturing toward some newly constructed small assisted-living units across the patio, nearly completed and almost ready to move into. I knew she was in denial, and somehow, I suspected that she knew it too. Her doctor had said that the cancer, originating in her appendix, had already metastasized. He told me that she had less than three months to live. As she spoke, she pointed and smiled with a dreamy look on her beautiful face, a glimmer in her Robin's-egg blue eyes, her skin as fine and as pale as pink vellum.

"That's where residents at Rayner's live after they recover. Some people think I'm not in touch with reality, but I know how I feel. So much better since you came. It must also be the treatments they've been giving me."

I was saddened. I'd been told that the only recent treatment they'd administered was by a dentist that Frances had seen the week before, and even that was only palliative.

"Cheer up, lovey ducks. You seem very far away. What is it? Tell me," she nudged with sincere interest.

I decided to tell Frances what had happened the day of my arrival, that clear sharp memory that had stabbed me in the heart when I'd first opened the door to her room, that brief moment when I knew she hadn't recognized me.

"It happened so fast, it was so vivid, so real. My mother's mother, my only living grandparent, was coming to Los Angeles from New York City to live with my sister Carole. She was about your age at the time and I was eleven. I was so excited to finally have a Grandma, that most captivating of all beings whom everyone speaks of with nostalgia. Warmhearted sights and stories and sweet smells, cuddles and caresses, white hair like cotton candy, that's what a Granny meant to me."

"The day my mother and I went to pick her up at the airport, I could barely contain my elation. I wore my prettiest dress, my black patent leather belt and Mary Jane shoes. As we walked toward the gate, Mother said, 'There she is, your Grandma Bessie.'

"I took off running as fast as a I could, crying out, Granny, Granny. But as I came closer, she looked right through me as if she didn't know or care who I was. It was as if I were made of jelly jar glass. My heart shattered as she walked brusquely past me toward Mother."

I couldn't help but tear up.

"That was the memory I recovered in that moment, deadly."

Frances took my hand in hers, looking deep into me, not through me.

"Oh, my lovely ducks. I'm so very sorry for that. But of course, you are absolutely right. It took a second for me to recognize you, with your long grey hair and all those packages and envelopes overflowing your sack.

"Your memory reminds me how queer the mind is, full of surprises, all wrapped up tight, unimaginable and unrecognizable until something unexpected presents itself like a mirror looking into the soul, and reminiscence takes over."

Frances was full of passion and sympathy. She gave me a big hug that wrung out all the hurt feelings of being left out in the rain, of being unloved, unremembered, unwanted. I told her that without her body of work, her personal interest in mine, and her generosity and wisdom, I never could have come this far. She looked distant for a moment, and then she returned.

"I'm just concerned that nothing I've written will survive once I'm gone. You know, I might not survive, don't you?"

I nodded.

She'd been the Grandmother I never had. To her credit, and my benefit, she had never given me specific instructions about what to say to my patients, convinced that I needed to find my own way of expressing my observations to them.

"I think that the important thing is to be fluid, spontaneous, real and natural. And if you can grasp my scheme of understanding, without being overshadowed by my personal style, your own formulations will spring up in your mind like seedlings in the sunshine. I think of our discussions as the soil in which your own individual understanding will continue to grow and blossom, and I imagine that your thoughts will germinate like plants, that you will be able to say things in an authentic and organic way that will prove to be meaningful to each of your patients and to the analysts who read your papers and books one day, and you will help them all to flower brilliantly."

Was she telling me that I was a part of her legacy?

I remembered how difficult it was for me to leave her that day.

I recalled sitting and waiting, just a month later, with Vickie Hamilton in her home in Brentwood. It was the eve of November 11, Remembrance Day in England. We received the sad news that it was over. Frances was gone. But her work remained, alive and still growing, in the many conferences all over the world that to this day are all created to honor her work and her memory.

Those recollections occupied me on the train to London in December of 2016.

CHAPTER 24

SO MANY PEOPLE FROM THE 'LIST' have graced our lives since Frances died, one month to the day after I left her side. What stuck with me most, and what shaped my life indelibly, were some of her disturbing last words.

"I am concerned that nothing I've written will survive once I'm gone."

At the time I couldn't respond to these words. Nothing I could have said would have assuaged her fears. But, a year after her death, I founded the Frances Tustin Memorial Trust and in some small way, was able to make sure her fears would not materialize.

The Trust became an Internationally respected organization, a living monument to Tustin's work and a source of remembrance and continuance of her groundbreaking model for the understanding and treatment of autism. For twenty-two years before my retirement, it grew into a source of encouragement for the explication, extension and expansion of Tustin's seminal ideas. In 2018, after I had failed to establish the Trust in France, the torch was passed to Alina Schellekes, one of the younger former prize awardees, to be co-sponsored in Israel by the Tel-Aviv University.

On this visit to London, Ted and I were guided through the new wing of The Tate Modern Museum and treated for lunch at the Stately and very British Oxford and Cambridge Club by our friends George and Pramila. They had been guests in our home for dinner, years before as friends of JoAnn's, and we had kept up a lively connection ever since.

I read my paper on that night after a quick bite with the President of the Society, a fitting fare thee well and what I expected was the end of my professional career in that same city in which I had found my professional mentor. The following day, we visited the National Gallery with our dearest friend in London, Maria Rhode. She too had been very close to Frances, even before I had. And Maria had stayed with us in Los Angeles years before to present her award-winning paper, one of the first to earn the Frances Tustin Memorial Prize. We three had lunch in a charming cafe in the museum before Ted and I left for St. Pancras Station to catch the *Chunnel* home to Paris. I felt that this was only a taste of how it would be for us in the future, when everything, every place and person was so geographically close.

As lovely as it had been to see a few of our good friends, visiting a glamorous British club, and seeing wonderful art in London, I had missed our new home, and hoped that this would be our last trip away for some time. The Christmas holidays in Paris that year were cheerful and bright, even while the country was still chinning itself up out of the recession. With Jeff's help bringing up all of our Christmas decorations from the *cave*, we trimmed our nine-foot-tall Douglas fir tree, and our home was dressed up in its full, festive attire.

Just before the holiday, we invited some of our French friends for a real Italian Christmas meal. It was our first dinner party since the move. Richard and Claudine lived in a lovely penthouse filled with Medieval and Renaissance *objets d'art* in *Charenton-le-Pont*, a suburb on the South East border of Paris. They had transformed their rooftop into a magnificent glass sunroom, adjacent to a garden filled with white birch trees in built-up wooden planter beds surrounded by flowering shrubs and containers bursting with radiantly colored geraniums of red, pink and white.

I laughed as I remembered the first time we visited them for dinner. It was one evening after the four of us had attended the *Opera Bastille* and had enjoyed a performance of Wagner's *Lohengrin* together. Line number eight of the Paris *Metro* from the Opera traveled directly to their stop in *Charenton*. Trotting after Richard from the train to the escalator that took us to the street, he apologized for the long walk we would have to take to reach their home from the Metro.

When we arrived at the top of the escalator, we were surprised as Richard turned left and opened the first door on our right, belonging to their apartment building. Now that was door to door service! They also took the same line to visit us, exiting at *Madeleine*, barely around the corner.

We were mad about Richard's playful and enthusiastic way of entertaining, his love of sharing all that was his kingdom, and his pride in Claudine's ever artful cuisine. Claudine cooked and served, blithely skipping through her well planned and beautifully executed evening. She was one of the most joyful people I'd ever had the pleasure to know, and she was also incredibly patient with my beginner's French.

We had made the Uhls' acquaintance twenty-five years before our move to Paris, when they had come to visit Los Angeles with our friends, Alain and Monique Gibeault, whom we had known for nearly eight years. Alain had served on the site visiting committee with three other analysts, one from São Paulo, one from San Francisco and the most senior from Quebec, all sent as emissaries from the International Psycho-Analytical Association to examine every aspect of our small society and its institute, including the work of every senior analyst and candidate in training, attending each and every class and business meeting to determine if our society was qualified to become a direct component of the International, skirting membership in The American Psychoanalytic Association.

Because Alain represented France, all assumed that he would need a French speaking intermediary, and so it happened that Ted was assigned to be his *chaperone* throughout the visit. They had not realized that Alain had been born in French Canada and was fluent in English. Nevertheless, he and Ted bonded instantly with their common languages, so much so that the two of them even got lost one day, having lunch at the beach in Santa Monica.

This was at a time when cell phones were virtually non-existent, and no one knew how to reach them. When Alain failed to show up to administer an examination of the work of one of the candidates and his supervisor, there was sheer pandemonium until I was able to locate them, enjoying a *tête-à-tête* at Gladstone's by the Beach.

Each evening that week, we took Alain out on the town. I suggested one night, when I realized that we were still driving around after midnight, that he might need to get some sleep before his early morning meetings.

He replied, "Sleep? I can sleep in Paris."

This sounded both absurd and yet familiar, since Ted and I always felt the same way each time we were in Paris. We could always catch up on our sleep in L.A.

When, in the Summer of 1995, Alain and Monique and their friends Claudine and Richard attended the International Psycho-Analytical Congress in San Francisco, we invited them to stay with us as they passed through our city during their travels in the Western United States. Because the Gibeaults spoke English and the Uhls did not, we offered to host Richard and Claudine and their teenage children, while arrangements were made for the Gibeaults to stay at the home of another colleague who lived very close by, one who spoke no French but graciously offered her guest room.

From the start, we experienced some unusual vibes between us and the Uhls, when in our pajamas we managed to converse in French well into each night of their visit, with the help of Ted's translations. Since that time, the six of us would have a reunion nearly every year in Paris before the move.

However, for this night in our own Parisian apartment, the Gibeaults were out of the country, and we decided to introduce our *Charenton* friends to their neighbors. Albert and Laure, who lived a short walk from the Uhls, across from the *Bois de Vincennes*, the beautiful woods with a splendid lakeside terrace restaurant, and two islands that floated like gigantic tortoises on the water, each filled with Canadian geese, peacocks and pea-hens under the shelter of grand trees and along with many colorful flowers, all in their glory in the warmer months.

Since both Albert and Richard were analysts in the same Society, we thought it was time that they meet one another. Laure was a talented ceramicist who had been a free-lance museum curator in her working days, and Claudine had recently retired from her practice as an obstetrician and gynecologist. She now spent her days playing her grand piano in that marvelous sun-room and enjoying their grandchildren at home, in the countryside of Burgundy and abroad. Richard worked furiously if infrequently whenever he was in town, in order to support the splendid sailing yacht on which they traveled the Mediterranean and various adjacent seas.

Before entering our dining room, we sat in the living room for an authentic French *apero* of Champagne and small *blinis* with *crème fraiche*, *salmon fume*, and black caviar to top them off. Ted lit our small wood burning fireplace for the first time. It drew quite well, blazing away as we chatted and nibbled in the living room.

The fire and the small *hors d'oeuvres* and *Champagne* had both warmed us up and stimulated our appetites for our Italian dinner, complete with tortellini soup, *cotechino* and lentils in a bed of *zabaglione* sauce, an Italian cheese board, and my specialty, a home-made *tiramisu*, all accompanied by a fine *Chianti San Felice*.

The week before our *féte*, our little rue had been lit up with strings of holiday decorations, crossing back and forth, up and down the street, right under the level of our windows. The greeting *"Joyeux Nöel à rue Vignon"* in red lights was suspended on each end of the street. Ted was the proud and smiling host at the head of the table, and I was ecstatic to be able to fill our home with good friends and good food in such a merry atmosphere for our first holiday season in our own home in Paris. I was even able to stand on my own two feet, relatively operational for the first time in months.

By February, Doctor Charming proudly announced that my foot was mended, after checking the X-rays and examining it for any pain. He said that I could walk without the crutch, but that I must wear cushioned sport shoes. He also gave me an *ordinance* for a *podologue* to make insteps to protect the newly mended bone and to take some pressure off my knees."

I was heartened by the news and couldn't wait to shed my air cast and to begin to regain my strength again, after so many months as an invalid. The good doctor insisted upon one more thing.

"Be careful. You must return to walking very gradually, *peu en peu*, little by little."

I nodded my understanding and promised to be a good girl and I made an appointment with the young and talented *podologue* to be fitted for my insteps, just two doors up the street from our home. This is an example of one of the most awesome things about living in a big city, especially Paris, the city of shop keepers and small private medical cabinets. Nearly everything one could need, any service or shop, a yoga and Pilates studio, an aesthetician, hair and nail salon, *la pharmacie, la labratoire*, even the *radiologue* where I would go for my annual mammograms, were all within the quarter of the *Madeleine*.

At the *radiologue*, I discovered a truly a modern miracle. They had a mammogram machine that doesn't turn your breasts into *crêpes*, both vertically and horizontally. And the results were conveyed on the spot by the radiologist, and an immediate follow-up ultrasound exam would be carried out right there and then if anything looked the least bit suspicious. Throughout my adult life in Los Angeles, even the top practitioners in Beverly Hill hadn't offered such discomfort-free dream machines. The x-rays machine at our dentist's office was another state-of-the-art contraption. You simply stepped up, rested your chin with your forehead leaning against a plastic pad to steady you, and the scanner rotated around your jaw and, *voilà, c'est tout.* A full extra-oral computerized radiographic series in less than two minutes, replacing the semi-torturous, intra-oral, bite-wing technique yielding the 18-24 pictures and *beaucoup* radiation customary in Los Angeles.

These were some of the procedures and conveniences I couldn't have imagined. When I questioned my dentist about this new technology, she explained that the French government requires that all technicians and physicians update their equipment every ten years.

Quelle Vie!

Roxanna, the *podologue*, not only made me a set of padded arche supporting and specially configured inlays for my sport shoes that changed my posture and relieved me instantly of all pain in my hips, knees and back, but she also custom constructed an appliance that looked as if she were crafting it from silly putty. It was meant to protect my severe hammer toe and to shield the big toe next to it from a blistering friction. For the first time in memory, I felt no pain no matter how much I walked, neither in my joints nor in my feet. This magical wonder brought with it some danger I should have anticipated but didn't.

Instead, this freedom enabled me to be swept up into a sudden whirlwind of activity, with visits, one after another from three of our favorite L.A. friends, one from Seattle and two from New York. It was as if we were on a carousel of museums and restaurants and, of course shopping. French friends were also around on and off throughout the pre-springtime, and concerts at the *Theatre Champs Élysée*, the *Philharmonie*, the *Maison Radio France* and the opera and ballet at both the *Palais Garnier* and *Opera Bastille* were plentiful.

We relished some time with friends Caroline and Howard, who belonged to the screen and theatre set, living not only bi-coastally but also bi-continentally, with homes both in Paris and in the South of France, in L.A. and sometimes even in New York City when Caroline was teaching young actors at NYU. They brought into our lives, along with their friendship, a special bit of glamour whenever we'd meet in restaurants like *La Closerie des Lilas* or when we'd cook for each other in our Paris apartments. Theirs was located in the illustrious quarter of *Montparnasse* on the left bank. We loved them and were grateful to have friends from such divergent worlds, far from our own life experience.

Richard and Claudine treated us to a day trip away from *Paris* to the village of *Yonne* in Burgundy not too far from their country home. While Richard was away skiing, we returned the pleasure by treating Claudine to an art exhibition, lunch and piano recital at the *Foundation Louis Vuitton*, the magnificent Frank Geary creation that appeared like an enormous sailing ship amidst the woods and gardens of the *Bois de Boulogne*. For me this place provided consolation for the loss of two of our L.A. favorites, The Walt Disney Concert Hall, also designed by Frank Geary, and The Getty Center Museum and Restaurant, close to the top of the mountain range high above Western Los Angeles.

As we neared Springtime, we visited our dear friends Didier and Bernadette, who prepared a gourmet luncheon for us in their home in *Caen*, Normandy. Their daughter was present too, and the time passed like a gull on the wing, so quickly that its beauty barely had time to register in memory. We stayed on in the harbor in *Honfleur* for two nights, the town where Erik Satie, one of my most beloved French composers, had written his mesmerizing music for solo piano.

His house is a museum that sends shockwaves through the senses. As if cut in half, the design and décor on one side of the floor is utterly unlike the other. One was clearly intended and decorated for normal daily use, while the other was a bizarre scene, way beyond the ordinary imagination, perhaps more like a child's wonderland. Upstairs is a white room with one window through which Satie must have gazed while he sat at his white piano, creating his jazzy phrases, unique harmonies, and enigmatic melodies. Like the name of the liquor that our hotel *Absinthe* was named after, at times this Satie experience seemed like a highly alcoholic, psychoactive and even hallucinogenic experience that one cannot forget.

In contrast, a nearby serene and delectable luncheon, underneath the trees and alongside one of the shallow tributaries of the Seine was utterly pacific and paved our way to the glorious gardens of *Giverny* and the cozy home that had belonged to one of my favorite artists, Monet.

When May arrived, there were two special events in our lives worthy of memorizing. Early in the month, we were granted our first *Titres de Sejour*. Visiting at the time, Lana waited hours for us outside the *Préfecture de Police,* so that we could celebrate together as she recorded on her iPhone all of our gleeful after-moments in the delightful *Café Deux Palais,* just across from *St. Chapelle.* At last, we were legal residents, although our cards had to be renewed annually until, after five years of good behavior and no infractions, we'd be eligible for our *Carte de Residence* that carried with it ten-years of freedom from paperwork.

The second memorable affair was the wedding of our Jeffrey and his beloved Michelle. We had hosted a birthday and engagement surprise for Michelle, which was nothing less than an indescribable work of art and a labor of love, planned and executed in creative splendor by our Jeffrey. It had taken place in the dining room of our home the previous November, with just the four of us and Ziggy in attendance.

In Contrast, the wedding was held in the elegant *Mairie de Saint-Denis,* across the square from the *Basilica.* This noteworthy basilica had been the burial site of the Kings and Queens of France and was located in this northern suburb of Paris and named after the Christian martyr and the Patron Saint of France, St. Denis, who had served as the first bishop of Paris in the third century.

Jeff's and Michelle's nuptials were planned as a small-yet-royal event, taking place on Jeff's birthday, late on a Saturday morning. The handsome couple and their entourage paraded up the sweeping white marble and crimson carpeted staircase to enter the large hall where the ceremony was officiated by no less than the *Maire* of the town. Jeffrey honored Ted by requesting that he sign as one of the two official witnesses.

We were happy to be able to contribute, as our wedding gift, a sum that would cover the reception dinner which was a tradition that had to be honored in their community. For *Filipinos,* there was no such thing as eloping, and rarely did they have parents present and able to gift such a celebration. All those in the very large congregation of the bride and the groom had to be wined and dined, if somewhat modestly.

The evening, attended by nearly one hundred family, friends, and acquaintances was held at an all-you-can-eat Asian buffet, with dancing and entertainment, including western square dancing and singing in costume, compliments of some very talented personal *compadres* of the bride and the groom. The photography was endless, as was customary, and the best part of the event was the stunning and delicious, three-tiered wedding cake, along with gift bags for all.

The end of May promised more festivities for us and some travel throughout France in June as well. However, I had carelessly disregarded the warning of Doctor Charming. Jumping into my new freedom from air-cast, crutches and the like with both feet and a bit too much enthusiasm, I ended one day walking up the rain-drenched and incredibly slippery and steep steps of the *Grand Palais* to attend the *Taste of Paris*, a four-day gastronomic festival featuring French chef demos, tastings, workshops, gourmet vendors and champagne bars. Shortly after we'd arrived in the hall, I felt as if a chisel had been driven with a sledge-hammer into my left foot. Sure enough, it was yet another fracture of the fifth metatarsal, this time in the other foot and once again, owing to my habit of too much too soon. This time the X-ray revealed a more serious break, further back toward my ankle. My foolhardiness kept me largely in a wheelchair and took a full year to heal.

"It's a good thing that you are not a centipede, my dear," my friend Monica said, with her usual sharp wit and the adorable laughter of a hyena.

"You will have no more feet to break after this one."

Ted was determined not to let this bad break spoil our lives. When our Swedish friends arrived from *Mälmo* to visit us during Paris Fashion Week in June, Ted was indomitable, insistent upon wheeling me all around the town in the chair, which enabled us to show Susanna and Ülf some highlights of Paris.

We were astonished to find that they had never seen many of the sights before, although they'd been to Paris several times. Thus, on their first day in Paris, after we had enjoyed brunch together at *The Westin Vendôme* where they were guests, we went gaga over the haute-couture being paraded about by models and displayed on mannequins all about the hotel lobby. Entering an exclusive-looking area, filled with formal gowns in the middle of the lobby, Susanna inquired about the price of a dress.

"Dear Madame, these dresses are for buyers only," a woman with an official badge advised us.

"But I *am* a buyer," Susanna declared.

"*Desolé, mais oui Madame* are you prepared to buy one-hundred of this design," the woman inquired, apologetically.

Susanna and I laughed at our *faux pas* until our sides hurt. It was now obvious that this was a space for professional buyers only. At that instant, a real pro stepped in between us, asking Susanna where she'd purchased her outfit. Susanna was wearing a mainly green, very trendy Gucci ensemble, that was genuinely drop-dead gorgeous, especially on this tall, tanned, Slavic beauty with long silky black hair falling below her waist.

Before Susanna could respond, the buyer had taken photos of her outfit with a mobile phone and had texted the pictures to a colleague at another location, instructing him to buy a quantity of this same design.

Susanna definitely qualified as a *fashionista*, especially fond of *Gucci*, and always dressing Ülf in matching *Gucci* garb for men. It was now apparent that when they had visited Paris in the past, they may have come here just to shop. We walked our friends all the way from their hotel, through the gardens of the *Tuileries*, under the *Arc de Triomphe du Carrousel*, and past the facade of the *Louvre*. We headed South toward the *Pont des Arts* to cross over to the left bank, and to continue the walk by the river to the *Cathédral Notre-Dame de Paris*.

Unfortunately, the bridge was closed off with barriers of chain link fencing on both ends. Not to be thwarted by yet another barrier, *Sir* Ted pulled the end of the barricade towards us, leaving just enough room, for our friends and himself pushing my chariot, to squeeze through. As we proceeded over the bridge, we looked around and realized that there must have been a fashion show or some grand party on this site the previous night. The *chiffoniers*, probably at a nearby café for le dejeuner, had been in the midst of cleaning up the trash.

Since there was no one around, we took advantage of tentatively 'owning' the bridge. At the center of the *Pont*, we snapped photos of each other and the surrounding sights from a very prestigious vantage point, posing without the intrusion of crowds of tourists.

All of a sudden, two men came running towards us.

"Le pont est fermé maintiennent, c'est dangereux, vous devez retournes très vite, s'il vous plait," one man shouted.

Ted set the brake on the wheelchair and took off, jogging toward the perturbed man who had called out his words of caution. From what we could tell, Ted said just a few words in French and when he returned, we were escorted to the other side of the bridge, with the gates parted for us to safely pass through. Our friends were impressed, but not nearly as much as when we strolled along the river and crossed over to the *Ile de la Cité*, approaching the cathedral, walking through the stunning *Parvis Notre-Dame Place Jean-Paul-II*. There for the first time, they set their eyes on the stunning bronze monument atop the tomb of *Charlemagne* sculpted atop his horse and accompanied by two armed footmen.

There she was at last, the most magnificent cathedral in the city. After a full inspection of this remarkable Parisian landmark, we walked past the City Hall and stopped for coffee and a snack in a nearby café and simply stared while we enjoyed the view and recounted all of our memories of this sacred landmark.

Much of the summertime was similarly active, when the weather was not too hot, in spite of my disability. Richard and Claudine chose a day without drizzle to drive us all out of Paris for a day in Burgundy to visit several ancient sites in *Vézelay, Tonnerre* and *Noyer*. With a dollop of chivalry, Richard shared the wheelchair duty with Ted, pushing me up the steep hills within each village.

An evocative souvenir of my experience of this period in my life took the form of a photo taken of me by Ted, left all alone by Richard in my wheelchair, a tiny figure in the middle of the great empty hall of that medieval hospital, *Hôtel-Dieu de Tonnerre*, also an amazing archeological museum for those who were able to walk up the stone stairs, which the others did while I waited below. The image Ted captured, was haunting indeed. It was me as an infinitesimal speck in the center of this vast space that had once been filled with hospital beds. It harkened back to my early years, constricted in my movement and left all alone.

Putting this one piteous moment aside, we enjoyed delicious traditional food in a restaurant in *Noyer*, a village filled with half-timbered houses, refined brick ashlar masonry, and countless pillars and pinnacles that seemed to jump directly out of a fairy tale. There were many cobbled lanes and small squares, made mainly of chalky, granitic rock pavement, and towers that were surrounded by the river Serein. I was truly in French heaven, in spite of the bumpy ride.

The still functional *Abbey in Vézelay*, built in the year 1150, was an exquisite example of Gothic and Romanesque architecture, famous for its relics of Mary Magdalene, better known as The Madeleine. It conveyed a sense of the spiritual as did the views from the hilltops all around. They were truly divine. By this time, I was such a pro on my crutches that I hardly missed a sight that didn't require climbing stairs. It's not easy to explain how I could have had such a memorable and fun-filled time while intermittently feeling downtrodden, small and broken. I'm sure the devotion of my friends, and especially of my remarkably caring and considerate husband, served to open up a space for pleasure as well as pain.

Around that time, Ted began to attend drawing lessons twice weekly at an atelier in *Les Batignolles* owned by a couple who were both professional artists and teachers. The Atelier was not far from home by Metro, bus or even by foot, depending on the weather and Ted's mood. From the very beginning, Ted discovered that he had real talent. His cousins, all of his friends and I were amazed.

One friend wrote to Ted, after receiving some photos of his early drawings from me.

"If you hadn't retired, he might never have discovered this hidden talent."

I sent a photo of one of his drawings in black and white to another friend who was an art connoisseur. She could indulge her good taste in just about anything she laid her eyes on. I couldn't wait to show Ted what she had written.

"These pears, with the cinnamon sticks and the star anise look so real, I can taste them. When we come to Paris, I'd love to buy the drawing to frame and to hang in a prominent place in my kitchen."

One by one, the responses of all who saw Ted's drawings, could be boiled down to a unanimous 'Wow!' Since Ted did not appear impressed with the compliments from others, one day I asked, "What do your instructors say about your work."

"Pas mal."

Not bad? I was beginning to think that my adulation, or that of anyone else, might constitute a burden of expectation for Ted. I decided to stop panting like a puppy dog to see photos of his work as soon as he walked through the door after class, just to lighten the load. He went on to produce more and more amazing drawings. Each afternoon Ted, whom I'd already dubbed 'Grandpa Moses,' would return home with photos of his work from that day replicated on his iPhone. I was astonished by his rapid progress. From day one his work, first with pencil, later on colored pencils, and afterward with pastels grew more impressive by the week. He'd begun with fruits and vegetables in still life ensembles, detailed landscapes, various animals, and finally had embarked on his much-awaited turn at portraiture.

When colors began to appear, there were dynamic drawings of birds with each feather coming to life on the page, flowers thriving petal by petal, and heirloom tomatoes each in their own idiosyncratic shape and size. All were arresting, even breathtaking. Ted's daring pastel still life drawings and portraits were some of his best works, and he seemed to be going toward even more difficult materials, subjects and techniques.

While Ted was in class, I'd work on my online French course and when Richard was in town, he'd take the Metro from his door to mine for a couple of hours of language study, which I named our *pas de deux*, composed of one hour devoted to improving his nautical English and the other spent remediating my French grammar and phonetics. Try as we might, he never could pronounce the "H" in English, and I continued to find it challenging to drop it altogether from my speech in French. We were a great team, until we went off the tracks. We began to devote more and more of our time together planning a trip on his Yacht along the Amalfi Coast early in the Spring of 2018. Richard would be taking his boat to Naples from Saint-Tropez, and Ted and I would meet him there, spending the preceding week in the City, with Claudine arriving by air to meet up with us three. This plotting of a week-long playdate for the four of us eventually took up all our study time, at least that which had been devoted to my French.

Meanwhile, Claudine worked to master her Italian and Ted prepared for our time on land in a new city, one he hadn't ever visited, happy with the thought of being in any part of Italy after so long. He visualized the colors of Naples, the vast differences in the tastes and the architecture. He was fully equipped with the language and Richard supplied him with an ample supply of Dramamine for our time on the Mediterranean. Richard and I were in charge of the logistics, me when on land, Richard when at sea. But Richard was such an incredibly enthusiastic, fit and vivacious man, it was sometimes challenging to keep up with his speed of thinking, planning and doing. He was always three giant paces ahead of everyone else, full of ideas, opinions and dreams, and always chomping at the bit to get going. Ted and I admired him for all of these qualities, and I hoped he wouldn't begin to feel that I was an albatross around his energetic neck during the course he was plotting for the four of us. We were nine months away from my current disability.

In the interim, JoAnn came in the late Fall of 2017. She gladly moved at my diminished speed and we three enjoyed each other's company, sometimes shop talk, at other times gossip, and art and food all the time. Amongst other activities, we all were treated to a ride on the enormous ferrous wheel that mucked up the Eastern border of the *Place Concorde* from late Spring through Fall. Since I was in a wheelchair, they treated all of us like royalty and we were escorted past all the crowds, straight into one of the gondolas. Free admission was the icing on the cake.

Ted and I had always hated this ugly scar on the *Place Concorde*, but we had to admit that the view was breathtaking while riding atop it. I was reminded of a story that Ted once told me about George Bernard Shaw, who had opined that the *Tour Eiffel* was beautiful from any place on top of it, where one does not have to look at it.

I didn't agree.

The *Tour* was one of my favorite landmarks as well as a reminder of the time I sat nearly at its feet on a park bench with Diane on my honeymoon, one of our few times alone together on that trip, and quite possibly the last happy time we experienced before she was discovered her husband's betrayal toward the end of their stay in Paris. It was the beginning of the end of their marriage and, I suspect, had a deleterious effect on our relationship.

Other memories overlaid that first. Although halfway up the tower was the romantic *Restaurant Jules Verne*, where Ted and I had dined for our 20th wedding anniversary on a clear night in November of 2002, with effervescent champagne, scrumptious victuals and vistas, no matter from which direction I caught sight of that Parisian icon that pierces through the clouds on a foggy day, it was always a shot of adrenalin to my heart.

Near and below the Tour Eiffel, Ted's 70th birthday was made exultant with Monica's and Philippe's company at the Chez François, a dinner club hiding underneath the *Aerogarde des Invalides*, with food that created hunger, French chanteurs that made us nostalgic, and a classy atmosphere providing the perfect backdrop for all of our favorite music from Charles Aznavour to Jacques Brel, Léo Ferré, Juliette Greco and Edith Piaf. We also took Marie-Claire, whose birthday falls on the same day as Ted's, to brunch at the *Westin Hotel Vendôme,* where their buffet is a challenge to any in Las Vegas, with the food alone occupying the space of three grand dining rooms, and seating overlooking a stately garden.

Guy, Marie-Claire's husband for over 60 years, was too ill to join us on that occasion. Both blind and deaf at one-hundred and two years of age, we felt that he was with us in spirit as we reminisced about the Christmas we had spent together with Marie-Claire's deliciously roasted pheasant with chestnuts, and a surprise visit, on our last day in Paris that year, to the splendiferous Château Vaux le Vicompte in *Maincy,* just fifty kilometers Southeast of Paris, and most certainly a place we would never have found on our own back in 2007.

Life was good in spite of my wounded pride, which was healing gradually and consistently along with my foot, as verified by Professor X and Doctor Charming every sixty days. On some occasions, when Ted wheeled me about the city in what I called my 'chair-riot', I felt like a toddler in a stroller. My whole perception of the world was from below looking upward, which in Paris is not a bad POV to have on the world.

Before the real chill arrived that late Fall, we also took a short trip by car to visit with Didier and his family in their country home, not far from *Camembert,* not so much a town as it is a giant pasture full of remarkable cows that seem to smile, along with a quaint tourist office and gift shop.

We also took pleasure in discovering rare museums, an unanticipated treat. Museums in Paris were also especially wonderful during these times when, because I was officially *handicapée,* and Ted was my attending person, we were both admitted *gratuit* and were never once made to wait in a queue.

Further interruptions in my *pas de deux* with Richard came about as we neared the Winter holidays and thereafter when Richard's inevitable ski trips gobbled up much of the Winter. However, he always kept in touch, mostly with photos taken by his companion and guide, a true necessity because Richard liked to ski where no other tracks existed. He'd climb up the sunny side of the Alps and ski off *piste*, down a slope covered with virgin snow on the other side, where no other human dared to whoosh such steep and uninterrupted runs.

One email bore a photo of Richard marching uphill, skis strapped to his back in an X-shape. The caption he had written was, "Sometimes I think that I make life unnecessarily difficult for myself,"

I replied, "I think it's your cross to bear!"

Such teasing went on between us because, between the skiing and the holidays, Richard and Claudine were nearly absent from our lives, taking time to enjoy their grandchildren, especially in their family home in the *campagne* in Burgundy, or in *Thonon les Bains*, along *Lac Leman* and across from Geneva, Switzerland. I am a generally happy person, but at these times I was saddened that Ted and I had remained childless. Nevertheless, we'd enjoy the beauty of our time together outdoors, even as the chill of December began to shorten the days. That Winter it snowed and Mother Nature's pure white powdered sugar actually stuck to every surface, including the tippy top of the *Obelisk*. It was joyful, even though our geraniums nearly suffered an icy death in their window boxes.

Christmas was a special time again in 2017. We attended the services at our neighborhood *l'Eglise de La Madeleine,* and my new language made a most promising debut when I discovered that I was able to sing all the carols in French, and for the first time could understand the sermon, pronounced with sparkling clear diction by the head priest.

As 2018 approached, we anticipated watching the New Year's celebration of fireworks and the *Lumiere* projected onto the *Arch de Triumph* on television, snuggled up with Ziggy on our reclining sofa. By February it snowed even more than it had before and was cold enough that the snowflakes stayed for days on the steps of the Madeleine, on the park lawns, on the roofs of cars, on the streets and sidewalks, and even in our geranium planters, this time around, finishing off our beautiful red flowers for good.

Unfortunately, as that month entered its second week, we headed into some hard times. Ted was diagnosed with a hernia, most probably exacerbated by all the pushing, pulling and lifting he'd done without complaint while I was wheelchair bound. The day after Valentine's day, we went to the hospital. Ted was in good spirits, dressed in a white surgical cap, a black gown with white trimming, and white booties worn over his thigh-high black pressure stockings with lace trim at the top. He was still clowning around in his room, when they fetched him with a gurney to be repaired.

Ted came through surgery still in a cheerful mood, but when we returned home, that night we noticed that Ziggy was not his usual self. He'd stopped eating and was drinking liters of water. The next day he had stopped drinking altogether. It was his kidneys. We knew this would happen one day, but his blood and urine had been religiously tested every six months and had been normal, so we had hoped for the best.

He still looked so good, but in his eyes one could see that he clearly didn't feel that way. Failing kidneys cause nausea and there's no going on without undue distress. We couldn't let him suffer. Our vet, with whom we had been in close touch, agreed to come to our home with her nurse to euthanize our boy with a minimum of fear or tension. They even brought a soft blanket for him to lie on. It broke my heart when I laid my eyes on it. I knew this would also be his shroud.

We put our arms around him as he stretched out on the blanket in the comfort and security of his familiar environs and closed his eyes peacefully and forever. Doctor Tournier was very dear.

"You can hold him as long as you wish, we'll wait in the other room."

If I'd had my way, I would never have let go of his little body. He had been so beautiful, gentle and kind. I knew there would never be another like him. His death seemed peaceful and painless for him, which was really what mattered. For us, his loss was deeply unbearable. Our Ziggy had truly worked for and enjoyed his time in this, the most beautiful place in the world. His death deeply resonated with those of all my other furry children, especially all those I'd held in my arms or lap while the life drifted out of their bodies, like the sweet smell of honey-suckle dissipating on the slightest puff of wind.

It's one of those flaws in the so-called grand plan; Our beloved animals, so sweet and innocent, so essential to our daily existence, do not have nearly enough lifespan to wrap around our own. After a while, Ted and I felt obliged to let our Siegfried and his entourage go on their way.

The nurse gently wrapped Ziggy's body, enfolding him with each corner of the blanket on which he lay, one by one like the corner of a puff pastry, and with a sense of ceremony and grace. She then lifted him up close to her body to carry him back to the clinic, on foot.

"*Courage, au revoir et à bientôt,*" Dr. Tournier called out, as she followed her assistant in solemn procession down the staircase.

I could hear the lump in her throat. I understood that her last expression carried her sincere hope that we would, one day, find another feline friend to love. We sent them away with our gratitude, closed the front door, sat down on the living room couch still warm from Ziggy's weight, and had a good cry in one another's embrace. The sadness I felt that day made nearly all other recent sorrow pale by comparison.

Why do people use the word 'good' to describe a cry, I wondered what is so good about goodbye.

CHAPTER 25

EARLY IN MARCH, we were invited to speak and to visit Barcelona, Spain. It appeared that since word had spread that we had moved to Paris, we were receiving invitations to present papers and to teach in places where psychoanalytic societies that had been unable to afford to bring us to Europe when we lived in Los Angeles, could now afford to reimburse us for our expenses and offered a modest honorarium.

As it was left up to us to choose, we reserved a beautiful hotel in the old part of town on the Plaza just across from the *Cathedral of the Holy Cross and Saint Eulalia*, also known as the Barcelona Cathedral. This Gothic landmark was the seat of the Archbishop of Barcelona, Catalonia, Spain. It was constructed from the thirteenth to fifteenth centuries.

I fell in love with our room from the moment we walked in. It was enchantingly elegant, old fashioned and spacious. I flew to the windows to open them straight away. I took in a deep breath of cool, fresh air and looked down on the street scene.

"I can hear the singing and see dancing in the plaza below."

I called to Ted to join me for the view, so festive and foreign. We watched as the twilight fell over the city and the old-fashioned streetlamps generated a romantic atmosphere in our quarter. This ancient part of town, with its artisanal shops for clothing, jewelry, and art, and the small yet sophisticated restaurants on its slightly hilly streets, was as beautiful as I had imagined it would be.

"I wouldn't mind going astray in all of this," I said to Ted, with *besitos*.

We were a short walk from *La Rambla*, the place to go for open markets, shops and night-life, Catalonian modernity at its best.

"I just can't get accustomed to seeing these buildings that took so long to construct, nearly as long as it took to build all of America. It makes me feel so small and our former country of residence so insignificant, especially these days," I added, with reference to Donald Trump.

I was troubled by every text we received on election night, just six months after leaving the States. Disbelief and horror invaded the minds and hearts of our friends when the results of the election were announced.

"You escaped just in time," one friend wrote.

Others expressed thoughts, in texts and emails, that conveyed their assumptions that we had moved because we had seen this catastrophe coming.

"You were so smart to move to Paris when you did."

If not omniscient, we were lucky. It was painful for us to witness from afar the incompetence and hubris demonstrated by this unscrupulous real-estate czar-turned shoddy reality TV host, lacking even an ounce of reality in his ignorant, overweight carcass. We only subjected ourselves to the details of his rapid destruction of America and her democracy when we couldn't resist watching YouTube for the local news and commentary, or while reading reports of the shock and awe running through the governments and the peoples who had been our allies in Europe.

Meanwhile our friends and countrymen and women were forced to be subjected to bombardment by it every day. In America, it was wall to wall Trump, unless you chose to live in a cave in the side of a mountain in the Rockies. I was so grateful to be in France, governed by what seemed to be intelligent leadership with a conscience. We had the sense that President Macron would do what he could, as hard as it might be, to bring the country into the twenty-first century. He seemed to be attempting to moderate and modify with a sense of the real and would surely stand up to dictators rather than writing them love letters.

In France I felt safe and cared for much of the time. People were affable and sentient. They remembered you from one day to the next. As retirees, we had the time to meet and chat with strangers in the *Marché* or in a café or a restaurant or shop, although Ted and I were not what you would categorize as members of the café society. However, we did meet a few new people and made some new friends in Paris over time.

We also met lovely people in Barcelona, as was always the case when we traveled abroad to speak by invitation. Perhaps that was partly owing to the sense that they already felt they knew us from my writing and Ted's teaching. Now that we lived in Europe, we might return to visit our new friends, and these new friends might visit us in our home in Paris. Everything seemed so close and congenial.

A couple we had just met on the day of the conference, Antonio and Esther, took us to the Mediterranean Sea shore, where we sat outside in perfect weather, and ate fresh seafood to our hearts content. We gabbed about psychoanalysis, but quickly retired that subject in favor of learning more about this interesting city from two of its natives.

On the first night, after the conference and its festivities were over, we were on our own, strolling *La Rambla* and searching for a great place for small bites of delicacies called tapas. The following day we hopped in a taxi and headed for *La Sagrada Familia*. Along the way, our driver pointed out the many buildings that this famed architect had designed. They certainly were unique to this part of the world; Nothing was quite like the Sagrada style. In Barcelona, we soon found that all Taxi drivers were amateur guides and loved to showcase their city.

On our last day, we visited the *Fundació Joan Miró*, a gorgeous contemporary museum of Miró's art, surrounded with flowers-filled gardens. I was put in mind of the first time we previewed our house on Fairburn Avenue. We had a glimpse of some of what may have been the largest, privately owned, collection of original canvases by

Miró. Each painting enveloped its own wall, too much for the eye to take in without the perspective necessary to really appreciate these special works of art. Between the art and the oversized furniture that had clearly been purchased for a house twice the size of that one, it took some imagination to realize what a treasure the house was and how it might look without what amounted to 'too much beauty.' I can still hear Ted's words.

"We'll take the house, if we can stipulate that the sale includes all of the art on these walls."

Ted enjoyed playing with Michael's head when he made it clear that he also wished the sale to include the oversized, antique silk, French *Aubusson* carpet that completely covered the sprawling master bedroom floor. Ted did have a talent for the absurdly comic.

After leaving Miró in a setting suitable to the size and subject matter he had painted, we discovered the *Museum of the History of Barcelona,* near our hotel. After that visit, we returned to the seaside to enjoy our last *Paella.* In spite of the beauty and joy of Catalonia, unlike other times, we dreaded this return home to our apartment, now a sadly empty place. Perhaps for the time being, less than a month after we'd returned home from Spain, we re-packed our bags and flew to Naples for that long awaited and meticulously planned adventure. We stayed in a stunning hotel with a panoramic view of both the marina where Richard and Claudine would anchor their boat, and beyond to Mount Vesuvius, still an active volcano. This was the amazing sight we'd wake up to each morning from our bed.

We had a glorious week exploring the city with and without guides. Beguiling walks, climbing up to and through the preserved ruins of Pompeii, a visit to the *National Archeological Museum,* and explorations of hidden mountaintop treasures like *Chiaia, Borgo Marinari, and the Castel St. Elmo* with its new art museum and unending vistas over the city were actually doable for me, while I exercised great care and used a cork-handled cane for balance. The *Castle del Ovo* stood imposingly just behind and above our hotel.

Ted and I sat on the terrace of our hotel and indulged our palates until our friends arrived on their sailboat, the *Tastevent*, a nifty play on the word *tastevin*, a small silver cup that the French use to taste wine. The Uhl's sailing ship was indeed a relatively small vessel for tasting the wind, which can vary in the Mediterranean Sea depending on the convergence of synoptic patterns, temperature, precipitation, wind currents and their extremes.

We set sail with Richard and Claudine around the Gulf of Napoli and down the Amalfi Coast. My love of the sea made being a guest on this beautiful 'vessel for tasting the wind' all that I could need to keep me happy for the week. As we left the harbor, I was reminded of my first experience when my friend Leslie and her brother took us to sail his new sixty-foot catamaran to the mainland from Hawaii when we were fourteen.

Deep sea fishing on the South East Atlantic coast with Father was always exciting, and at nineteen, the many weekend sleep-over fishing trips off the Santa Rosa Islands near Ventura kept our freezer filled with some of the best black cod and red snapper off the coast of California in the late sixties..

As the *Tastevent* picked up speed, there were reminiscences of more recent times, too. A rough ride on the choppy Ocean in the beginning of Spring in Australia. I was on a relatively small, three-day live-aboard boat on our way to deep sea snorkel on the Great Barrier Reef off the coast of Cairns. For some strange reason, I thought this would be a good way to work off my jet lag before a four- day speaking engagement in Melbourne. In Neptune's tropical heaven, I'd rise and dive into the ocean each morning at six o'clock, so far offshore that no land was visible. On my first dive, I had panicked and returned to the boat many meters shy of the 300 I had to swim to get over the reef itself.

I was both humiliated and fearful that I might end up spending the whole three days in the high and dry safety of the boat. But I finally acclimated to swimming the open seas as soon as I shed my wet suit, which had given me a new and unwanted experience, a horrifying case of claustrophobia. I preferred looking like a Beluga whale in a tank suit, rather than a beached sea lion.

My diving buddy and I were an odd couple. She was a tall and slim Quantas hostess, 30-year-old with long red hair and freckles, and I was a nearly sixty-year-old, 5'2" shrink, with cropped silver hair, and skin that hadn't seen the light of day in over forty years. Together, we accomplished six one-hour dives each day, with an hour in between to refuel. I'd fall into my bunk at 7:30 each evening after dinner, sleeping like a baby in a cradle, rocking gently on the wind-driven waves of early September in the South Pacific.

A couple of years later, this time with Ted by my side, I was thrilled to be on the other end of the Northern Pacific, off the West coast of Vancouver Island where we spent one day aboard a high-powered motor-boat, mostly whale watching out at sea, and another in a rowboat looking for bears on the small islands within the coastal inlets of Tofino.

Not too long after that, Ted, JoAnn and I took a three-week road trip to Alaska. There were calm moments on Lake Lucille when Ted took us out on an electric party-boat that he bravely skippered all by himself after dinner for a half-dozen hours until well after midnight. We were awe-struck by the sight of flocks of amphibious private planes, landing, taking off, parked off the docks of the homes surrounding the lake. Watching them maneuver with ease on the still waters at dusk was like watching large seabirds do what came naturally. We also took an all-day cruise from just outside Girdwood, South of Anchorage, to see the magnificent glaciers calving in Prince William's Sound, which had almost entirely recovered from the devastation caused by the Exon Valdez in 1989.

A lovely visit with JoAnn's cousin Alex and his family in Homer brought unexpected surprises. We had enjoyed a lovely BBQ and drove the gravel road to the longest spit I had ever seen in order to watch the sun go down, and we drove back to our B&B where we spent the night before taking the ferry boat to visit the Kodiak bears on the island of the same name. Just before bedtime, Ted realized that he had left his warm, seaworthy jacket at Alex's home, so we called and made arrangements to retrieve it at five AM. Since we were three sharing one bathroom on the floor of the B&B, I volunteered to wake up in the dark, take my shower and dress first, and to drive the nearly two-hour round trip to Alex's home.

Traveling East on my way there at the crack of dawn, I saw ahead of me a mother moose and her twin calves. Both the car and my heart came to an abrupt halt. This unusual family were taking their time to cross the road, stopping to look me over in the process, with the sun just rising behind them. My only regret was that I hadn't brought a camera and was unable to share that unique image with my fellow travelers.

As nautical experiences go, the most daunting was that twelve-hour ride on unexpectedly stormy seas, between the spit in Homer at the Southeastern tip of Alaska to Kodiak Island. The 30-foot swells were just a wild rollercoaster ride for me, as I stood outside with other stalwart types under cover from the downpour. I enjoyed the ferocity of the ocean as I had never experienced it before, and savored the freedom to smoke, while poor Ted and JoAnn sought safety below decks in their cabins, both afflicted by a severe case of *mal de mer.*

Luckily a few days later, on the ferry back to Seward on the Southwestern mainland of Alaska, the brilliant blue seas were calm, the sky bright and sunny, and we all enjoyed watching the gymnastics of schools of bottlenose dolphins, and the enormity of the playfully breaching humpback whales, frolicking in calm weather, rare so near the beginning of Fall.

All this to underscore the fact that I could have remained on Richard's boat forever, and I would have been as content as a barnacle. But my foot had passed muster with Dr. Charming, and although I still used a cane to keep the weight off of the foot and to enhance balance, swelling was a bothersome problem from time to time. Nevertheless, Ted and I were still able to take part in each excursion off the boat.

Our friends put up with my diminished velocity, and generously shared many of their favorite spots with us. The islands of *Procida,*

Ischia, and *Capri* were breathtaking just to sail around, and down the coast we stopped and visited small villages on the *Gulf* and even further down the *Amalfi Coast.*

Field trips to *Isilo la di Ventotena, Campagna Tyrhenian, Forio, Positano* and *Amalfi* were deliciously diverse in landscape and flavor from those of Northern Italy, where we had visited many cities more than once, and where Ted had lived. There were evenings when Claudine became our gourmet Chef, after shopping with Ted for fresh provisions on land during the day. These meals, prepared in Claudine's galley and shared on board the boat in the fresh air of their outdoor dining area, were special times for us to be with our friends.

Once docked in the marina in *Naples,* we invited our friends for a last dinner at the seafood restaurant on the terrace of our hotel. We still had a few days before returning home and were thrilled that there was enough time to visit the *Tile Cloister* of *Santa Chiara Majolica,* built in the 1730's, walk up and down the *Via Parthenope,* and to enjoy just one more lunch on the terrace atop the *Grand Hotel Vesuvio.*

We returned to Paris near the end of the first week in May 2018, just in time for the two-year anniversary of our arrival in Paris and our scheduled visit to the *Prefecture of Police* to renew our residency cards. But on June 1st my whole life was turned upside down, by choice and necessity. I had decided, with Ted's encouragement, to sign up for a three-month course in French on the left bank. The course took place five days per week, and seven hours per day, throughout the end of August. The *Fondation de Robert Sorbon* was a private school for the study of French civilization and language, located in a relatively new, air-conditioned brick building close to cafes, and conveniently situated across the street from the bus stop for my return trip home.

Each day I'd leave the house early in the morning with my back-pack over my shoulders. I'd walk across the *Place Madeleine* to catch the bus, with only one change just before *Montparnasse,* arriving at the edge of the 14th on the *Boulevard Raspail.*

At seventy, I was of course the eldest in my class, including all my professors. We were a real international group. About eight of the students spoke fluent English. There were three Chinese girls. Two were nineteen-years old attending a university on the East coast of the States, spending their Summer vacation in Paris to learn French, while using their weekends and holidays to trip around and about Europe. The third *Chinoisee*, a bit older, was a lovely model living in France, hoping to advance her career.

Two women, one thirty and the other in her fifties, were from Brazil. The younger woman was married to a Frenchman, while the elder hoped to emigrate permanently, if she could obtain work papers. There was even a professional Soccer player named Malindu from Sri Lanka, of all places, and a very young Korean boy who was always the first in the room each morning and was nearly always asleep with his head on the desk at the start of class.

My first day, I was headed next-door to a little Italian restaurant for lunch, when Fleta, a thirty-two-year young woman from Texas asked if she could join me. I came to learn that she was a mathematical prodigy and could always find freelance work, but she had yet to complete her Bachelor of Science degree at a university in the States. She expressed her interest in psychoanalysis, and I hoped that she might eventually ask me to point her in the right direction, since she was unquestionably a lost soul.

Tsiminon, a Vietnamese woman, also in her early thirties, spent all of her breaks Skyping with her three-year old daughter, whom she had left back home with her parents and whom she visibly missed. My knowledge of the psyches of children so young made my heart break, appreciating what that toddler might be feeling without the warmth of her mother's physical presence. Tsimi, as we called her, had been sent to France by her family with the hope that she might develop a market in Europe for their coffee business.

Catalina, a lovely Italian woman, and Pouria, a young man from Iran, were both twenty-years-old. Ski, pronounced like sky, was a twenty-something woman from Maryland. She was simply adorable, with shoulder length blond hair and a sweet provincial look straight out of the American fifties. An Australian woman, Laura, was as brilliant as an artfully cut diamond and miles ahead of everyone in our class, even in the art of French conversation. She was a talented fashion designer who had lived in Milan and New York, and now was here and hoping to remain so.

Most of our Professors were nothing less than excellent. We had one for grammar, reading and writing, and a second for phonetics, which was taught at lightning speed only an hour per day in a special language lab. I seemed to be doing well in *phonetique*, and although my written tests earned good scores, my capacity to converse was still limited, although improving.

During Bastille Day there was the usual long weekend. Although Ted and I would ordinarily have watched all the festivities on TV. We were delighted to hear from our favorite Northern California friends, who had a home on the Ile Saint-Louis and were here in Paris for the holiday. They said that they had a surprise treat. The mystery stimulated our appetite for a new adventure. Joel and Carol picked us up late in the afternoon and we drove to the *Palais de Versailles*. A *degustation* by Michelin three-star Chef Alain Ducasse at his newly opened restaurant *Versailles-Ore* on the first floor of the palace was first on the list of surprises. This grand indulgence of several dishes, each one paired with its own wine, was followed by a special live theatrical event in the courtyard, just off a small secret area of the Palace.

The characters in the play were all lit up individually, as if for Christmas, and the palace walls served as a backdrop for Lumiere-style projections of an ancient story about the gods and the planets, acted out and accompanied by the strains of French Baroque music, and ending with a bang, a pyrotechnic salute to the Sun-King himself, a majestic treat and very special company with whom to share our independence.

A month later, Ted and I got away alone during the long weekend holiday dedicated to the Assumption of Mary in mid-August.

We took the train to *Chartres*, a charming town just an hour south-west of Paris, famous for its Gothic Cathedral, *the Notre-Dame de Chartres*, built in the 13th century. It was reminiscent of the Notre Dame de Paris, but not nearly as grand. In the evening, we enjoyed their *Annual Lumiére*, consisting of dazzling projections that made every building light up with colorful, ever changing and imaginative animations, such as people laying the stones of the church, those who were climbing the front of other buildings and peeking into windows, acrobats flying across the facades of still other landmarks.

The walk through the town in the evening after dark was no less than spectacular, and during the day we found the village to be quite *sympa*. We stayed at a hotel in the center of town and it was just the break we needed from the hordes of tourists in Paris.

Upon returning to class for the last month of the semester, we were surprised to meet the new instructor, our first male teacher. Coincidentally, Antoine was born in *Chartres*, had studied in the States where he'd earned his PhD, and had written his dissertation on Stendhal as a biographer. He had just returned to France and had taken up the post of our previous teacher, who had left us for her Summer *vacance*.

Antoine made that last month of class endurable, with his ingenious ways of helping us to practice conversation in teams, teaching us French songs and projecting French YouTube videos to aid us in exercising our comprehension of the spoken language in the most painless and enjoyable modalities, none of which had been used by other instructors.

Antoine had also arranged for us to meet for our final class in the 4th *Arrondisement*, where he took us on a walking tour of the secret gardens of the Marais, a quartier that had preserved the narrow streets and traditional architecture of medieval and Renaissance Paris. With Ted's help, that evening after class the whole group, including the students and nearly all of our professors, met at our home for aperitif, tasty finger food, both *sucré* and *salé*, and of course beaucoup de Champagne for all. We each took photos to send to

THE MOST BEAUTIFUL PLACE IN THE WORLD

one another, a festive tribute to our accomplishments and a show of gratitude to our dedicated and ever-patient instructors.

I'll not forget the moment when Raquel, the older Brazilian woman who was fluent in English and was definitely the bubbly type to begin with, drank so much *Champagne* that she lost all inhibition and jumped into my lap, throwing her arms around my neck.

"I Googled you," she fermented with kisses and hugs.

"And you're famous!"

I blushed and was pinned under the weight of her exhilaration, while everyone had a good belly laugh. What fun we had that day. My age, rather than being a fault, felt like it had made me the person I was always meant to be. I wondered if it might just be that the most beautiful place in the world is a 'state of mind,' not just a geographical location. This may have been the most important lesson learned that Summer.

CHAPTER 26

IN SEPTEMBER WE FINALLY MET with dear Monica and Philippe for dinner after their long Summer absence. We'd missed them terribly as we did most of our French friends who sought out the sun for six weeks, leaving us alone with only tourists. The next weekend we visited their home in Montmartre for the first time, since I was finally able to negotiate stairs. Their home, a four stories high private house, had Mona's consulting room on the ground floor, their bedrooms on the next two, and the top floor housed their kitchen, dining and living rooms. Just like Mona, their home was artsy, colorful, courageously teeming with eclectic, exotica, and a playful array of furnishings, *objets d'art* and paintings. Owing to Phil's talents, it was also immaculately and expertly maintained, and had the envied climatization. This visit would begin Ted's campaign to install a cooling system in our apartment later that year.

We had time until October to get caught up with the exhibitions that were about to close and discovered one more that was altogether a new find. *Le Musee Maillol* was a small private gallery with an interesting permanent exhibition of sculpture by its namesake, and a rare temporary exhibit of the painter and photographer, Foujita. We entertained at home and enjoyed our leisure time until we flew off again to Munich.

We found this capital of Bavaria, to be a city filled with a variety of Nazi era memorials, as well as light-hearted sights and sounds, and the delightful fragrance of fresh fried schnitzel in beer garden restaurants blooming with flowers.

Outside dining was made possible by the mild weather. We had spent five weeks over two separate trips to Berlin on the occasion of two important conferences and found that we were of two minds when it came to the history of Germany and the Jews. On the one hand, most Germans were apologetic, ashamed and aware of the existence of contemporary antisemitism and the possibility that Nazi-ism could reappear, without cautionary regulations and social consciousness. On this eve to visit yet another German city with a history, I was reminded of one occasion, long ago in 1972, when a young couple had purchased some acreage near Dennis' and my ranch and had built a fine home.

We stopped to introduce ourselves to our new neighbors in this sparsely populated community, and they returned the visit soon after. We had a few laughs concerning the distribution of animals that had been abandoned in the valley where we lived on opposite ends. Coincidentally, city dwellers would drop off their unwanted pups at Rudolph and Shirley's place, where they were more than welcome to stay, and all unwanted and often pregnant city cats were deserted in front of our place, where our big barn was more than adequate to house all commers. On this visit, the husband at the age of thirty, asked us to forgive him. He realized that we were Jews and because he was born in Germany to parents who had followed Hitler, he felt guilty and insisted that he personally owed us a heartfelt apology.

Ted and I had a similar experience while visiting *Wannsee* in Berlin, where the young guide, while apologizing to our group of mostly Jewish colleagues who were clearly offended, also confessed that he had once felt free of responsibility for the Holocaust, until one day in University he had suddenly realized that although his parents were not even born before WWII had ended, his grandparents had been active in the Nazi Party in their day. He too felt the desire to make amends.

Later, on that trip, we visited Dresden, a stunningly restored city that had been completely demolished during the war. During Lunch with our colleagues, a woman from Frankfurt jumped up from her seat and raced into the next dining room. She had heard the sounds of the same songs that were sung by Nazi's who would lift a mug of bear to the Nazi cause. The singing was silenced, and she returned, apologetic, and explained that the room had been filled with elderly Germans who had clearly survived the war as Nazi sympathizers if not worse.

"We dare not ignore even the slightest signs of the return of those horrendous attitudes. We must always intervene, never allow complacency to exist for a moment."

This time in Munich, Ted and I stayed in a small hotel in the *Altstadt*, the ancient part of town not far by foot from the *Marianplatz*, a large square near the city hall and the Palace, with a famous clock that enacts historical events on the hour. The *Staatsoper* was the epitome of elegance and had marvelous acoustics. Museums like the *Glyptothek*, that housed a collection of ancient and modern sculpture, as well as the *Propyläen*, a gateway in the style of the Propylaea at Athens, leading to the *Alte Pinakothek* that contained one of Europe's great collections of paintings, were enough to make us vow to return someday. But the awareness of what had occurred under Hitler's reign, even in this city filled with beauty and culture and intact architecture, never faded.

On a lighter note, the long-awaited treat was our visit to mad King Ludwig's *Schloss Neuschwanstein Castle*, a lengthy bus trip from the city, high in the mountains of Bavaria. Ted had always promised to take me there ever since we began to travel together. He used to say that it was modeled after Disney's castle in Fantasyland. The guidebooks even referred it as "Disney-like." Indeed, it was fantastic, perched high above the village atop a steep mountain.

Naively, we thought that a bus tour to the castle meant just that. But the bus stopped at the base of a 1.5-kilometer mountain trail. Only those who could endure a treacherous one-hour climb bearing a sign that read 'Danger' were privileged to complete the visit. One couple, a good twenty years younger than we had just returned, having missed their tour of the castle. They told us that shortly before reaching the entrance, they'd begun to experience altitude sickness.

This report was less than inviting, so we remained content in the village, strolled through the charming paths along the swan filled lake, taking photos, browsing the shops, and having lunch in a Bavarian beer garden, while the other tourists walked up the steepest and longest part of the mountain upon which the legendary citadel floated against the sky like a white cloud. Back in the city, we enjoyed yet another taste of German comfort food in our local haunt, the *Franziskaner Hofgarten*, where they served Ted's favorite beer, *Franziskaner Weissbier*.

After a week, we were on our way to a conference in the Polish resort of *Sopot* on the Baltic Sea and near Gdansk, where the declaration of Poland's independence from the USSR had begun in 1980 with strikes by the laborers in the Lenin Shipyard led by Lech Walesa who would become the first President of free Poland.

We were escorted by one of the conference organizers, a lovely young therapist, who drove us directly from the airport to the hotel where the conference was to take place. We arrived in *Sopot* not knowing what to expect. It was our first time in Poland. Our initial surprise was finding that a vast number of locals spoke English. Our room in the conference hotel, just a 150-meter walk away from the Baltic seaside, was a stately suite surrounded by woods.

The ballroom where the conference was held bulged with attendees, who poured out the doorways into extra seats set in the corridors. Alina and I were the main speakers for the event and clearly carried an attraction for the analysts and analytic-therapists who lived in the tri-cities area of Northern Poland. Alina was already a known quantity, since I had recommended that she be invited to Warsaw the previous year, when I was too incapacitated to accept their kind invitation.

The Polish professionals adored Alina and already knew my work, so the crowd was not a total surprise. Nevertheless, I was flabbergasted that these people in a country that had been squashed under the thumb of communism for so long were oriented to psychoanalysis in such large numbers.

Our friends, Ülf and Susanna, also came from southern Sweden, just a ferry ride across the Baltic. I was delighted that they attended the conference, so that we could enjoy some sightseeing together. The food was upscale and not our grandparent' heavy Eastern European dishes, even in the cool Fall weather, especially by the sea in *Sopot* and *Gdynia*, and by the harbor in *Gdansk*.

Such visits to far-away places, opening our eyes and minds, meeting old friends, and making new acquaintances, brought back fond memories of other foreign adventures we'd enjoyed in Denmark and Sweden before our retirement. Being so near to those Scandinavian sights, just a short ferry ride away, reminded me of the friendly people, distinctive architecture, the dark, delectable breads and of course Ted's favorite fish, Herring.

I adored Copenhagen for so many reasons. Eighteen-years before our visit, I'd been approached at the International Psycho-Analytical Congress in San Francisco by a junior analyst named Bent Rosenbaum. He asked if I was Judith Mitrani. When I replied in the positive, he commended me for my work and pronounced himself a fan.

By 2013, Bent was in charge of the committee that invited guest speakers from abroad to the Danish Psychoanalytic Society. I was on Bent's list. We were thrilled to receive the invitation, which was coordinated with the Swedish Society. We would speak in Malmö and Stockholm, as well as in Copenhagen.

For Ted, all the varieties of herring prepared in every conceivable way alongside the hefty whole grain and seeded breads was heaven. For me, being close to water, even the waters in the large canal across the street from our hotel, was rapturous. I had always felt that Mother Nature's liquid environments were a promise of eternal life itself. A good swimmer, I was a kindred spirit with Hans Christian Anderson's *Little Mermaid,* whom we met in the form of a bronze sculpture sitting on a boulder in the bay. More magical figures, with legs rather than fins, gave us a night at the Royal Copenhagen Ballet with Prokofiev's *Romeo and Juliette* with a glorious *mis en scene* to compliment the choreography and the score.

One of the most unusual places in Denmark was the spectacular *Louisiana Museum of Modern Art, right* on the shores of the *Øresund* Sound in *Humlebæk,* just a half-hour-drive North of Copenhagen. The art was cutting-edge, the ultra-contemporary architecture thrilling, but a walk down the grassy knoll for a view of the sea was for me, a religious experience. Bent's company, along with my Dutch friend Josina, and an unexpected visit to the seaside home of Isak Dinesen, made the day unforgettable.

To travel from Copenhagen to Stockholm, we opted to take the six-hour train ride all along an early spring landscape, with ice floes rolling down the rivers as we raced along. Upon approaching the city, the harbor was still not yet defrosted, and featured lots of swans and ice, all vying for space. Throughout our stay, we enjoyed bouts of light snow fall on and off between partly sunny days.

Nydia and Ingmar, new friends introduced to us online by our Australian colleague Julie, had arranged to meet us in front of a famous park alongside a row of restaurants, to have lunch with some friends of theirs who were our colleagues and to explore a sector of the city that was outside of our comfort zone in the old town. Sun filled the sky, a first since we'd arrived. We hadn't met Nydia and Ingmar before, but they walked straight up to us, offering warm hugs and handshakes.

"How did you know it was us," I asked.

"Well, because only someone who doesn't live in Sweden would sit on the shady side of the bench on the first sunny day in Spring."

I could see her point. The benches were all doubles, back-to-back. One side facing the sun, the other away from the glare. Of course, coming from Los Angeles we chose to face away from the bright warmth and were not at all tired of the cold air. After a hearty laugh, the four of us were off to a great start. We met up with their psychoanalyst friends and after a long walk through the city by the water, we parted, just long enough for us to visit two museums, before joining them for dinner in their lovely home.

When we lived in Los Angeles, such trips were possible thanks to our reputations as analysts as well as to the graciousness and hospitality of our hosts, who made special efforts for us wherever and whenever we were invited to speak from Japan and Australia, throughout Western Europe and Israel, on both coasts of Canada, and in many cities in the United States. In spite of all the struggles early on, we looked back at what now seemed to be a charmed life, traveling on the backs of our own talents and our devotion to the profession we loved.

CHAPTER 27

IT BECAME EVIDENT THAT, now that we actually lived on the continent, we could enjoy visiting places where we could just be tourists. Much of our life in Paris felt as though we were still tourists there too, albeit with new benefits. There was the ease of home ownership, always a place to come back to, or to just hang out in, as well as a few pitfalls and responsibilities.

Soon after we arrived back from Poland, it was time for Lana to visit once again. Unlike in Los Angeles, we enjoyed ballet and Opera we had never heard of. *La Dame aux Camelias*, a ballet in three acts, adapted from a novel by Alexander Dumas was on the agenda for Lana's visit. This was a special treat, performed at the Palais Garnier, a short walk from home. I could say that phrase, 'a short walk from home' a million times and never get used to the idea. Afterward we went to what was then one of our favorite brasseries, *Le Grande Café Capuccines*, all decked out in the Art Nouveau style that included ornate iron work with the flamboyant and asymmetrical use of floral and vegetal designs, along with richly colorful glass works of art, both on the walls and ceilings.

During Lana's visit, we also attended concerts at the *Maison Radio France* and a special chamber music concert, organized by Sinfonietta's *Music by the Glass*, in the *Musée Gustave Moreau* another new find, with the soiree upstairs seated amongst an interesting collection of art in what had been a private home,.

Lana left just before Ted's 70th birthday and our departure on his long wished-for visit to Athens. We arrived in Greece by air on November the 25th, a day before Ted would become a septuagenarian. The Royale Olympic Hotel upgraded us to a suite with a view that was to die for, both from inside the room and from the terrace that spanned its full width.

We could see the *Acropolis*, a hilltop citadel crowned with ancient buildings, including the colonnaded *Parthenon* temple. Directly in front was a large park that afforded us an eyeful of the *Temple Olympian of Zeus*. We dined that first evening in the restaurant in our hotel. Ted was already gleaming.

I had arranged for a guide to show us all of the important sights as we ascended the face of Mount Acropolis on marble stairs still slick from the early morning rain on Ted's birthday. He was proud of me as I climbed up each step with care, not wanting to turn his dream into a nightmare for both of us. We explored the ancient ruins to his heart's content, all the way to the top while he and our guide discussed history.

After we'd exhausted the ruins and the views from the crest of the *Acropolis*, our guide walked us part way down the back side of the mountain and started us on our visit to the *Acropolis Museum* before taking her leave. Completed in 2007, this stunning example of contemporary architecture made of stone, glass, and marble, housed a collection of antiquities barely contained in its astonishing 25,000 square meter space.

That evening we dressed to the nines. I had arranged a birthday dinner for Ted at The Hotel Grande Bretagne, one of the most sophisticated hotel restaurants in Athens. Ted was jubilant as his wishes came true, one by one.

"I love you," He murmured, reaching for my hand across the table.

"Happy Birthday, you are now officially a septuagenarian."

I was secretly grateful that we'd made it past the stats, the markers that modern medicine has deemed as pointing toward a long and relatively healthy life. Would we be amongst the lucky few who would die natural deaths?

The following day we visited the *Ancient Agora*, both the museum and the ruins of the marketplace. We discovered a quaint restaurant on a steep hillside, with a warm fire lit in an ancient clay chimney near our table at the end of the room. The day after, we arrived by foot to the Roman Agora and Hadrian's Library. We ended what was another special day slumming it for the evening in the brightly lit Pláka neighborhood, filled with authentic Greek restaurants with roomy terraces, and shops of all sorts on the crisscrossing, narrow, winding alleyways.

The most humorous was a shop selling T-shirts. One read *Oedipus: The Original Mother F - - ker*. But Ted thought a pair of hand-made silver earrings would suit me better. I also saw a playful dress, ankle length black jersey with colorful appliques of animals and people sewn onto it just below the bodice, all the way to its hot pink hem.

"But it's not *my* birthday."

"It will be soon enough. And besides that, happy 38th anniversary!"

Ted kissed me and gave me a great big bear hug. I felt so lucky to have a husband who was so generous, kind, loving and thoughtful. I hoped we'd be forever together. He was still showing me the world, just as he had right from the beginning of our life together.

"What would I do without you?"

The next day we walked all throughout the archeological site and the museum of Kerameikos, another marvel of Greek antiquities. We chanced upon an unusual gallery of contemporary art known as the Frissiras Museum. We learned that it had opened in 2000, the only museum for contemporary European art in all of Greece. The paintings were almost all figurative, and the 4,000 pieces in the full collection were housed in the newly remodeled, four-floor contemporary building, and rotated every few months. Ted took so many photos of the art that I was certain his phone would run out of storage before the cloud could snatch his data for safekeeping.

The next day we woke up late for a change. It was our wedding anniversary. After breakfast, we walked for a while and took a taxi to a far-away place by the sea, one that our Greek friend Anesto had strongly recommended. We had met Anesto through Nicolas when he and I were both Nicolas' students. Garbi was a restaurant in the town of Vouliagmeni, perfect for a leisurely lunch. This was the most glorious day since our arrival, with cerulean skies and puffy white cotton-ball clouds. Just we two were there, late in the afternoon for most diners, unless you counted all the cheeky seabirds, each one sitting on the back of its own chair, hoping for a handout.

Our driver had offered to wait for us, insisting that he had something to show us on the way back. Ted shrugged his shoulders and smiled.

"Thank you, but we will likely be a couple of hours. Are you sure you want to wait that long?"

"No problem for me Sir," our driver replied shaking his head.

"I'll be right outside whenever you're ready."

We sat at a table by the open windows, right next to a narrow walkway by the sea, and enjoyed an imaginative three-course meal, including delicious desserts that the chef brought out for us when we ordered our coffee, although we hadn't ordered any.

"These are my newest creations, so they're on the house. Please."

We showered the young chef with compliments for the attractive plating, the freshness, the creativity and the plentiful portions of his delectable dishes, every one.

"We promise to return, and to tell all of our friends in Paris, and everyone in the U.S. not to miss *Garbi* when they visit Athens."

It was so sunny and cool that we couldn't resist taking the liberty of a short walk, with our arms around each other, along the water after lunch. When we returned to our taxi, the driver smiled, opened our doors for us and whisked us away further uphill to Lake Vouliagmeni, then down the other side of the mountain to our hotel. All the way there he indicated special features as we passed. He even stopped for us to get out, to see and to photograph the view of the entire city from a parking lot, where a young couple dressed in wedding attire were being filmed by a drone.

Once in our room, we took a nap. When we woke-up we sent for a pizza from a nearby local hangout we'd seen while walking. It was the first and only pizza we'd had in Athens, made with feta, olives, and peppers. We decided on an early night and went to bed with smiles on our faces.

For me, this had been one of the best trips ever, partly because I'd never had a great desire to visit Greece and was knocked off guard by the splendor of the historic sights and the wonders this ancient country had to offer. But most especially because I hadn't seen Ted so consistently happy and deeply content in a long time.

Our penultimate day was spent exploring the ruins of The Temple of Zeus in the park across the road from the hotel. From our room, we never could have guessed how vast the park was and how enormous was the temple itself. Even the pillars that had fallen, lying in thick round slices. They were like stone dominos that had toppled over and were now overlapping one another on a bed of grasses. They were huge compared to the human beings who had originally constructed this monument to the god Zeus. I'd read that Zeus was best known for the lightning and thunder he hurled. In the Greek myth, his winged horse Pegasus carried his lightning bolts and he had trained an eagle to retrieve them. He was credited with controlling the weather, causing rain and huge storms.

We were glad to be staying within sight of this temple, a tribute to such an important Greek god, one who had graced us with good weather throughout our entire visit in Athens at the very end of the Fall season. We were sure that this location had brought us luck and very little rain during our waking hours.

For our last night in Athens, we were invited for dinner by Anesto's wife and son, at a small typical local Greek restaurant in the neighborhood where they lived. Although Anesto had been relocated to London and couldn't be with us, we still had an enjoyable time together with good homecooked food and local wine and texting him photos of the evening. It was indeed a fitting close to a once in a lifetime adventure.

We were happy to be going home, full-up with new memories to last a until next time.

Our first evening back in Paris, we were alight with joy to see our little rue all dressed up with Christmas decorations and colored lights. The next day Jeffrey brought up our tree and its ornaments from the cave, and we were soon ready for our next memorable event. Michelle was very pregnant, and we'd offered to host her baby shower in our dining room just a week later. Jeffrey had, as always, creatively decorated the *salle manger* with his usual *joie de vivre*. The couple were expecting a baby girl and had invited us to name her. The stained-glass window in the dining room was trimmed with pink and white balloons and covered with a sparkling white sign that read, in glittering bold pink letters, WE CAN'T WAIT TO SEE YOU, BABY G. WE LOVE YOU!

The words 'Baby G' were bookended by wings, and an angel's halo hovering above the head of the cherub. The table, set with pink and white dishes, glasses and napkins, tablecloth and place markers, provided gifts for all, pink baby bottles attached to keychains and filled with pink and white candy-covered almonds. The cake was pink and white too, and there were dozens of cupcakes to match.

Each guest brought a special homemade Filipino dish for a pot-luck dinner, and we provided the pink Champagne. The letter 'G' stood for the name we had been honored to offer Jeffrey's and Michelle's baby months before. We suggested the name Geneviève, after the patron saint of Paris. They loved the full name, Baby G for now, and later Jenny for short. We thought this venerable French name, besides being charming and meaningful, might come in handy while they were in the process of becoming legal residents in France.

The room was filled with kisses, laughter, and plenty of what we used to call 'Kodak' moments that Jeff and Ted took advantage of with all gladly mugging for the cameras. Now we just had to count the days until the arrival of this much-loved *petite fille*. Michelle was due to give birth right after Christmas. While we all held our breaths waiting, other less joyful developments had been gestating and burst out in a French society accustomed to revolutionary tactics and frequent strikes.

The first we had seen of the yellow vests was around mid-November, just before we left for Athens. Thousands of people, who called themselves *Les Gilets Jaunes*, flooded the cities from the suburbs all over France, disrupting traffic and often unwittingly becoming camouflage for those who were known as the *Casseurs*, the masked vandals in black who built barricades, broke everything they could with the paving stones dug up in the streets, fractured windows and set fire to cars and motorcycles, as well as to their own barricades. It all began in protest of the increase in the tax on petrol.

These *manifestations* often turned into riots, until *Police* and *Gendarmes* moved in to protect precious monuments, private property, and to break up crowds in historic areas before they became completely unmanageable. Sometimes tear gas, and in extreme cases, rubber bullets were deployed by defenders of the peace. Fire hoses were also used to break up the more violent manifestations, compliments of the *Pompiers*. All hands were on deck, so to speak, in order to safeguard French cities, the people, and private and public property.

The first time we were personally impacted was when we called an Uber to take us to the airport for our flight to Athens. By that time there were already so many *bouchons*, like corks in bottles, made up of the demonstrations, as we used to call them in the States. It was unclear if and when our Uber would reach us. This was when we learned that living around the corner from a monumental square could be nightmarish at times of civil unrest.

At the last minute, we texted our driver, the fifth one we'd been handed-off to, and suggested that we walk with our luggage to the intersection where *rue Vignon* empties into the larger *rue Tronchet* and wait there for him to pick us up. Luckily, the highway and the airport were not yet blockaded.

By the time we returned home, the manifestations had been limited to Saturdays, at which time traveling on foot was the only reliable mode of transportation. So many buses, cars and taxis were tied up in a traffic *confiture*, stickier and trickier than anything I had ever seen in the States since the Vietnam war.

The Gilets Jaunes took their name from the yellow safety vests that French drivers are required to carry in their glove boxes and must wear in case of emergencies if they need to evacuate their cars. We'd learned about gilets jaunes while studying for our French driver's licenses, which we'd discovered were required in order to be able to drive after the end of our first year as official residents in France. This requirement had never crossed our minds, since our California Driver's licenses had always been sufficient while driving in France and they were still valid.

We'd been driving for a total of over one-hundred years. Surely, the French would accommodate us.

CHAPTER 28

WE BEGAN OUR RESEARCH into where and how to get a French *permit conduire*, and were dumbfounded, with an emphasis on the 'dumb,' as we realized that it was not a matter of reciprocity. No simple exchange. The process wasn't going to transpire overnight. Getting a French license entailed attending classes in person and taking written tests online as dress rehearsals for the actual exam to prove proficiency in the regulations, signs and signals known as Le Code.

In order to be eligible to take both the theoretical and the oral/practical exams, we had to prove to our instructors that we were in fact ready to pass. All of the schools in this profitable business made sure that their track record of students who passed would afford them a competitive advantage.

Naturally, the oral aspect of the test was of great concern to me. No matter whether or not I could comprehend or speak French, I'd be asked at least five questions about the operation of the car, in French of course. I was then required to have enough linguistic skill to be able to use a combination of words and mime to answer these questions before I could even pull away from the curb.

In this last section I was instructed, in French of course, to carry out certain operational maneuvers, with the examiner sitting next to me in the passenger seat trying desperately to keep a straight face when I was unsure, for a split second, which way was *à droite* and which was *à gauche*. I also ran into what I came to refer to as a 'trick instruction,' the one where the examiner commanded "*tourné à droite"* just before I came to a street on my right that happened to bear a sign indicating no entry.

All our friends said, *bonne courage! Bienvenue en France,* as I recounted my latest discovery: that driving, like so many other things in France is not like driving in America. The wonder was that we had managed all these years to survive and to avoid maiming or killing anyone without knowing the rules of the road and the meaning of signs and signals, which vary in great numbers and significance in France.

To be honest, many of the road signs were intuitive and, in the end, not so difficult to learn. But I'd never known panic until I was driving at 50kpm, which is slow, and saw a sign I'd never seen before. Even more impressive, the 'right of way' is to driving a car in France what the 'catechism' is to practicing Catholicism. Not paying attention to and often yielding to whatever was on my right was a deadly sin.

Not unlike in California, each 'sin' comes with a fine, but in France, the price tag also costs points. This point system is not a game. It is serious business. For the first three years you're given six points. Each moving violation diminishes points rapidly until one can no longer drive or may be sent to jail or even have their car impounded if the violation is serious enough. Sometimes an infraction is considered to be so grave that one may be required to go back to school and take the tests over again.

That said, if you make it through the first three years, you're awarded an extra six points for good behavior, which gives you twelve points to worry about. The bright side of this system is that the death rate per million cars on French roads is half that of the United States.

As for the driving schools, the upside is that the school makes all the arrangements for the tests, if and when they deem you are ready to take them. They supply the code book and the practice tests online, as well as the cars and instructors to actually practice driving. Unfortunately, the books and sample tests presented a problem for me, since I hadn't learned the vocabulary for driving and mechanics of automobiles. The solution was to pay four times what Ted with his fluent French paid so that I could attend the only school in Paris that had something resembling English speaking instructors, which really meant German instructors who spoke English in an accent as thick as a knockwurst, English books, and English practice tests online, or so they advertised.

The school was located in the far western suburbs, nearly an hour's drive away by Uber, which made the cost of attending classes in person skyrocket. I realized after the first class that if I studied the book provided in English, and repeatedly took their English language practice tests online, I could study at home and skip the Uber fare.

Unfortunately, the English language website had been hacked, and would crash halfway through each test, making it impossible for me or the school to know how well prepared I was. As might be expected, they did nothing about this situation in spite of my pleas and their promises to attend to the glitch. What might ordinarily infuriate, inspired me. As they say in France, *faute de grives on mange des merles*, which literally means if you don't have a thrush eat a blackbird, perhaps a caveman's equivalent to making lemonade out of lemons.

As such, I was determined to teach myself to use the practice exams provided in French, not only from my school but from Ted's as well. I also discovered many practice exams that existed on the internet in French, free for all. This unexpected break derived from a near calamity, led to my learning more French while studying for my driving exam than at any other time.

The only problem that remained was that although I could talk code until the smiling cows in Camembert produced cheese on their own, I couldn't have one moment of adult conversation about what happened over the weekend without stuttering.

Yet another complication concerned the nature of the cars in France. The automobile we'd left behind in Los Angeles was a sixteen-year-old, top of the line, Mazda 626. It was in like-new condition, with relatively few miles on the odometer, but it didn't possess any of the accessories built into every new car since 2000.

We had no idea how to start these new cars that were more like computers let alone where the brakes were or how to apply them. The cars at the schools were hybrids, and everything was foreign to us, in the broadest sense of the word. Even with all these obstacles, by 2018 Ted and I were each set to drive a car in France.

These memories of my trials and tribulations of learning the responsibilities and earning the right to drive in France takes me off course, perhaps behind and off center as if glancing in the sideview mirror. Surely my unconscious detour is not unlike the many detours that had to be taken in the more than ten months of dealing with the *Gilets Jaunes* and their violent and dangerous colleagues. As someone once described it, I was a shrink who had run away from American insanity, seeking French sanity, and running into a very different kind of craziness.

On Saturday December 22, 2018 during that incredible invasion of *Les Gilets Jaunes*. we were awakened early in the morning by what sounded like a boisterous group of people speaking loudly and laughing. The commotion was coming from downstairs in our generally serene courtyard, just below our bedroom. I jumped out of bed to have a look out the window. I couldn't have been more taken aback than when I saw at least a dozen yellow vests camped out and making themselves at home, sitting on the benches and chairs, using the French wrought iron patio table we had brought from L.A. and contributed to the building, eating croissants, drinking café, and breaking into the toilette in the garden shed to relieve themselves. Some were even climbing the trash cans to see if they could escape over the wall into the street behind ours.

I called 112, the equivalent of 911 in the States.

How did they get beyond our security and through the Port Cochere I puzzled while awaiting a live response? The voice on the other end of the phone sought clarification.

"Bonjour, quelle est votre urgence, Les Policiers ou Les Pompiers,"

Les Policiers, *s'il vous plait.*"

When the policeman came on the line, I tried to explain the urgency but just as I struggled to the end of my sentence in my less than poor French, I watched as the police with their helmets and shields ran into the courtyard, rounding up the Gilets Jaunes and herding them out through the port, back into the street.

I scurried to the front of the apartment and looked out the kitchen window. Below I saw 150 or more of these yellow vested trespassers, all squeezed together and held in place on either end of the street by 200 or more police on one side, 200 or more gendarmes on the other, with each side backed up by ten or more navy blue gendarme and white police vans. Mingling amongst the group were various newscasters with big boom microphones and cumbersome cameras. Ted and I both hung out the window to watch the show. It seemed for all the world that both the police and the gendarmes intended to hold the group of yellow vests hostage for a while, perhaps to teach them a lesson.

A female newscaster from *BFM Paris* television, holding a heavy boom microphone extending some two meters away from her body saw us in the window.

"*S'il vous plait*, may we come up to film from your apartment."

I hated to be a party pooper, but I was compelled to say *Desolé non*, unwilling to allow a crew of strangers into our apartment with their equipment, a major violation of home, the one and only sacred and safe space remaining in town. To our delight, the authorities sequestered the Gilets Jaunes until dark, when both captives and captors—all worn out—dispersed without much fuss. Surely, they were happy to be able to go on their way, to get off their feet, and to have a decent bite to eat.

The chaos continued on Saturdays, although the remainder of each week was mostly normale. These days, Paris is mild in the Winter compared to the way it had been before we became permanent residents. We spent the crisp days before Christmas walking through the *Tuileries*, with its perfectly manicured skeletal remains of what had been enormous green chestnut giants, on to the *Louvre*,

244

or through the *Parc Élysée* to the *Grande Palais* and a visit to the Christmas market along the *Champs Élysée*. We even prepared a festive Christmas Eve dinner for Monica and Philippe and their adult daughter Sarah. I dressed up, danced to the music as I served the meal, and fell asleep that night with sugar-plum fairies, all wearing yellow vests, in my head. Ted said I smiled in my sleep. I had noticed the previous week that there were some great seats available for the ballet on New Year's Eve. Bernard and Bianca, with whom we usually celebrated the Nouvelle Année were out of Paris that particular year. For the first time, we were on our own. I made a suggestion with excitement and trepidation, fully expecting Ted to nix the idea. I tried to cajole him.

"Let's get tickets for Swan Lake for New Year's Eve at *Le Théâtre des Champs-Élysées*. We've never been out on New Year's Eve in Paris."

To my surprise, Ted proclaimed it a *bonne idée*.

As that day progressed, we were chagrined to realize that getting from here to there by Uber might be impossible. The midnight celebration was to begin at ten-thirty with colorful and vibrant projections onto the Arch de Triumph and crowds of revelers all the way up and down the *Champs Élysée*. The police were out in full force, and all roads around the *Élysée* were blockaded for safety and crowd control, including the *Place Concorde* and the entrance to the *Champs Élysée* from every direction. We were stuck.

The only way to get to our destination was to walk the four kilometers to the Théatré and back again. Forever an optimist, I swore that we could do it. Crossing over the *Champs Élysée* at *Rond Pont* to walk up *Avenue Montaigne* to the theatre, we were cheered on as throngs of people walked in the middle of the street, happily bundled up, the vapor of winter chill emerging from their mouths, indistinguishable from smoke. All conversed excitedly. There were no cars or even buses permitted for a large radius all around the Champs Élysée.

With all glittering like diamonds and festively wreathed, the walk was an extra special holiday treat. I adored each and every Christmas holiday season in Paris as if it were my first. The ballet simply added a particularly exultant touch to the last evening of 2018, like *crème sur dessus du le gâteau.*

As we stepped out after that divine performance, I felt the dazzle of all the trees on both sides of the Avenue that twinkled as if entwined with crystals. Walking back home, it was after eleven-thirty by the time we reached *Ronde Pont.* Crossing the streaming masses of people on the *Avenue des Champs Elysées*, already celebrating with Champagne, seemed a little precarious. Nevertheless, Ted held my hand tightly and we made it through to the other side, without mishap.

There we found a triangle of grass with two empty park benches. We realized that the big screen within yards right in front of us would give us a magnificent view of the *Lumiére* and fireworks at midnight, a wonderful discovery when we were certain that we couldn't make it home to watch the show on television. So, we sat down on one of the benches and snuggled together against the chill. We had the best of being in the midst of the *fête* and just enough security, serenity and space with no one in front of us to block our view. All that was missing was a thermos of hot cocoa.

This was a once in a lifetime experience for us, even though we'd spent many a New Year's Eve in Paris even before we moved here. This one seemed special, with all of the happy sounds of the crowd, just far enough away. The nippy cold of the season was felt on our faces, but unable to penetrate our warm winter coats and gloves. After the finale, we began our walk to the *rue du Faubourg St. Honoré*, a short cut to the *Madeleine* and home. Before long, we were stopped by the Police. They explained that after ten, no one was allowed to walk past the home of the President.

"*Desolé*," I said, fluttering my eye lashes, shivering under my head of thick silver hair and displaying my cane and a sad face.

The policeman grinned.

"*Je vous accompagner devant l'Élysée*," he generously offered.

"*Oui, merci, trés gentil*," Ted gratefully replied.

The two men had a chat on our way past the 'forbidden zone' on the *Faubourg*. They reminded me of Humphrey Bogart and Claude

Rains at the end of the film, 'Casablanca'. It was as if it were the start of a beautiful friendship. Like so many of the French, when the policeman asked us where we were from, and we answered 'California,' he responded with a heartfelt, *Ah, bon!*

"J'ai visité Los Angeles et San Francisco, et j'aime beaucoup la Californie."

He was originally from *Lyon*, a city that we had wanted to visit. We parted amiably with *mercis* and *trés gentiles* from us to him, and several *bonne années* to one another before continuing on our way toward home sweet home.

When we finally arrived at one-thirty in the morning, our evening of merriment was made all the merrier as we listened to Jeffrey's message. Michelle was in the *Hôpital Paris Saint Joseph* and had given birth to their beautiful baby girl, our little *Geneviève*. We could look forward to a perfectly joyous New Year's Day.

When we woke up, I made eggs Benedict and sliced up some fresh melon on the side. We rushed off to have a peek at this new little wonder, only a few hours after her birth. We arrived, the first to greet Baby G and her proud parents. She was beautiful and, like both of them, had thick black hair the likes of which I'd never seen on a newborn. She was asleep in a small cot abutting Michelle's bed. This is quite a departure from most American hospital maternity wards, where babies are kept in a communal nursery and brought to the Mother for feeding. Sometimes, if the nurses are not too harried, they'd bring the baby upon request of the mother.

"She's gorgeous!"

Michelle was lying on her bed, unsmiling, wrung out.

"Yes, Madame, and she weighs seven pounds."

"And she has lots of hair, Madame." Jeff added, picking up a lock of his own.

"That she does."

I dared to ask Michelle if Baby G was nursing yet.

"No, Madame, we feed with bottle."

Jeff explained that Michelle had a fever after giving birth and the doctor had prescribed medication to suspend her production of milk, for the baby's safety. How sad this was, as I knew Michelle had looked forward to breastfeeding. Geneviève stirred and began to fuss. She was right on the verge of crying when Jeff took the bottle, already prepared, and placed it so that the nipple was touching Baby G's lips. As little as she was, she grabbed hold of the nipple with rosie lips and sucked vigorously. But, after a while she began to fuss again, and then she let out a cry, at first slightly muffled, becoming a tiny wail.

I risked making a suggestion and asked what I hoped would be a stupid question.

"Perhaps she'll be happier in your arms Michelle, especially when she's eating and even afterward until she falls asleep. Have you tried to hold her?"

"No, Madame, not yet."

My face fell and I choked back a cry. Had no one ever told them that a baby needs to be held while feeding, not left one off in a cot or cradle or crib? I was reminded of a film I'd seen in graduate school, one that demonstrated all the wrong ways to mother a new baby, a time when most problems with bonding and relationship begins. The most painful to watch was one clip of a baby whose parents had propped the bottle up against a pillow in the cot, and when the baby was a bit older, on a couch, making it possible for the baby to literally feed itself. With Michelle, I knew this was not neglect, but a lack of knowledge about humane infant care.

"How about you Jeff," Ted asked.

"No, Sir. I'm not sure how. But our cousins and aunts and some friends are coming, and they will show us, Sir."

I wondered if Jeff hadn't wanted to bother us for advice or assistance. After all, we were Sir and Madame, not his parents. He had grown up without much attention, the tenth of ten children of parents who died when he was young. Too young. However, the tragedy was even greater, when so many Filipino parents had to go abroad to work and never had the opportunity to raise their own children. I was close to tears, trying to think of something to say that would do more good than harm, when Ted came to the rescue.

"Would you like me to show you now?"

"Yes, Sir, I would like to hold Baby G."

Jeff was enthusiastic as Ted demonstrated, picking up the baby while explaining each step, with special emphasis on the importance of supporting her head and holding her close to his body. Jeff reached out, standing as close to Ted as possible, as if to become an extension of this trusted and experienced elder.

"Now I will try."

Jeff was a natural. He just needed to observe this man whom he looked up to. Ted had also always been a natural with both newborns and children of any age, which was an innate quality and an intuition and thoughtfulness that was rare, and that may have created a firm foundation for his professional development and his success in the practice of child analysis.

Jeff held his baby girl firmly and gently, with particular care for her head and neck.

"The nurse, she came in and picked her up, but she just let Baby G's head hang."

My heart stopped.

Clearly, Michelle was given no pre-natal education. None had been offered by the hospital. The nurses were strangely unprepared, although they were the suppliers of prenatal care for the mothers. I felt badly that we'd not been pro-active with Michelle and Jeff by offering books or sending links for online education. YouTube video demonstrations were plentiful and most extremely helpful. They were a fitting tool for this younger generation, all of whom use their smart phones for just about everything everywhere. There may have even been an application for the basics of childcare.

I decided that there was no time like the present to remediate the situation. I pulled up a chair on the other side of Michelle's bed and held her hand, while I gave her some gentle, motherly advice. No, I hadn't ever been a mother, but I was the proud aunt of four nieces and five nephews since I was age four.

My sisters each saw in me a potential source of reliable childcare, and they made sure to educate me well and at a very early age. I knew that putting a baby to the soft bare breast of its mother or another caretaker, even while bottle feeding, was soothing and a great source of comfort for both members of the nursing couple, especially when breast feeding wasn't possible.

Between Ted, Jeffrey and me we managed to help Michelle hold her baby and I caught a wonderful image of the three of them cuddled together on the bed, just as it should've been. I was just beginning to reach Michelle, or so I thought, when a dozen Filipino women—the aunties and cousins and friends, most of whom I had met when we had Michelle's baby-shower—flung open the door and frenetically scampered around the room, kissing and hugging both Jeff and Michele.

Soon, all attention was glued to Baby G. Although she was back in her cot, contentedly fast asleep, they were all very excited to 'meet' her and did everything possible to rouse the newborn from her slumber, especially to see her eyes. It was clear that the 'clan' was the trusted source of counsel on the subject of childcare. We were simply ornamental, especially for Michelle. After all, they were her family, raised in the same way that she herself had been reared.

Jeff, on the other hand, wanted to talk more with Ted. The three of us bowed out of the hen party. Jeff walked us to the Chapel on the way out of the hospital. He was proud to show us the *crèche,* which was especially moving and where we took photos of Jeff with each of us and of the two of us together before we parted.

If I had been religious, I would have said a prayer for the three of them.

CHAPTER 29

THE NEXT DAY, Philippe took us on a road trip to the town of *Senlis* in *Picardy*, close to Paris. We visited the *Royaumont Abbey in Asnières-sur-Oise*, which was founded by King Louis IX in 1228, and restored in 2018 after a long and embattled history. We also savored a flavorsome *dejeuner* together and strolled the streets, filled with mouth-watering *fromageries, chocolatiers*, and *pastisseries* and took home samples from each.

Life couldn't have been any sweeter and I was reminded of so many other small villages we had visited on our first trip to Normandy nearly thirty years ago, visiting other small villages and learning about the making of cider and Calvados and the ancient battles that had taken place there too.

More reminiscences were created when we traveled to *Caen, the largest city in Normandy,* where on St. Valentine's day Didier and Bernadette and mutual friends Bernard and Bianca who had a large house close by, dined in their new apartment in town. I thought their apartment a wise move to the center of town, as they too grew older, but I still relished the memories of the elegant 18th century, four story home they had lived in on a lovely slope overlooking the city. Their elegant period furnishings had looked as if both were created simultaneously. At that time, when we had first visited their old home, we too were living in our upstairs-downstairs older home, which was not made for old joints. I already felt, even back then, like the Tin Man in the *Wizard of Oz*, always in need of lubrication just to keep walking, let alone climbing four flights of stairs.

A week later, we took pleasure in our customary reunion, this time in Paris at Monique and Alain's, who had invited Claudine and Richard to join us for dinner at their lovely home facing the *Cathedral Jean d'Arc* where we could hear the bells of the church ringing, much to my delight. Church bells always reminded me of those in the Cathedral Basilica of Saint Mark in Venice, Italy where our hotel room was less than 25 meters from the side entrance and the Bells left their imprint on my heart with each day of each visit.

The next week we were invited to an intimate recital of a young and energetic piano trio playing in a private home. This chamber concert made us homesick for our friends Howard and Yvonne with whom we would attend such intimate concerts at Cal Tech in Pasadena. We missed them dearly especially since they were two of our dearest friends and in the category of those we feared we might not see again.

Ted had missed the live theatre we frequented in L.A. But I was determined to attempt to find enjoyment in French live theatre, some of which even offered supertitles. One of the most memorable for me was a stirring performance of *Peau D'Ane* at the *Théâtre Marigny*, located in the *Élysée* park, a theatre within walking distance of home. I was able to obtain an English translation of the play, which helped carry me through the dialogue.

Later that week we attended the Van Gogh exhibition at the *Ateliers des Lumières,* a new and indescribable venue that had been an iron foundry from 1835. In 1935 it was converted into a tool manufacturing company that operated for 60 years and in 2013 an art officianado named Bruno Monnier developed *CutureSpaces,* using 21st Century technologically to enhance the exhibitions of both classical and contemporary art immersed in music and dynamic computer-generated video transformations. I was beginning to feel like life in retirement as we'd always imagined it might be possible.

On the January $22^{nd,}$ 2019 it snowed, remarkable since global warming had noticeably hit Europe. It lasted three days and stayed on the ground for a prolonged visit. This kind of event relieved my fears about how climate change might spoil our pipedream of living in a spot on the planet that had four distinct seasons. The hard chill didn't last, and Winter failed to suspend our exploration with friends. Our visits to places like the ornate *Gothic Bourg-en-Bresse Cathedral*, and the *Musée National de la Renaissance in Ecouen*, also a day-trip from home, went unhindered even under cloudy skies.

The sculptures, tapestries, decorative arts, and my favorite *stand-straight-up-inside* fireplaces were impressive, bringing on a deep regression to early childhood, a time when anything gorgeous, large and unusual induced in me a profound state of awe. Memories of my father escorting me to The Barnum and Bailey Circus, The Hollywood Chinese Theatre in its original glory, The Los Angeles Rodeo, swimming together in the Pacific Ocean, Disneyland in its opening months, and the Griffith Park Observatory were each awesome, early encounters. In adulthood, especially satisfying was the company we were in, our long-time friends the Uhls and the Gibeaults.

Around this time, Ted asked me what I wanted for my seventieth birthday. The usual request would have been for an overnight stay at Disneyland Paris, which I hadn't yet visited. Much to his surprise I had changed my mind. I glanced down, shyly.

"I'd like to spend a week in Lyon."

Ted nearly jumped off his chair with glee.

"Excellent. What made you decide on Lyon?"

"The food, the architecture and the marionettes and you want to go there, too!"

I was always happiest when our desires crossed paths.

Arrangements were made, and before we knew it mid-March arrived. The *Cour des Loges in Lyon* in the *vieux* section of town was a birthday wish come true. The hotel was set within a 14th-century *traboule*, an enormous courtyard where the breakfast was served in style each morning. It reminded me of an ancient version of the hotel *Jeu de Paume* in *Chantilly* where we had stayed years before, with a similar setting for breakfast. Our renaissance suite was filled with antique furnishings and hand painted frescoes, and the typical

Lyonnaise specialties in both hotel restaurants could easily have sufficed. Ted's favorite dish was *quenelle*, dumplings made of ground fish in a delicious cream sauce, sexy and light weight clouds oddly resembling their Jewish cousin, *Gefilte* fish. Mine was *Bresse* chicken with morel mushrooms and herbed cream, chicken unlike any other in France.

The point in Lyon where the *Rhône* and the *Saône* rivers cross is marked by a striking specimen of contemporary architecture, *Le Musée de Confluence*, with views of both sides of town set on the shores right where the waters coalesce. This one-of-a-kind museum was dedicated to the anthropology and science of nearly all species from the beginning of Earth's history. There was nothing like it in memory.

Besides this most recent exhibition hall, we spent a day at the Musée des Beaux-Arts, second only to The Louvre in Paris and within walking distance of our hotel and exploring *Les Quartiers Saint-Jean* and *Saint-Georges*, that made up the old town of Lyon, was enchanting and brought back so many memories of other "old towns" in major cities in Europe that we'd been fortunate to linger in for at least a week at a time. Perhaps because I was born in Los Angeles, I most enjoyed lodging and strolling in the oldest part of any town and within walking distance of the Romanesque *Cathédrale Saint-Jean-Baptiste* and the Gothic-Byzantine *Basilique Notre-Dame de Fourviere* on the very top of the hill overlooking our part of town.

Le Parc de la Tête d'Or was the perfect place for walking off rich food. It was named for a golden statue of Christ that, according to legend, was buried there by the Crusaders. Nestled on the left bank of the *Rhône* River, this park was a haven of tranquility in the heart of the city, and a splendid place to rest my feet.

The last place we visited was *Les Halles de Lyon*, a covered market featuring everything one could wish to buy, both prepared food and all the ingredients one could dream of cooking with at home, plus a number of small restaurants spread throughout the *Marché*. We stopped at one that specialized in seafood platters. Even our four eyes, let alone our two stomachs, could not possibly take in the tastefully arranged *grande plat pour deux*, with countless lobster tails, gambas, oysters, *coquilles St. Jacques, moule* and crab. Nevertheless, we were on holiday and gave it the old college try.

We stopped at one of the cheese booths, and Ted chose several varieties to take home the next day on the train, and we flagged a taxi to return to our hotel. The driver was entertaining and *trés sypa*. I noticed a photo of a beautiful white German Shephard hanging from his rearview mirror. When I asked about his dog, he told us the story of the breed.

The white coated Shepherds were known in Europe as early as 1882. They were preferred by sheep herders because they were easy to tell apart from the dark European wolves, and the aristocracy of Austria favored them because their coats matched the *Lipizzaner* horses they bred, and the white dresses worn by high-born women. Unfortunately, in 1933 the breed's standard was amended in its native Germany when the Nazis deemed these dogs to be inferior and banned them from the registry, eventually demanding that all puppies with white coats be destroyed after birth until they literally disappeared from Europe.

Those now in Europe are known as White Swiss Shepherd dogs and are a cross between an American born male white German Shepherd and a female from England, both imported by a woman in Switzerland in 1967. I was so intrigued, I had to ask our driver questions I could not have formulated in French.

"*Parlez-vous* Anglais ?"

"Oui, un peu."

I had come to learn that this response usually means that the person understands much more English than he speaks; Certainly, much more French than I spoke.

"You must miss your *chienne* when you are driving all day," I said.

"*Mais, non,*" he said with a grin on his ruddy face.

"My dog, she is always with me, she is behind you now."

As the car pulled up in front of our hotel, we looked behind and saw this quiet, well behaved but very large beauty, who had been there all the time. When we got out, our driver took us to the hatch-back door. As the hood raised up, we were formally introduced to *Lila Blanche*, tail wagging as if welcoming us to sit on either side of her to pose for a photo, which we did with great pleasure, stroking her lovely fur and scratching behind her perky ears. She snuggled in between us and licked our hands and cheeks.

We laughed, as the taxi drove away. We'd both had thoughts of kidnapping her.

I was sad to leave Lyon. We had such a wonderful visit and there was much more to see. It was early in the season, which meant that the stately opera house and the *Musée des Arts de La Marionnette* and the *Théâtre Le Guignol de Lyon* where the marionette company performed a traditional puppet show, were all still shuttered until mid-April. I was so looking forward to a real puppet show with such fond remembrances of years as a child with 'Punch and Judy.' The trees had just begun to leaf out and the gardens were mostly empty of all but the earliest blooms. We just had to come back one day. But when?

There were countless times we'd uttered those same words about innumerable places in so many countries, and even those we'd neglected for a time in Paris. Perhaps there was simply not enough life left in us or in anyone or anything for that matter. Even monuments were sensitive to decay and destruction. The catastrophe of April 15th, 2019 was an unforgettable example. We were at home preparing dinner in the kitchen when we heard alerts from BFM Paris TV ring out on both our cell phones, sitting side by side on the counter. I was closest, so I looked over to see what the breaking news was about. We had planned to watch Macron's speech on TV later that evening, one in which he was expected to announce the outcome of *"le Grand Debat"* with citizens throughout the country. His intension was to address the increasing violence connected to the *Gillets Jaunes* protests in a conciliatory attempt to begin to heal the nation. In view of what was expected, *this* headline was utterly not.

"Un incendie est en cours à la Cathédral de Notre Dame de Paris."

The Notre Dame, on fire? It had been around six-thirty when the alarms had sounded. As we watched the roaring flames and black smoke rising from our Lady that evening on television, I gasped as we saw the fall of her beautiful spire that concluded the collapse of the roof. By eleven o'clock, when the fire was all but put out, we could see three-hundred years of artisanal construction, and nearly a thousand years of French history, reduced to ashes and blackened walls. The drone view from above revealed the portion of the church under the roof that had been most impacted by the fire. It was the cross itself, a transverse vessel that had separated the choir from the nave and had formed the arms of the crucifix.

I was in tears and disbelief.

It was *déjà vu*, or at least horribly reminiscent of seeing the fires near the top of the World Trade Center in NYC on September 11th, 2001. Watching this implosion felt as if countless personal Parisian memories had been incinerated. I tried to recall our first Christmas eve in the Notre Dame before we were married, where Ted stood beside me, singing the mass in Latin, much to my surprise. I recollected being young enough to climb the many stairs to the bell tower on our visit that year, and the photo I'd taken, indelibly printed in my mind, of Ted kneeling like a choirboy in prayer on the narrows steps of the spiral that lead to the roof now gone. I remembered meeting the present-day hunchback of Notre Dame, an African immigrant who happened to have a bad case of kyphosis, and who had proudly shown us his modest quarters in the belltower, confirming that he was in charge of ringing the bells, years before they were mechanized.

Ted had told me the story of Archbishop Lustiger, who'd been born Jewish but converted to Catholicism in 1940, having been sheltered by the nuns in a convent from the Nazis during WWII. We both laughed at the thought of asking him to officiate at our wedding ceremony in the cathedral. He later became a Cardinal under Pope John-Paul II, and in 2007 we thought once more to engage him, this time to renew our vows on our twenty-fifth wedding anniversary, which we celebrated in Paris. Unfortunately, he had passed away earlier that same year.

I had vivid images of leading Diane and her husband to the top of the Notre Dame on our honeymoon, and the photos we took of each other with our favorite gargoyles on the rooftop. The stupendous views of Paris from that roof that was no more had constituted some of my favorite Parisian souvenirs.

I recalled the glory of watching the transformation of this gothic icon from an imposing sooty grey to the color of *Chantilly crème* for the occasion of the millennium celebration. I could still hear in my heart the many concerts and masses we'd attended in this magnificent church throughout the years, even as recently as 2017 when a fabulous group of youthful choristers performed a piece of performance art, rendered in both voice and movement, with singers appearing from all sides of the audience surrounded in the center of that same transept, now gone as we had known it, forever.

We paid our homage to what remained of her ladyship two days after the fire was completely extinguished. While sitting close to one another in the terrace of a café facing what remained of her elegance, we realized that we were being showered by her ashes, still raining down on the crowds, some of whom had brought flowers, others kneeling in prayer for her to rise again one day.

CHAPTER 30

OUR ATTENTION TURNED AWAY from the tragedy, about which we could do nothing but grieve, toward our next adventure that had already been deep in the planning before we had arrived home from Lyon. It was one trip we had dreamed of for many Summers. For us there were countless reasons to travel to Norway in the Summertime. The cool air from twenty down to zero degrees Celsius, the beautiful fjords and the deep blue North Atlantic Ocean, coupled with the lush green mountainous terrain was just what the doctor ordered for two heat intolerant Parisians. We'd made all the arrangements and could now enjoy ourselves until mid-July.

For most of our Parisian friends, being chronic tourists in Paris was incomprehensible. But we had foreign friends to entertain and our own hunger for all the wonders of the city were a challenge to keep up with. In May, we experienced something entirely age-inappropriate and out of character for us. We bought two tickets to see Hugh Jackman perform at the Accord Arena. I hadn't attended this sort of spectacle since I was a teenager, screaming with the Beatles or Joan Baez and Bob Dylan when they performed in the Hollywood Bowl in the early sixties. Ted had largely stayed away from such crowds and the noise one has to tolerate before the concert begins. In this case, there was a DJ with a keyboard of controls that produced killer rock music, mostly heavy metal that blasted out of several three-story tall speakers, with the same volume as an Apollo spaceship taking off from its launch pad at The Kennedy Space Center. I was catapulted by this blast from the past, unable to sit still in my seat.

As far as I was concerned, dancing is the only response to this kind of noise.

Of course, poor Ted was like a newborn in a terrible state of over-stimulation. He put his fingers in his ears, scrunched up his sweet face until it turned a bright shade of red, lowered his head to his chest and completely zoned out, as if he had physically left the scene by an act of sorcery, until all noise ceased, and Jackman came onstage.

Happily, for me, Ted and I almost equally enjoyed Jackman's performance, his singing and dancing, and the self-effacing jokes that he'd make about his life on and off celluloid and live Broadway theatre. Afterwards, I promised I'd never subject my love to such horror again. From then on, my dancing to loud rock would be limited to those times when I'd bake or cook or clean house, and when he was at the atelier creating beautiful art in virtual silence.

Of course, classical music was my preferred accompaniment to writing clinical papers for presentation, which to my surprise were still being commissioned by various psychoanalytic societies in Europe for 2020. My first thoughts of retirement included writing on the topics of retirement and termination in analysis. I had so many experiences that I had thought at the time that this would keep me creatively productive and might be useful to my colleagues and beneficial to their patients.

But for many reasons, my inspiration for anything remotely related to my previous career was dissipated by events beyond my control. The question that I could not answer sufficiently was how does one write for the benefit of the profession and its therapeutic aims in the age of internet technologies, social media, and unchecked violations of intellectual property rights? Such abuses not only rob the author of royalties, but more importantly, they may lead to unintended violations of both the patients' and the analysts' privacy, when distribution becomes available for less than the equivalent of $40 to anyone outside the realm of the once confidentially-constricted and hermetically sealed inner circle of the profession.

Rather than to continue writing for professional journals, I spent some time and energy cooperating with publishers toward our goal of resolving this problem, one that emerged so rapidly and insidiously that it had only recently been brought to the attention of anyone involved. What most people were not aware of was that fact that contemporary writers of clinical scholarly and professional works, whether they be published in books, anthologies or journals, don't earn a fraction of the money paid per article sold over the internet, illegitimately, and without the permission of either the author or the original publisher. More than the financial aspect, it was the lack of moral integrity that was discouraging. Thus, I went on to enjoy my life in Europe, and to drop the term 'fairness' out of my vocabulary of expectations. It only took a total of twenty-odd years of personal analysis to face the fact that there is no such thing.

But there certainly is goodness in the world. That feature had not yet been expunged. In May 2019, we renewed out residency cards for the third time, and were free to travel by train to the city of *Tours* in the *Vallée de la Loire.* Jane and Marc, new friends whom we had 'inherited' from our girlfriend Dale in L.A., had a wonderful home in *Monthou-sur-Cher*, with a more-than-hospitable guesthouse in which we were invited to spend the week. What a wonder to make such good friends, a much more valuable commodity than a guest house *gratuit.*

Marc was born in Belgium and Jane was as American as apple pie. They lived in Bangkok half the year working in the legal field, and in France during the other half, give or take various visits to children in the States or in other parts of Europe. They were fun and funny, caring and charming, intelligent, interesting and interested conversationalists. Ted and I spent quite a bit more time with them than we had any right to expect, especially in the evenings after we would return from visiting the great chateaux of the valley, as many as we could cram into a week's time.

It wasn't that we hadn't done this before. In fact, over thirty-seven years earlier, for ten days of our month-long honeymoon in

France, we strayed from Paris and drove throughout the valley visiting most for the first time. But that had been in December of 1982, when the trees were all bare-bones if beautiful, and flowers were found only indoors in hotels and restaurants.

On this visit in the springtime, there was thick green foliage on all of the trees and a myriad of flowers of every variety, color and variegation blooming in beds, in boxes, in hanging pots, and creeping through and draping over gazebos, pergolas, pavilions and trellises everywhere we went. And during all those many years in which we'd been absent from the valley, nearly every Chateau had been renovated, some beyond recognition. This was the meaning of the word picturesque.

The *Chateux des Amboise, l'Aumone, Bracieux, Chambord, Cheverny, Chaumont,* and *Loches* were as if new to our eyes, and the walks through the gardens took the lion's share of our time each day. Most of these grand castles had recently become home to wonderful Michelin Star restaurants where we enjoyed a gourmet *dejeuner* and continued on our visit without ever leaving the grounds. We were also escorted by our hosts to a collective wine tasting event in a nearby village, and we sent home two cases of *Vouvrey Brut,* a dry sparkling wine, perfect for the ubiquitous *apero.*

We also had our share of fright.

One day, I was driving our rental car when I realized that we'd passed our turn-off for Jane and Marc's. The roads were narrow and lined on both sides by deep and wide drainage ditches, laid out along the endless agricultural terrain. Every so often, there was a dirt road that could be used as a turn-around.

As soon as I'd caught sight of one, I turned right in. However, as I was backing out, I failed to heed Ted's warning, turning the wheels in such a way that I ended up with one right front wheel deep into the ditch, and the remainder of the car precariously tilting straight up in the air. Ted and I were barely able to extricate ourselves. I called Marc and yelped.

"So, I drove the car into a ditch."

"Where are you?"

I could tell Marc was trying not to laugh.

"Near you, I'm sure. I think we just passed your street when I tried to turn around."

"I've got you. Be right there."

Just then, a woman in a pickup truck stopped to see if we were okay. Although she could do nothing to get us out of our predicament, she insisted on waiting until someone arrived to free us. Three more people stopped to see if they could do anything, all just before Marc and Jane arrived. One woman even offered to drive home and return on her tractor to tow us out of the ditch.

By then, Marc had been on the phone with a friend of his, the son of the Mayor of *Choussy*, Thierry Gosseaume. The Mayor had a king-sized tractor, the proper rigging and plenty of experience with this kind of calamity, which I imagined happened all too frequently, especially to tourists. I drifted back in time to the seventies on my own farm in Thousand Oaks.

My place was located around a sharp right-hand curve in a narrow rural two-lane road lined on both sides by similar agricultural drainage ditches. At least twice a week, I would hear tires screeching followed by the sound of a loud metallic 'ka-chunk' at the roadside. I immediately knew what it was. I'd run out the front door, hop on my Kubota tractor, and drive down the thousand feet of asphalt and through the gates to the rescue.

Somehow the sight of my pre-fab house on top of the hill, the large center-aisle barn halfway below, and three acres of green pastures filled with white horses, plus a huge redwood slab that had the name *Four Freedoms Arabian Farms* carved into the wood and arching over and under an Americanesque flag with red and white stripes and a blue field of white stars circle an Arabian horsehead, was just enough to highjack a driver's attention from the road, long enough for them to run their cars into the gulley on the right side of Moorpark Road.

The scene before my eyes was so familiar, but this time I was the one being pulled out to safety. This total stranger, the Mayor no less, came with his big chain with hooks on each end, one end wrapped around and attached to the bucket on the front of his over-sized tractor, and the other end hooked to the undercarriage of the car. Monsieur Mayor was such an expert that the car was salvaged without the slightest scratch.

We said our *mercis* to Mayor Thierry and Ted offered to pay him for his trouble. However, he simply said *Da rien, bonne courage,* and drove off into the setting sun, a big smile on his handsome face. This good Samaritan had saved some careless tourists and possibly the reputation of the town. We followed Marc and Jane back to the farm, and they offered us a glass of wine to take the edge off the after-effects of our harrowing experience. The four of us sat outside and enjoyed the beauty of the landscape all around us on their farm.

"We stopped at a large Marché in the village and brought two kilos of wild *cepes* and other mushrooms of all varieties."

"We can make a good supper with some of these," Jane replied as she examined the bags filled with brown button, chanterelles, enokis, girolles, morels, oyster, porcini and shitakes.

"I think these might go with whatever we have on hand."

I bashfully winked. It was the least we could do for all the trouble we'd caused.

Beyond our wildest dreams, Jane created four courses, each one using mushrooms of one variety or another, along with fresh herbs from her garden, and combined with butter, cheeses, pastas, poultry and cream. This was some of the best food we'd eaten, and the company was equally delectable, even though I was nearly teased to death about my driving.

All laughed in good spirits, with me not at me.

CHAPTER 31

THE NEXT MORNING, we said our goodbyes early. Jane and Marc went off to do some errands before we'd had our breakfast. We tidied up the cottage and placed our luggage in the trunk of the car. It had been such an unexpectedly delightful week that we were sad to be going home.

On the way to the train station to return the rental car, we stopped at a sign that announced *Max Vauché Maître Chocolatier*. In a patch of grass there stood an enormous bronze sculpture that resembled one of the three Musketeers with a placard that read *Baron du Vallon de Bracieux de Pierrefonds*. We drove into the parking lot and were unable to resist sampling the vast array of chocolates of all kinds, shapes and colors. These were most certainly artisanal sweets and included a wonderful sugar free assortment. We took a selection with us back to Paris.

On the train home we shared photos with each other on our iPhones to stretch out the holiday a few hours longer. We were three plus year into our new life in France and yes, still tourists with many memories to compare with visits to the same or similar place three to four decades ago. I felt that we were in perpetual vacation mode, unsure of the day or date and without care.

We arrived home just a week before the Baptism and official naming of baby Geneviéve. It was a wonderful occasion for all, with the exception of Baby G. There were very few people present at the ceremony in the church, where two other families were also having their babies' Baptism in the native language of the Philippines. Baby G had not one but two Baptismal dresses, neither of which felt very comfortable to her, as indicated by her blood-curdling screams and the deluge of tears that flowed, no matter who held her. She wasn't too happy about having water poured over her head by the priest, a ceremony that signifies purification or regeneration, certifying admission into the Christian Church.

I was as bewildered as Baby G seemed to be about why a six-month old infant would need to be purified of anything in order to gain acceptance into the Catholic community. But then again, I wasn't raised in the world of original sin. In the Jewish religion in the States, only money can buy entrance into the community synagogue or temple. I also couldn't help but wonder why Baby G's naming, which was already endorsed and registered in France would be in need of further endorsement by water-torture.

The evening, in yet another all-you-can-eat oriental buffet, was a dinner reception in celebration of the newest member of the church. It was neither joyful nor soothing for the guest of honor. In spite of her tearful if wordless appeals, Genevieve was required to pose with each of the seventy-five or more attendees in a special area decorated as usual by her talented Daddy. No one seemed to mind that she was not happily mugging for the camera, perhaps because they had all been through this ordeal as infants and for them, it was part and parcel of an infant's life.

The best photo I took of the occasion was one of a smiling mommy Michelle and daddy Jeffrey supporting a sleeping Baby G laid out in front of them across Michelle's pretty white dress, with Baby G in her own white lace-trimmed gown. The only thing I could think of that could be worse in the Jewish religion, was the *Brit Milah*, the ritual of circumcision for baby boys, one that allegedly dates back to a pact made between God and Abraham. Baby girls in the Jewish religion are exempt and are only subject to purifying rituals after they begin to menstruate.

Amen, hallelujah, amen!

Life in Paris resumed its normalcy after Baby G's special event, with Ted returning to his drawing, now with pastels even more vibrant than his renditions in colored pencils. We also dined at the home of our friends Caroline and Howard in their fifth floor Montparnasse apartment where we were treated to a homemade meal of seafood and fish and the most beautiful rainbow I'd ever set eyes on in the skies right outside their windows. I decided to take this as a sign that our trip to Norway, only a month away, would be all that we had imagined.

We were packed and ready to go. This was more complicated than one would think, both in the planning and the doing, partly because we were looking forward to temperatures that ran anywhere from twenty degrees Celsius to zero or below. We also needed attire appropriate for everything from boating and hiking in the wilderness to fine dining, both on shore and off on the cruise ship, where we'd be spending an entire week journeying from Bergen in the South of Norway to Cape Nord, within the Arctic Circle. We'd be away from Paris for three weeks traveling by cars, buses, fjord boats, trains, a cruise ship and airplanes.

Since our trip to Japan in 2001, we hadn't had such a complex adventure. The differences between these three weeks in Norway and those spent in Japan were innumerable and the similarities, surprising. In Japan, we were invited guests of a foundation that supported all psychoanalytic activity in the country. In Norway we were on our own, a sheer pleasure trip, one of the few that was solely of our choosing. Like Japan, we knew relatively little about what to expect in Norway. But this time we had to do our homework. There were no offers of hospitality nor honoraria to cover unforeseen expenses.

In Japan, we had been looked after by the Secretary of the foundation, Dr. Okinogi. In one of dozens of letters to us over the year's preparation for our visit and the conferences, he wrote that people had nicknamed him 'Okinogi Travel' for his expertise and willing generosity in making all arrangement for 'distinguished' visitors. In contrast, for our trip to Norway I was appointed chief travel agent, arranging for flights, an all-day 'Norway in a Nutshell' adventure, our hotels, luggage transfers, and a cruise by ship from the sunny, temperate South of the country to the freezing Artic North and back again by air, as well as hiring local guides in both Oslo and Bergen, and securing tickets for some concerts during the Greig Music Festival.

Although our Norway holiday was the most extravagant we'd ever undertaken by ourselves, our trip to Japan, with all first-class flights, trains, hotels, guides, receptions, restaurants, and performances of Kabuki Theatre in Tokyo and Miyoko Odori in Kyoto were just part and parcel of what was known as 'Japanese Hospitality' during the years of good fortune in Japan and it all felt like a dream from beginning to end.

In Kyoto, we spent the only day that we had all on our own strolling up Philosophers Walk during the height of cherry blossom viewing. People were so friendly and proud of the natural beauty of the season, and anyone who could speak a few words of English would inquire if we were enjoying the cherry blossoms. We ate lunch in a modest restaurant where the owner took us outside to choose what we wished to order from various photos pinned to the window. Few outside our professional circle in Japan spoke our language and, with the exception of a couple of essential phrases like *Kon'ichiwa* for hello, *sayonara* to say goodbye, and *domo arigato gozaimus* to express a thank you, we didn't speak theirs either.

Back inside the modest eatery, sitting across from us on the floor in traditional style was another couple with a baby boy no more than a year old. The sight of the serene caring and attention with which this child was handled by both parents taught us much about the Japanese culture and its regard for the next generation starting at a tender age.

We also visited both The Silver and The Golden Pavilions, each with their Zen and Shinto shrines, only accessible via very long peaceful walks through endless, perfectly manicured, Japanese gardens and past the limpid pools that interspersed throughout. We were left breathless on all accounts. This was the one and only day of the whole trip during which we could recall having to open our wallets.

In Norway, everyone spoke English and most without the slightest bit of an accent. All were amazingly friendly, and wherever we went we saw tall, blond families with young children. They seemed, for the most part, to be unusually happy and as carefree as the Eloi in H.G. Wells' *Time Machine*. The difference was that there were no Morlocks to harvest them at night in this garden realm that was anything but dystopian.

In Japan, although we were treated like royalty, with only three days of work to interrupt our 21-day vacation break, it was clear that most Japanese had what we in France or in the USA would call a difficult life. Our colleagues' spouses were not permitted to join in any evening festivities, even if they themselves were colleagues.

Young people lived at home throughout and even after university, since living on their own was often prohibitive. This also meant that marriage and even co-habitation was postponed. One of our young escorts, a university student Aniko, described her living space as four *tatami* mats.

"What is that in square feet?"

Our guide explained the facts of life in Japan.

"In Japan, the size of a room is often measured by the number of *tatami* mats, about 1.6-square meters in each rectangle. These are twice as long as they are wide. Alternatively, in terms of traditional Japanese area units, room area or floor space is measured in terms of *tsubo*, where one *tsubo* is the area of two *tatami* mats, a square."

My hand went to my mouth, in Japanese style, as my jaw dropped. I just could not imagine living, sleeping, bathing and cooking in such a confined space. It was no wonder that only the very well-to-do entertained in their homes. In Norway, although we did not have the opportunity to visit anyone's home, as we had been accustomed to during professional visits in nearly all other countries including Denmark and Sweden, we were able to ascertain that the price of a very nice home in Oslo is less than one-third the cost compared to Paris or even to West LA.

In Norway, we found that both space and comfort were affordable for its residents. People lived well in this country with its philosophy of 'capitalism with a conscience.' Norway was famous for having the highest living standards, and its rich economy fueled by oil and gas exports retained by the government, was one of the major reasons why this was so. It not only made the country extremely efficient and stable, but it also helped ensure that it will continue to be so for many years to come.

Some swear that Norway is the best country in the world in which to live. It has one of the lowest crime rates and is also ranked highly for its literacy rate, educational levels, and individual material wealth. Also, Public art is fostered and supported by the State, and infrastructure of all kinds is well maintained. Like the Japanese, the Norwegians pride themselves on the beauty and cleanliness of their public spaces.

Unfortunately, like in Japan, travelers find Norway a very pricey place to visit, especially if one wishes to stay in quality hotels and eat meals in choice restaurants throughout their stay. All the same, the refreshing atmosphere within Norway's large cities, with their primary colored and quaint old-fashioned wooden houses, their exquisite contemporary architecture, art and history museums all in stunning natural surroundings, add up to an experience of sheer joy.

This was especially true for us. We were seeking a brief change from the heat of Summer in the city, and the hustle and bustle of our new hometown. We had saved for this sort of foreign exploration for many years, and now we had both the time and the resources that enabled us to enjoy it.

We counted our blessings.

CHAPTER 32

OUR FLIGHT FROM CHARLES DE GAULLE to Oslo-Gardermoen on July 16th took three hours. Since we were arriving near midnight and only staying two nights this first round, we chose the mid-range Comfort Hotel Karl Johan, within walking distance of the train station that we would be departing from. The room was more comfortable than expected for what we thought would be the equivalent to Motel-6 in the States. The terrace restaurant, surrounded by a gracious garden, was open and perfect for a late-night snack upon arrival.

The next day we strolled down the main shopping area of Karl Johan around the center of the city and through the park that leads to the harbor where we discovered an Opera House like no other we'd ever seen. It was a wonderful spot for lunch with endless views of the main Fjord. It was also the first time we'd arrived at an opera house off season without disappointment. *The Norwegian National Opera and Ballet* was by far the most visionary and esthetic example of contemporary architecture I'd ever seen in person or in print. Frank Lloyd Wright would have been enchanted by such a structure, built for a specific function and in a form that was designed in harmony with the people and their environment, a philosophy termed *organic architecture.*

Jutting out into the harbor connecting land with water, this glass, metal and white granite building with slanting rooftops made of a glistening milky marble coursed straight into the sea, inviting people to walk on them, to enjoy the spaces, and the views of the city. The whole configuration appeared as if it were an enormous glacier of ice and snow, sliding into the Fjord or perhaps emerging out of it.

This public space was created by an architectural firm called *Snohetta*, which had won a stiff competition for the project. The opera house was like no other I'd seen. Both the glorious wood and golden interior spiral features in the main lounge, and the exterior filled with explorable wonders were always open to the public, day and night.

As we sat on the terrace to enjoy a delicious lunch and fresh sea air, I briefly thought I could live here forever.

A short distance away and behind us, we could see the fabulous Barcode Project, where a group of young architects had created a series of mixed-use, residential, high-rise buildings. Each one had a strikingly individual contemporary façade, with varying gaps between each building that created a look approximating that of a barcode, the source of the project's nickname. It gave the city a verticality previously unknown and it contributed to Oslo's one-of-a kind skyline.

Out to sea, not far from the terrace of the opera house, floated an incredible glass and stainless-steel sculpture called *"She Lies,"* created by Monica Bonvicini, an Italian sculptress. It evoked the power of both ice and water and was anchored to a concrete platform that was tethered to the harbor floor, enabling it to turn and change direction and orientation based on the activity of the currents, tides and winds. Its movements were a reminder of nature's constant capriciousness. Here we found so much more to love about Norway, and we'd hardly been here a day. It was not easy to tear ourselves away, but we knew that we'd return to Oslo for a week at the end of our trip.

At our hotel, we removed our backpacks from our luggage and filled them with some essentials and valuables to carry with us for the next day's activity. Vidar from the porter service arrived at six in the morning to pick up our luggage to transfer it to The Clarion Hotel Admiral in Bergen while we took the *"The Nutshell."* It would be impossible to carry our luggage with us, considering how we were to be traveling throughout that day.

The Nutshell is a once in a lifetime mad dash from Oslo to Bergen. Most people take two days back and forth and consider this *visiting Norway*. For us it promised to be a good preview of what we'd encounter on the cruise, and the most thrilling and scenic route to our next destination, where we would stay for five days before boarding our ship for the North. After breakfast that morning we walked to the Central Train Station and got onboard a modern train from Oslo traveling to the high mountain station of *Myrdal*. The views of the forests and Fjords were indescribable.

My only thought was, there is a God!

From *Myrdal* we boarded an old fashioned, narrow gauge train. It reminded me of the train from Flagstaff Arizona to the South rim of the Grand Canyon. But instead of a long ride through a rocky desert landscape leading gradually uphill to a pine forest, this fantastic journey took us through lavish green and heavenly blue land, sea and skyscapes, past the astonishing *Kjosfossen* waterfall, through small tunnels and along exciting mountain switchbacks. We caught sight of what appeared to be some historical buildings and *beaucoup des fromages de chèvre*, on the hoof.

Nearly an hour later, we arrived at the village of Flåm, right on the waters of *Aurlandsfjord*, the largest tributary of the longest Fjord in all Norway, the *Sognefjorden*. I have to admit that I could never have begun to pronounce any of these names out loud, but I was fortunate that my iPhone could spell them. Since our three-week road trip through Alaska with JoAnn, I couldn't recall taking so many photographs, not only of these incredible sites, but of Ted's face that, throughout the trip, bore such a blissful, radiant, and rapturous expression that it made my heart rejoice. It was the most beautiful face in the world. I never had to say 'smile', not once.

We shared a surprisingly good pizza on the wooden deck of a tourist trap, because it had a vacant table with the best views of the fjords and the surrounding mountains, in spite of one of those behemoth cruise-ships that had wedged itself into a natural berth in the shore, unloading its five thousand tourists who flooded the town, making it an unappetizing prospect for exploration during our one-hour stopover.

When we heard the 'all aboard' we knew it was time to climb up the gangplank to the ferry boat that was to take us on our fjord cruise on the *Aurlandsfjord,* continuing to the *Naeröyfjord,* a very narrow fjord only 250 meters wide. This was a unique experience that reminded me of the days in my twenties when I would kayak for three days every Summer on the Rogue River, from Ashland Oregon 125 miles to the mouth of the river at Gold Beach on the Pacific. Like the Rogue, there were many waterfalls sliding down mountain peaks of melting ice, the tops of which were too high and far away for us to see. There were also small, idyllic farms in dramatic mountain settings where real people lived. Besides a more primitive mode of travel, in Oregon the Grizzly bears sat on rocky ledges in the mountain crevasses just below the falls, as if taking a shower after a fresh salmon supper.

After *Naeröyfjord,* we climbed onto our comfortable coach in *Gudvangen,* a bus that would take us down the *Stalheimskleiva* Road to *Voss.* From *Voss* we continued on the Bergen Railway to our final destination, at least the last before boarding our cruise up the coast. In Bergen we were welcomed to our hotel with a surprise upgrade to a suite with an all-encompassing view of the harbor, just across from the enchanting row of Bryggen houses with their primary colors that made them stand out on the *Hanseatic* wharf along the water. We could have remained in our room all day, as one by one we watched magnificent sailing vessels enter the waters appointed as the starting line of the 2019 Tall Ship Races that would climax in *Aarhus,* Denmark. The sight of fifty-eight resplendent ships from seventeen countries, all with sails unfurled, was a first for us.

There were many 'firsts' during our five days in Bergen. We attended two concerts as part of the Grieg Music Festival. These were a splendid but miniscule part of what we might have enjoyed, had we been able to arrive earlier and stay longer. In the town off the main square, where a giant bronze statue of *Ludvig Holberg* stood overlooking the seafood market, was a lovely small and understated church that dated back to 1830. There we heard Grieg's String Quartet in G minor, his Opus 27.

The next day we took a taxi to visit *Troldhaugen*, Grieg's charming yellow Victorian house and museum, way up in the mountains overlooking a fjord, not a place you would expect to find the ugly trolls it was named after. This was also the burial site of Grieg and his wife Nina.

The piano recital took place in an intimate concert hall that had been constructed after the composer's death along a path through the flowering gardens on the grounds of his home. A glorious view through a huge picture window revealed the small, red hut below where the composer had worked, surrounded by forests and the Fjords farther down, an ideal backdrop for the small stage and Grieg's own Steinway grand piano on which a selection of his sonatas, dances, and Norwegian folk songs were performed by a young and talented student from the *Greig Academy of Music*, a part of the music department of the University of Bergen. Although I had always been enchanted by Grieg's music, hearing it played in the same landscape that inspired his unique style and in this space, was like being touched by his spirit.

The next day we strolled the promenade and explored the alleys of the *Bryggan*. We ate seafood right in the center of the marketplace. It tasted as if it had sprung right from sea to salver. We took some lovely sweets up to our room and watched the *Bergen Opera Festival* performance of Bizet's *Carmen*, spectacular even on TV.

On our last full day in Bergen, we visited the *Rasmus Meyer Collection* in KODE 3, part of the seven extraordinary sites that made up what the Norwegians named KODE, one of the largest, multi campus museums for art, design and music in the Nordic region. Its collection of artists' homes, of which *Troldhaugen* was one, and four buildings in the middle of the Bergen city center, housed temporary displays of the works of contemporary artists, as well as extensive permanent collections containing works by Edvard Munch, JC Dahl, and Nikolai Astrup.

These museums also organized over 400 concerts annually and offered 900 acres of parkland and nature trails. Here we learned that this deceptively small city, nearly always taking a back seat to Oslo, was well worth another visit, or two or three. These were sights we had not given much thought to before we left Paris.

July 22nd arrived all too soon. It was time to board our Hurtigruten ship, The MS Finnmarken. She was not too large, as cruise ships go these days, but the spaciousness of our suite reassured Ted that he would enjoy this week on the water. Our cabin was near the bow and was decorated in aquatic blue and foamy white with a comfy living room and TV, a king size bed to float on in our dreams, and an ample bathroom with a large shower and unlimited potable water. There was stowage for all of our gear, and a private terrace facing the shore, all decked out with chairs and a table for two, for times when we craved privacy.

It's not easy for me to convey my sense of that next week on the voyage up the coast of Norway from Bergen to Kirkenes. It all seems like a dream now. If I look back at some of the photographs in my digital album, I will only be tempted to write what would amount to a travelogue, not a bad way to share the sights I beheld and to possibly encourage those who can and who may be inspired to venture out into this very special part of the world.

Instead, I will leave such descriptions to those who know these seas and sights much better than I, those whose business is hawking travel, or better yet, to the folks who live on this land of devastatingly mystical and scenic splendor. Rather than filling these next pages with what others more intimately familiar with Norway have already written, the novelists, the playwrights, and the poets, I will try to render an impression of what I saw and discovered in the sea and on the land, and about myself.

When we were clear of the port and set free all alone upon the North Atlantic Ocean and its Fjords, with only the wilderness, the forests, the skies and the purest of waters I can ever recall casting my eyes upon, I felt like we were embarking on a voyage through a part of the world where oceanic solitude is blessed for its purity, and peaceful sleep is always there beneath the dark blue waves, like a contented infant lying at its everlasting mother's breast.

Although I could not locate a source, I'm almost certain that someone has already written words like these. Google was no help to me in my quest to give credit, if credit is due another writer. But, in truth there was so much more than the ocean and its inlets. There were unimaginable shores, both verdant and rocky, mountainous expanses that showcased countless cascades born of melting ice, both large and small. And there were species of wildlife straight out of fairy stories.

All this was bordering the northern part of the Atlantic as it gave *naissance* to the many tributaries that paid homage to the sea they came from. In this reality there was poetry. Not poetry about, but poetry exuding from the waters, from the trees, the animals, and the people with leathery faces who dared live this life in the relative wilderness.

The skies were so changeable that they defied dates, places or times of the day. They were brilliant blue one moment, oftentimes streaked with white, grey or black clouds, cumulus, cirrus, stratus or nimbus, and many combinations that resisted this traveler's vocabulary. They were decorated by the sun, rising or setting, each event with its own color and cast, its own shade and hue, its own side effects, or even special effects, some dry, some wet, some foggy. Others shone with light so intense they hurt the naked eye, while still others seemed so dreamy that they seduced me to fall in love with life.

I saw farms where sled dogs were raised, and indigenous teepees were used as lecture halls. I visited a museum where antique instruments were not just on display, but were performed upon, at least one in each room by a dashing fellow turned out in such a way that he appeared to have ambled into the building out of Norway's 19th century past.

277

I glimpsed miniature marinas filled with fishing boats at rest, a *Vinturhus* with a life-sized Santa that stood on the porch and hand-crafted ornaments for sale within. I drank hot mugs of cocoa and mulled wine the farther North we traveled. There were small galleries with art I longed to have the space for back in Paris, and there were enchanted and brightly painted wooden dwellings that rose up here, there and far beyond, and huge racks where fish was salted and hung to dry in the sun for use as Winter sustenance.

Merely an eyeful sustained me.

Cheerful potted flowers in multi-colors filled me with astonishment as they sat on frosty steps leading up to the front doors of private homes. Reindeer both white and brown grazed by the side of the roads. They had inspired legends. There was one that was told by our guide. It contended that those animals that had proved themselves by leaping over and clearing the drying racks were honored by being sent to the North Pole to be trained to power Santa's sleigh, flying high above the houses below.

There were people on the ship and people on the shore, so many faces old and young, I couldn't keep track. There were many fellow travelers with whom I would have started a conversation and might have befriended if I could ever have imagined seeing them again. Others gave me no choice. They seemed to lack the curiosity to initiate or even to respond to an invitation to engage at the dining table on the ship.

In the end, we all seemed to remain strangers.

Names like *Trondheim, Sykkyven, Tromso, Stamsund, Brettesnes,* and *Skarsvag* became a blur of strange sounds. But I couldn't forget *Helgeland*, the place where we entered the Arctic circle. *Helgaland*, the Land of Helga. Was it about Aunt Helga who had asked, "Wanna go for a ride?" Was that why the name of that particular town was so easy for me to pronounce and to remember over all others? Could it have been possible that these foreign travels that so enchanted me, even our life in France far away from my Motherland, had assisted in bringing me back to my experience of my magical Aunt Helga once again?

Our final stop on the *Finnmarken* was over the Nordic cap in the small town named *Kirkenes*. We stayed overnight in our friendly hotel in the marina, with water on three sides. Ted had arranged for roses to adorn our dinner table and a fine meal to celebrate our last night surrounded by water before our flight back to Oslo the next day.

I had been filled with so many emotions on that ship. Often tears came to my eyes beneath my large, black sunglasses where they could well up in privacy. I felt as if I were under a spell much of the time, reliving an early childhood that had gone by too quickly or perhaps had never existed.

Perhaps it was the raw beauty everywhere I looked. I felt like a child out of time, either a lost child, one with a lost childhood, or a detailed memory that had mysteriously escaped without leaving a syllable behind. I was left with the certainty that I would do it all again, maybe going farther North next time, perhaps to *Svalbard* into the netherworld of the polar bear.

Who knows?

The two-hour fight to Oslo was, like LA to San Francisco, another trip where up and down converged even before I had a chance to notice. This time we stayed at the *Bristol Hotel*, a 100-year-old lodge in the center of town with a history that would fill a book on its own. Its architecture was a stunning mixture of Moorish style and traditional British furnishings. We were a bit disoriented as we entered the lobby, unable to locate a front desk. With sincere apologies, the staff upgraded us to one of the best suites in the house for our week-long stay, and we were given the royal treatment. The rooms were so voluminous and strikingly appointed, that we could have stayed a month.

Our first full day was spent with Marit our private guide who walked us through areas of public sculpture we'd never seen the likes of in any city in Europe. Frogner Park covered an area of 45 hectares with ponds and fountains, bridges and trees, flowers and most impressive of all, the world's largest sculpture garden created by a single sculptor, Gustav Vigiland. The sculptures were installed in two tiers. Those in the park below featured Vigiland's magnificent bronze fountain with 60 individual, life-sized reliefs, depicting all ages, relationships, stages, sexes and every imaginable activity engaged in by mankind in solos, couples and groups and in every possible combination.

If this weren't enough, dozens of marble steps led to an imposing 46-foot-tall Granite monolith with 36-life-sized granite sculptures that represented the circle of life. All together the park offered over two-hundred bronze and granite sculptures. The surroundings were exciting yet serene at the same time, and in order to really do it justice, I could have spent an entire week in this one park.

As if that were not enough for one day, Marit took us by taxi to a wooded mountain top, overlooking the side of the harbor opposite of that which we had visited when we first arrived for that brief day in Oslo before being swept away in the nutshell. These woods were called *Ekebergparken* and offered a breathtaking view of the whole city below. Marit shepherded us down the mountain as one by one we discovered monumental pieces of art standing next to, lying beneath and even hanging from enormous trees. Every major European sculptor in the past 130 years was represented in this project, situated in a National Heritage park covering over 25 acres and showcasing a total of eighty sculptures. We saw works by Renoir, Rodin, Maillol, Dali, Bourgeois, and many Scandinavian artists that I am ashamed to say I hadn't heard of before this visit. After seeing all we could, Marit led us to a wonderful garden terrasse half-way down the mountain for lunch, and left us to the astounding views and the fresh and delightfully presented food and wine, in perfect weather on a day I would never forget.

The next morning, all alone we visited Tjuvholmen Sculpture Park, with bronze life-sized replicas of native fauna, standing in fountains, in pools, in clumps of trees and in flower beds that added background to their realistic appearence. We strolled along the water until we arrived at the Astrup Fearnley Museum of Modern Art. This

newly situated and rebuilt museum was designed by the architect
Renzo Piano and had just opened in 2012. Piano was best known in
Paris for The Pompidou Center, which bore no resemblance to the
AFMM in Oslo.

The permanent collection and the temporary exhibits were all
interesting and some even beautiful. Most impressive were the enormous rooms flooded with endless natural light, especially at this time
of year. What I felt was most Norwegian in character was the way the
water flowed from the harbor, throughout the spaces between the
two halves of the museum that were joined by a bridge and provided
a public beach and swimming hole for all people, both young and
old. More public spaces, more blond couples with more small blond
children, and playful elderly folks as well, were all enjoying life in
this glorious weather on the weekend. They seemed as if they had
been the models for Vigiland's sculptures.

After a restful third day, strolling aimlessly, shopping and indulg-
ing in the best Japanese food this side of Tokyo at Alex Sushi, we
spent the fourth day wandering on foot far afield from our hotel.
We visited the *Munch Museum* and the *Viking Ship Museum,* and by
chance we happened upon another establishment, one we would
never have been aware of if we hadn't noticed a sign in this neighborhood of upscale mansions, pointing the way to the Norwegian
Center for Holocaust and Minority Studies. A long driveway paved a
path to a large and once elegant home. We discovered that research
at the center covered historical and contemporary antisemitism
as well as studies of genocide and violations of human rights of
all kinds, and the historical and current situation of right-wing
extremism in the world as well. A unique humanist center by any
standard.

The irony was that the museum was housed in the *Grande Villa*,
the former residence of Vidkun Quisling, who had been the head
of the Norwegian Nazi Party. Confiscated by the government after
Quisling was tried for war crimes and executed, the home was, right
from the start, dedicated to research, especially about the fate of the

Norwegian Jews who had been turned over to the Nazis, and those who had escaped to Sweden.

After this sobering experience, we were in much need of the balm of nature. We walked and sat for hours in the gardens behind the house and explored the paths that led to an exquisite beach on the fjord. On day five, we visited the Oslo Domkirke, a cathedral from the 17th Century with a magnificent organ, its pipes decorated by gilded acanthus leaves. The recital we'd come to hear was performed by Martin Setchell and included works by Bach, Vivaldi and a host of other composers. The Cathedral wasn't as large as one would have thought, as it was used for public State functions by the government and by the Royal family, but it had been faithfully restored, was mainly brick with a greenish bronze bell tower and a striking carillon that played some eighteen melodies that alternated with the calendar, on the hour and each quarter of an hour. Inside, the light streaming through the stained-glass windows accented handsome frescoes and paintings.

Having been so sushi starved in Paris, we decided to spend our last night dining at Alex's once again. This time we were given special treatment by our chef, who took our orders and recommended a terrific and mellow hot Saki. He also filled in between courses with the kind of delicacies we'd not tasted since visiting Japan. We also met a young couple who were sitting next to us, visiting from Los Angeles, where else? It was an evening filled with the unexpected.

We walked back to the hotel, some distance from Alex's, along a large park, one that we had altogether missed. We sat in the bar in the hotel lazing in comfortable velvet Queen Anne chairs with our Irish Coffees, dragging our feet into the late night, trying to delay packing for our flight home the next day.

In the morning at breakfast, we sat next to a lovely Japanese-American couple, also from California. They were our age and we chatted as long as possible. They were about to take The *Nutshell to Bergen* and the *Finnemarken* up the coast, and we all took photos and exchanged contact information. It was a nice coincidence, but we

282

were left wishing that fate might have enabled us to enjoy the entire journey together. Then off we went to the airport and home to our empty house.

It was time we started to look for a kitten, or maybe two this time.

CHAPTER 33

ON OUR RETURN TO PARIS, we were greeted by splendid weather, blue skies and mild temperatures. We enjoyed resuming being tourists once again in our own town. We walked to the *Petite Palais* one day to see the 'Romantic Paris' exhibit of exquisite paintings and had lunch on the terrace overlooking the garden, another recent discovery. On the next day, we took the bus to the *Jardin des Plantes*, and spent some hours walking through the Botanical gardens filled with my beloved floral specimens and exploring the habitat of the exotic plants located in a 19th Century hot house. It was unthinkable that this was our first visit. One place we had missed were the Huntington Gardens in Pasadena, not too far from L.A. These were reminiscent of the Huntington. We felt like one of our favorite places had rematerialized here in Paris.

On the bus toward home, we approached the stop for the Pantheon and decided to jump off and visit. It had been renovated since the last time, over twenty years before. Entering the building, we were struck by the majesty that had been revealed after the removal of eons of dirt and soot from the frescoes and the marble sculptures throughout this magnificent neoclassical building, dedicated to the memory of many great Frenchmen since it was secularized after the French Revolution. It reminded me of our sweet Madeleine, but it had a spectacular dome on top and was as white as could be. The city had been cleaning the stones and pillars of the Madeleine since before we had moved into the 'hood' and there was no end in sight.

Behind the *Pantheon,* The *Church of Saint Genevieve,* had also been through a *ravalement de façade,* and although we did not have the time to go in that day, we put it on our list, which was still quite lengthy. Continuing to take advantage of the temperate weather, so rare in August, we spent the next day walking the *Promenade Plantée,* which begins just south of the Opéra Bastille, with steps leading up from *Avenue Daumesnil* above the *Viaduc des Arts.* Here the red-brick vaulted archways underneath the old railway tracks were restored and renovated, and the sixty-four arches now housed shops and galleries celebrating the art and crafts of the area, along with many quaint cafes.

We bought some gifts for loved ones with birthdays arriving soon and enjoyed the variety of the views of parts of the city we'd not explored from this position. I wasn't sure I would have wanted to live in the buildings along this walkway, where we could almost reach out and shake hands with the neighbors from the elevated park. However, this walk across the city to the East was filled with ponds, garnished with lily pads, flowers bedded in patches like an American quilt, various kinds of deciduous and evergreen trees, and artistic and humorous graffiti decorating the walls behind stone seats in niches along the way, perfect for 'Kodak moments' as we Americans called them, fifty years ago, before film was replaced by digital cameras. I wondered how it was that in nearly forty years in Paris we had failed to explore these jewels that bedecked the most beautiful place in the world.

Lana finally came for her annual visit and we three attended a baroque concert at St. Chapelle surrounded by monumental stained-glass windows to die for. We also visited the Victor Hugo Museum for the first time and discovered an authentic if funky Mexican restaurant in the 2nd *Arrondisement.*

When our friend Dale and her business partner Melissa arrived soon after Lana had left, we'd arranged a semi-private visit to l'Hôtel Lauzun on the Quai D'Anjou along the river on the Ile St. Louis. This was a treasure trove of Parisian history, housed in an assemblage of recently restored, richly carved, artfully painted, gilded and mirrored interiors from the time of Louis XIV, one of the few so well restored by the city of Paris, in what had been a private mansion built in 1658 on the Island. It had a storied history of owners, each one further embellishing the interiors, until the French revolution, when the upper floors were divided into apartments for rent to artisans. Baudelaire had resided there from 1843, wrote *Les Fleurs de Mal* during his residence, and founded a club whose members experimented with Hashish. Who knew?

After our tour, we walked over to the other side of the island to see the back of the Notre Dame where the damage caused by the fire was most apparent. We spared our friends our experience of the horror we'd witnessed on that sad night in April, and Ted and I took them to lunch in a typical bistro on the island, without ruining all our appetites.

After the Fall gust of visitors, and while enjoying our usual weekly musical events, we were both completely taken up by a frantic search for a kitten to enliven our holidays and our everyday life for the duration. We'd had enough of returning to an empty home without a small furry friend to greet us or to share with us our daily routines and our frequently long stretches of time at home.

After Ted's 71st birthday, with the installation of his much longed-for custom-made cedar wood 'dressing'—better known as a walk-in closet in America—and the celebration of our wedding anniversary, I turned all my attention toward a number of small animal rescue organizations in Paris under the umbrella of the national SPA, *Secours et Protection des Animaux*, which in English means 'Save and Protect the Animals.'

When we signed up, every day we'd receive at least one or more ads with multiple listings in great detail for the species of animal we'd requested. Each had several photos and a detailed description, written in the first person (or shall I say first cat) to inform us of his or her attributes, age, color and breed, needs, flexibility, talents, must-haves and those situations that would be unthinkable. For example, translated one read,

"Bonjour, my name is Princess. I am a six-months-old female and I came from a family of four. I am an attractively marked European shorthair type, with lovely calico coloring and big green eyes. I am beautiful, soft, sweet and very cuddly. I love to play with toys and humans, but I would like to have a family of my own without other pets or small children that might pull my tail or bite my ears. I have had all of my vaccinations, and I have already been sterilized and treated for pests, and I have had an ultrasound to ensure that my heart and kidneys are congenitally in good health. I am patient with having my nails clipped and with having my fur brushed. I will need to be allowed the run of the house, because I am very social and feel badly when I am left out. I hope we can meet soon."

I would have thought that, with so many animals in desperate need of a home, enthusiastic future adoptive 'parents' with a safe and roomy apartment, plenty of experience and a track record, and with love to offer would be welcome. But I ran into many *bouchon* on my way to find a kitten that we'd be permitted to adopt. it wasn't that we were picky about the kind of kitten we wanted. We would take almost any color or variety, as long as it was a short hair. And the only criteria we were hoping to meet was to adopt either one female or two sisters, with the idea in mind that two together might be better off in the early months when we were out for an evening or afternoon.

The first ad that I responded to on the attached form was answered that same day.

"Bonjour Madame Mitrani. Je m'appelle Madame Lamontagne de Parvendu."

"Excusez-moi," I answered, in French.

"Parlez-vous Anglais" I asked, with my fingers crossed.

"A little," she answered tentatively.

Hoping my old perception was still valid, I plunged in.

"Oh, thank you."

"You ask about the chatton, Princess."

"Yes, I did. She is adorable. Is she still available for adoption?"

"Yes, but I must ask some questions."

She spoke in a stern tone of voice, very French, very official, very proper.

"If I may, how old are you and your husband?"

"We are both seventy."

The form I had filled in required that I write something about the two of us and our situation and location. I always underscored the fact that we were Americans, retired in Paris, that we had a pet-sitter to stay in our home if we went away for more than a few hours, that our apartment was 150 m² and that we had always had cats throughout our nearly forty years together. This seemed to raise red flags rather than green lights.

"Madame, are you not aware that cats can live twenty years? If you cannot remain in your home, if you have to enter a nursing facility, you will not be allowed to take your cat with you."

She suggested that we foster a cat or some kittens, or adopt an older cat, perhaps five to ten years at a minimum. We were dumb-founded. Who would have thought we would encounter such age-ism in Paris? There were some agencies that turned us away because we lived in Paris, which was outside their department. We never expected delivery service and would gladly have taken a train just to visit an available kitten. In desperation, once we commuted out into the suburbs to see a two-year old female tabby. Unfortunately, her disposition spoke of a neglected if not abused animal, and although it broke our hearts to leave her there, we did not take her home.

Prospects grew even dimmer after another ad was answered by a young woman who had two kittens, sisters twelve weeks old. Both fit our profile. We were horrified when we arrived to find at least fifteen cats of all ages in one room with a loft, all fighting and hiding, and the little kittens were feral, which was not at all surprising. How could we adopt them if we couldn't even find them let alone catch them?

After various other disappointing experiences, we had thoughts of purchasing a purebred Bengal or two from a reputable breeder in

Calais. Just as we were approaching the deadline for that option, we heard from the Society who had one of the kittens we'd inquired about the day before. Mickey was a six-month old male, silver and charcoal tiger striped tabby, living in Normandy. If this sounds familiar to the reader, one can imagine how familiar this scene seemed to us.

The person who contacted us, Joanna, spoke English. She was born in Finland but had worked in London for ten years. She questioned us thoroughly and, much to our surprise, told us that she was picking up a kitten for adoption by a young woman here in Paris. The kitten was being transported from Normandy by train to *Gare St. Lazarre*, close to us. Since Joanna worked in an office in *Place Madeleine*, she offered to have the people in Normandy bring Mickey as well, and she agreed to deliver him to our home to meet us.

"There's no obligation to take this kitten as he is still a bit shy at first, but I think he will settle in well if given the chance."

Joanna was so accommodating that we agreed on the spot to give Mickey a shot. On the evening of December 4th, we eagerly anticipated Mickey's visit. When he and his escort arrived, we were thrilled. He was so much more handsome than we could have imagined from the blurry black and white photos on the email. His fur was as soft as mink, and his little face was irresistible, with large green eyes set wide apart, a small quizzical muzzle, and lovely charcoal stripes on a pale silver background, symmetrically spaced all over his body. His mascara rounded his eyes ending in two black brush strokes that flared out and down each side of his face, like war paint on a little Indian.

It became clear right away why someone had named him Mickey. Instead of a meow, his immature vocal cords made only a sweet little squeak. We were given the option of changing his name, but Mickey Mouse it was. He was still a bit too shy for us to know how we'd all get along, clearly stressed out by the long trip and all the space he was given to wander in, but we agreed that we'd keep him for the week, and if he began to settle in a bit, we'd sign the adoption papers.

Joanna thought this was a wonderful idea. She suggested we keep him in the area of the laundry room where his food, water fountain and toilette were for a day or so. Then we could open up the door to the adjoining bathroom, and the next day to the master bedroom. This worked like a charm, and by December 8th, Mickey was ours and he was the master of the house.

Once given the run of the apartment, Mickey was excited and playful, exploring the Christmas tree and every piece of furniture. Those suitable for cuddling up in and on had been claimed. He said "Meow," and I knew that meant "All Mine". He followed us everywhere and cozied up with us at night while we watched TV. Sometimes he would camp out in his own padded swivel chair, next to Ted's side of the reclining sofa, and at other times, he stretched out on the hand-knitted throw between the two of us, nuzzled in snuggly, kneading and purring until he stretched out on his back, fast asleep.

Mickey even located choice hiding places, suitable for times when the doorbell would ring out like Big Ben, which he knew meant strangers were about to invade. Although Mickey liked to watch everyone, he was no watch-cat. His favorite hideout was also a great lookout. It was situated behind the carved wooden cartouche at the center of our very tall Louis XVI style hutch, which stood on four legs on the buffet that dominated our dining room. From that spot, Mickey could see out to the front door, into the living room, through to the study, and he could spy on anyone who entered the guest bathroom or passed through the dining room into our bedroom, all without ever being detected. He had definitely located the most unusual 'catbird seat' one could have imagined.

It took many days to ascertain how Mickey had ascended and descended this acme of the apartment. Finally, our curiosity was satisfied. To climb up, he first jumped on the top of the dining table, then up a step higher to level of the buffet. From the buffet he jumped to the top of the door to our bedroom and took one step up and onto the top of the hutch. Getting down was a bit more complicated. He'd jump to the top of the bedroom door and climb down backwards using the wooden moldings that edged each of the twelve mirrored lights as paw-holds, until he could push off safely to the floor, stopping briefly on the buffet and the dining table. This was one ingenious youngster.

It was a wonderful Holiday season with Jeffrey, Michelle and Baby G and as she approached her first birthday, we inaugurated her new nickname, Jenny. We took turns posing around the Christmas tree for photos, and for dinner I made a *Cassoulet,* and we had a beautiful cake that Jeffrey retrieved from the sugar free patisserie in the 17th.

We also hosted what we then considered to be a large dinner party for our friend Marie-Claire and the lovely American couple she had introduced us to. Jane and hubby Clair had journeyed to Paris from Houston Texas twice yearly for many years and were fast becoming two of our favorites; our age, bright, educated, not psychoanalysts and terrific raconteurs. We added another new friend, Frances, to round out the table that night, one whom we had inherited from our friends Desy and Henri in Dana Point, California. It was a lovely celebration, so enjoyable to dress up the table in the family linen, Limoges, crystal and silver.

It wasn't quite our old annual Christmas Eve party, with forty friends and a large buffet dinner, nor was it our annual New Year's Eve afternoon matinee at the movies with a small group of friends, king crab legs, Caesar salad, *Champagne* and American style sweet *petit four* at our house afterward. But we were thankful for all we had.

It was the start of a new year together in the most beautiful place in the world.

ABOUT THE AUTHOR

JUDITH L. MITRANI, PHD was for over three decades a Training and Supervising Analyst at The Psychoanalytic Center of California, which has honored her with Emeritus Status. A Fellow of the International Psycho-Analytical Association, Dr. Mitrani's work has been published in nine languages and has been the recipient of The James Gooch Essay Prize, The Windholtz Prize for psychoanalytic writing and The Rozsica Parker Prize. She is the author of many meta-psychological and clinical papers published in both American and international peer-reviewed journals as well as the books *Framework for the Imaginary: Clinical Explorations in Primitive States of Being* (first published in 1996, and re-issued by Karnac in 2008), *Ordinary People and Extra-Ordinary Protections: a post-Kleinian Approach to the Treatment of Primitive Mental States* (New Library of Psychoanalysis, Routledge, 2000), and *Taking The Transference: Essays on Psychoanalytic Technique* (Karnac, 2014). She is also co- editor of *Encounters with Autistic States: A Memorial Tribute to Frances Tustin* (Jason Aronson, 1997) and *Frances Tustin Today* (New Library of Psychoanalysis, Routledge, 2015) with her analyst/husband Dr. Theodore Mitrani. Judith Mitrani was the founding Chair of the Frances Tustin Memorial Trust from 1995 until 2018, and she supervises and lectures internationally on psychoanalytic technique. Since her retirement from clinical practice in Los Angeles in 2016 she has become a resident of Paris, France.

ACKNOWLEDGEMENTS

WHEN WRITING A MEMOIR, even one that is time-limited, it not only takes a community of supporters but a personal willingness to risk reliving a lifetime complete with all the feelings it entails. In this respect, writing this book has often felt like undergoing my third analysis, and for that experience, I think I'm grateful. This book is also responsible for helping me through the first year of the pandemic and its many challenges. As for my community, alongside all the characters who played various parts in these chapters, some held significant roles in the birth of the book.

My brilliant and droll friend Virginia Detterman was the most expert and exuberant proofreader one could wish for and probably the only person who will ever read the manuscript four times with such sustained enthusiasm. Others gifted me with more than encouragement, helpful critique, and inspiration. Among these were Svetlana Bubnova, Marie-Claire Busnel, Cathy Cohen, JoAnn Culbert-Koehn, Jeffrey Eaton, Terrence Gelenter, Jonathan Gluckman, Mark Greenside, Yvonne Hansen, Monica Horovitz, Howard Lovy, Warren Poland, Jane Puranananda, Maria Rhode, and Arnold Steinhardt.

I am endlessly indebted to the unique and talented Liz Dubelman, who actively cheered and steered my project toward the finish line and beyond. And much appreciation extends to Alex and Karl (and others at Publishing Push who shall remain nameless) for contending with my whimsicality throughout this project's artistic and technical development.

Finally, everlasting gratitude goes to my beloved husband, Ted. Besides contributing the original cover photography that affords the readers a first impression much more significant than my words alone, he also allowed me the freedom to write my heart out each day, never complaining when my eyes glazed over with emotion that never entirely made it to the page.

Made in the USA
Coppell, TX
29 August 2022

82239263R00178